VIRTUAL
REALISM

Other Books by the Author

The Metaphysics of Virtual Reality

Electric Language: A Philosophical Study of Word Processing

Translation of Martin Heidegger's The Metaphysical Foundations of Logic

VIRTUAL REALISM

Michael Heim

New York   Oxford
oxford university press
1998

Oxford University Press

Oxford   New York
Athens   Auckland   Bangkok   Bogotá   Bombay
Buenos Aires   Calcutta   Cape Town   Dar es Salaam
Delhi   Florence   Hong Kong   Istanbul   Karachi
Kuala Lumpur   Madras   Madrid   Melbourne
Mexico City   Nairobi   Paris   Singapore
Taipei   Tokyo   Toronto

and associated companies in
Berlin   Ibadan

Published by Oxford University Press, Inc.
198 Madison Avenue, New York, New York 10016

Oxford is a registered trademark of Oxford University Press

Library of Congress Cataloging-in-Publication Data

Heim, Michael, 1944–
Virtual Realism / Michael Heim.
p.   cm.
Includes bibliographical references and index
ISBN 0-19-510426-9 (cloth)
1.   Human-computer interaction.   2.   Virtual reality.
3.   Computers—Social aspects.   I.   Title.
QA76.9.H85H47   1997
303.48'34—dc21   96–42035

9 8 7 6 5 4 3 2 1

Printed in the United States of America
on acid-free paper

Dedicated

to those minds at large

who find no home

in the established schools

Hexagram 20 (Wind over the Earth) suggests Observing: Observing means being alert, careful. Above is the wind, penetrating. Below is the earth, soft. So make progress gradually, with proper timing. Advance without impetuosity, with alert observation. Be swift without being hasty, move strongly but with firm foundation. Advance with flexibility. A pearl hangs in the black void, illumining the whole world as though it were in the palm of your hand. Be attentive. Observe.

—THE TAOIST I CHING (CLEARY TRANSLATION)

Preface

Virtual Realism is an art form, a sensibility, and a way of living with new technology. Since the advent of personal computers, our offices and homes have increasingly dimmed to display glowing, colorful screens. The bright, open space of modern art museums now plays occasional host to electronic exhibits housed in closed dark rooms. The networked nation increasingly incorporates the language and lifestyle of virtual reality into daily life. While computer technology introduces its distinctive style, the Information Society copes with rapid changes in economics, education, and politics.

These social and technological changes stir debate about the future. On one side are network idealists who promote virtual communities and global information flow. On the other side are naïve realists who blame electronic culture for criminal violence and unemployment. Between them runs the narrow path of virtual realism. In *Virtual Realism*, I explain the technology of virtual reality, examine several new art forms, and suggest ways of adapting the technology to create a more balanced life.

My aim is to point out the crossroads in current transformations and to find some guidance for walking the path I call virtual realism. For guidance I look to recent art works, cultural traditions, and my own experience working with computer inventors, art students in electronic design, and students of philosophy and Tai Chi Chuan.

My previous books deal with the merger of computers and human life. *Electric Language: A Philosophical Study of Word Processing* (1987) was the first treatment of the merger of computers with reading and writing. *Electric Language* describes the three shifts in the psyche when software guides reading and writing. It analyzes writing that has become automated (no longer in-scribed or printed in resistant materials); as well as productivity-based writing (as opposed to contemplatively focused on linear wholes); and writing linked through hypertext networks (as opposed to the private space of traditional books).

The Metaphysics of Virtual Reality (1993) measures the reality shift that occurs when human perception merges with computerized simulations to create virtual worlds. The virtual worlds of cyberspace hold both a bright and a dark side. *The Metaphysics of Virtual Reality* was the first book that explored both sides of that increasingly complex reality. Since the publication of *Metaphysics*, the dark side of VR (Virtual Reality) has become more apparent to the public as the initial euphoric advent of VR wears off. While much of the population still has ears only for professors at engineering institutions who speak of becoming digital and of rendering cities into bits, a growing number of people are beginning to look at the complex tradeoffs. Some, whom I call naïve realists, are willing to fight technology with a Luddite passion.

Both of my earlier books proceed from a premise of balance. By balance I do not mean a static equilibrium but a dynamic balancing process. I take history to be a dynamic balancing act, as I explain in Chapter 3 of *Electric Language*. The mass media, in their current configuration, do not encourage balance. Balance becomes a slogan or gets drowned in an overload of images and sounds. The individual is left to seek a refuge beyond the media. Books may still serve the individual who wishes to take a step back. Today, however, even the book industry leans toward commercial excess.

Electric Language approaches computers from the philosophy of language; *The Metaphysics of VR* from the ontological experience; now *Virtual Realism* examines the new aesthetics.

Virtual Realism steps back to meditate on the merger of computers with the human spirit. What does it mean to merge with technology? How do artists today design worlds where humans interact with computers? Can art preserve human integrity in the merger? How can this marriage maintain a healthy partnership to keep both sides of the equation in balance? Such questions occupy these meditations.

When I write of merging with technology, I do not want to cover the merger with overstatements like "humans have become cyborgs," or "we all walk around with technical prostheses." Overstatements have a value and a place, but so does analysis. I would like to turn a bright light on the connection between art and interactivity, cyberspace and nature, information and ecology, virtual environments and planetary health. But if analysis casts a light on these questions so narrowly that the big issues fall from view, then we must remember not forget the issues just to follow our own light.

If the reader finds me straying from my purpose on occasion, I most heartily beg for reprimand. I embrace the reader warmly who understands the dangers of overstatement, and I implore readers to plague me with corrections or push me for further suggestions.

Redondo Beach   Email: mike@mheim.com
Spring 1996   Website: www.mheim.com

Acknowledgments

More people contributed to this book than I can possibly mention, so I restrict myself to direct supporters of this work who either commissioned essays or provided conditions where this work could flourish.

The warm energy and open spirit of the people of Los Angeles provided an important backdrop for this freelance philosopher. The people of Southern California—especially those I know in Redondo Beach and Manhattan Beach—do more than tolerate fringe enterprises like mine; they positively encourage them. The shared assumption of Los Angeles is that old things need to be made new, and this entrepreneurial spirit furnishes fresh sunshine when I get bogged down.

Over the past three years, Richard Hertz and Peter Lunenfeld at the graduate program of the Art Center College of Design encouraged me to teach seminars for an enthusiastic and talented group of students in Communication and New Media Design. In the process of advising designers at Art Center, I discovered many things that never would have otherwise occurred to me. Many conversations and experiments at Art Center permeate this book. Special thanks to my teaching assistant at Art Center, Gudrun Frommherz, who worked with me on technical and conceptual issues. Material from seminars can be found on links at my Internet home page or at the Art Center web site.

From 1990–93, the Education Foundation of the Data Processing Management Association, in cooperation with Technology Training Corporation, sponsored a series of six national conferences in Washington, D.C. about virtual reality The job of organizing and chairing these conferences gave me invaluable opportunities to learn about the issues and research in the field. No doubt, that effort to make sense of an emerging field shaped many of the views in this book.

Alfred University in upstate New York hired me as a consultant in 1994–96 to organize a series of symposia about the future of printed books. "Text 21" was an NEH-sponsored series that explored a range of issues surrounding the print-to-digital transition. My thanks to Ben Howard, Paul Ford, and the entire "Text 21" committee who helped make the series a success.

Thanks to Marvina White and Tom Levin, who asked me to speak at the Princeton University Writers' Program where I could address again the issues raised earlier by *Electric Language*. The Poynter Institute for Media Studies and the Ringling School of Design brought me to Florida as guest lecturer for a week with journalists in 1994, thanks to Kim Elam and Pegie Stark Adam.

The Netherlands Institute for Design and *Mediamatic* magazine involved me in the planning process for their 1995 Doors of Perception conference which led to Info-Eco workshops in Amsterdam. The "InfoEcology" chapter of this book draws on discussions at those meetings, and the same idea led to my graduate seminar "InfoEcology: The Humane Adaptation of Information Systems" at Art Center in the Fall of 1995.

Thanks to Louise Dompierre, curator of the Toronto's Power Plant Gallery, who commissioned an essay for the "Press/Enter" exhibition and who sponsored my dialogue with Sandy Stone at the reception. Several illustrations in this book derived from Power Plant exhibits. Not far from the Power Plant I met Derrick de Kerckhove, Director of the McLuhan Program, from whom I continue to learn. Thanks also to the graduate students at the University of Toronto, who in March 1996 sponsored a talk on the significance of the Internet at a student-organized symposium.

The Banff Centre for the Arts in Alberta, Canada, commissioned an essay on VR (Virtual Reality) art works, which became another chapter in this book. The many artists I met in Banff contributed immensely to this work. Kay Kepler at *VR Special Report* magazine published some of my work from Banff and from other freelance projects.

Professor Ryosuke Ohashi, a fellow philosopher and Heidegger translator, commissioned a keynote lecture and essay for the workshop "Intercultural Worlds in the Age of Virtual Reality," sponsored by the International Institute for Advanced Studies in Kyoto, Japan. Discussions with this Zen master provided helpful corroboration. Scholarly help also came from the researcher Akeo Tabata, now at Kobe University and formerly in Tokyo. Mr. Tabata, Japanese translator of *The Metaphysics of Virtual Reality*, has kept me abreast of relevant scholarship. In Kyoto, I also met Professor Atsushi Aiba, for whose advocacy of my work in Japan I am grateful.

Vicki Cooper commissioned an essay for *UFO Magazine*, which led to many of the ideas in the last chapter of this book. The art curator Rob La Frenais brought me to Switzerland to talk about "VR and the UFO Experience," and his international participants at "The Incident" conference inspired me to rub art against science in order to get epistemology smoldering again.

Support also came from the regular workshops I taught at the California State University Long Beach Extension Program in Science and Technology. Most of these were hands-on courses about the Internet. For the opportunity, I thank the program director Mark K. Smith and my colleague Morton Heilig with whom I also taught a certificate program in virtual reality.

David James and Marsha Kinder provided support by having me teach a graduate seminar in "The Metaphysics of Virtual Reality" at the University of Southern California School of Cinema-Television in the Spring of 1995. Again, students helped me work out many valuable angles, especially about point-of-view. (They also teased me about my "yes . . . but" pattern of thinking). In the Computer Animation Department at the University of Southern California, Vibeke Sorensen invited me to lecture on the "Existential Foundations of Computing" which led to involving more students in the InfoEcology approach.

Michael Sexson invited me to Montana State University in Bozeman to speak about the evolution of symbols in the April 1994 faculty/student series "Literacy: Decline or Evolution?" David Levenbach at Arkansas State University brought me to his campus to speak about virtual reality to faculty and students. Daryl Koroluk of the Saskatoon Association for Computers in Education brought me to Canada to speak to the Association in November 1994.

The members of the Tai Chi Circle Redondo and those who participate in my Inner Body workshops provide valuable support and insights. Without concrete experiences with people and their lifestyles, I would be far less willing to say what it means to balance technology with the inner body. These people have, each in their own way, shown me the Tao of centered, balanced action. My deepest bow to them, and to my Taoist teachers—Mantak Chia, Michael Winn, George Xu, and Chung-Jen Chang—who have been kind, enlightening, and generous with their treasures.

Finally, no celebration of mutual support can be complete without the name that makes my ears tingle and my heart glad: Thanks, Joanna.

Contents

VIRTUAL REALISM

U R 101

Today we call many things "virtual." Virtual corporations connect teams of workers located across the country. In leisure time, people form clubs based on shared interests in politics or music, without ever meeting face-to-face. Even virtual romances flourish through electronic mail. All sorts of hybrid social realities have sprung up on fax machines and computers, cellular telephones and communication satellites. Yet most of these "virtual realities" are not, in the strict sense of the term, virtual reality. They are pale ghosts of virtual reality, invoking "virtual" to mean anything based on computers. A strong meaning of virtual reality, however, ties together these looser meanings. A certain kind of technology—"VR" for short—has become the model for a pervasive way of seeing things. Contemporary culture increasingly depends on information systems, so that we find virtual reality in the weak sense popping up everywhere, while virtual reality in the strong sense stands behind the scenes as a paradigm or special model for many things. The first step in virtual realism is to become clear about the meaning of virtual reality in the strong sense of the term.

We need to be clear about using virtual reality as a model because the loose or weak sense of virtual reality grows increasingly fuzzy as the face value of the term wears down in the marketplace, where virtual reality sells automobiles and soap. Car manufacturers use virtual reality in television commercials: "Climb out of that virtual reality and test drive the real road car that stimulates all five senses!" Newspaper cartoons and entertainment parks pump the popularity of virtual reality. Products on CD-ROM bill their 3-D (three dimensional) graphics as "true virtual reality." AT&T welcomes you into its "virtual world." The term now belongs to the universal vocabulary. But movies and seasonal television shows should not stretch VR to a thin vapor. Because virtual reality belongs to an important part of the future, we need to understand it not only as an undercurrent affecting cultural developments but also as a powerful technology in its own right.

When we talk about virtual reality, we have to keep in mind that it is indeed a technology, not simply a nebulous idea. It's not synonymous with illusion or mirage or hallucination. Virtual reality is not a state of consciousness or a simulated drug trip. Virtual reality is an emerging field of applied science. But because virtual reality belongs to contemporary culture, it expresses and reinforces many of the broad experiences we share as members of a common culture. Our culture intentionally fuses—sometimes even confuses—the artificial with the real, and the fabricated with the natural. As a result, we tend to quickly gloss over the precise meaning of virtual reality and apply the term "virtual" to many experiences of contemporary life.

Confusion has its fruitful, creative side, and metaphors can mix things to illuminate. But if we are to truly understand virtual reality as part of the dynamics of cultural evolution, we have to focus on what exactly it is, and we have to put aside for a moment the loosely associated meanings and spin-offs. The point is not semantics but clarity of thought about where we are going and what skills we need to thrive. Unless we get a handle on the meaning of virtual reality, we cannot be realistic about the evolutionary challenge. Without understanding virtual reality as a technology, we can never become virtual realists.

So when we talk about VR, we must keep in mind its range of meanings. The central meaning of virtual reality and its many offshoots.

The many offshoots, only a few of which I've mentioned, belong to virtual reality as satellites belong to the planets they orbit. Many contemporary experiences—from using ATMs (automated teller machines) to visiting Disney's "Star Tours"—serve up, in a variety of ways, the experience of interacting with simulations. What we call the "automated teller machine" is not truly a bank teller but a machine that performs many of the functions of a bank teller. The "as if" quality—following the dictionary definition of "virtual"—qualifies the ATM as a virtual bank teller. So pervasive are these simulations that we find "virtual" describing everything from phone sex to the kind of non-committed gaze used while walking past store windows in the shopping mall. These extended meanings are all interesting, and even important, but we should not let the extended meanings confuse us.

Further confusion can arise when you delve deeper into the scientific writings about virtual reality. The terms researchers and software engineers use may vary. Since Jaron Lanier coined the term "virtual reality" in 1986, the label has stuck to the technology, but researchers tend to prefer a narrow sense of the term to designate specific projects. Researchers at the Massachusetts Institute of Technology, and at the University of North Carolina, for instance,

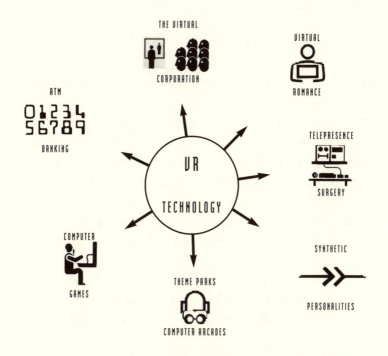

Figure 1.1 The Central Meaning of Virtual Reality and its Many Offshoots

avoided the phrase "virtual reality" in the early 1990s and instead spoke of "virtual environments." Military scientists prefer to speak of "synthetic environments." Researchers at the Human Interface Technology Lab at the University of Washington in Seattle refer to "virtual worlds." Japanese researchers refer to "Tele-Existence." In general, however, the phrase "virtual reality" still holds its own as an umbrella concept that continues to appear on grant applications as researchers concede the power of the term "virtual reality" to describe their holy grail.

We begin then with "VR 101," or "Virtual Reality for Complete Beginners." If you are already working in the virtual reality industry, please skip this chapter and begin with the next one about virtual realism. Virtual realism requires the capacity to reconstitute the real through computers, and it also means the maintenance of human identity as we install the technology into our lives and our lives into the technology. Before speaking of virtual realism, however, we must have a clear notion of virtual reality as a technology.

The Three "I"s of Virtual Reality

VR is first of all a technology. It is secondarily an experience that describes many life activities in the information age. What distinguishes, then, VR as a technology?

The "real" virtual reality—that sample of contemporary technology that provides the paradigm and that I abbreviate as "VR"—creates a very definite experience made possible by high-speed computers. Right now, in the 1990s, an experience of VR in the strong sense is rare among the general populace. That's because very few people today have access to super computers that can run high-speed graphics and that track human movements. As we know from past decades, however, yesterday's UNIVAC is today's five dollar calculator. The hardware on the shelves today does not offer a fully immersive experience. In the next ten years, though, we can expect a widespread and growing experience of genuine VR in a variety of contexts, from driver-training to computer-aided tourism.

Virtual reality is an immersive, interactive system based on computable information. These defining characteristics boil down to the "three I's" of VR: immersion, interactivity, and information intensity. Immersion comes from devices that isolate the senses sufficiently to make a person feel transported to another place. Interaction comes from the computer's lightning ability to change the scene's point-of-view as fast as the human organism can alter its physical position and perspective. Information intensity is the notion that a virtual world can offer special qualities like telepresence and artificial entities that show a certain degree of intelligent behavior. Constantly updated information supports the immersion and interactivity, and to rapidly update the information, computers are essential.

Virtual reality first emerged when computers became powerful enough to control several input/output devices that feed information in and out of the human body. The computers in VR systems need to track changes in the user's sense organs and to represent those changes in output that appears before the user's senses. A head turns left, and a tracking device passes this change to the computer which then generates the corresponding 3-D image so it matches the new angle of view. The hand wearing a fiberoptic glove reaches out to grab a virtual teapot, and the computer notes the physical movement and updates the teapot graphics accordingly—and perhaps gives feedback to the gloved hand. The changes in visual geometry must happen fast enough to make them appear to flow smoothly. 3-D graphics and surround audio system provide sensory immersion, and the system's fast response gives the feeling of being present in an artificial world where things can be touched, moved, felt, and handled.

The computer's lightning calculations make the interaction possible, but just as important are the immersion devices that belong to VR systems: light-weight visual displays that work like miniature televisions but engage the eyes stereoscopically; or four-wall projection panels that display real-time 3-D graphics; tracking devices or cameras to detect the position and orientation of hands, feet, and head; audio reproduction that pinpoints the precise location of sounds in 3-D auditory space; and sometimes haptic feedback devices that respond to the forces applied by muscles. All these devices and more underlie virtual reality systems.

Devices for immersion have existed from time immemorial. Theaters and religious rituals have historically used different types of immersion experiences, from baptism by water to theater-in-the-round. The decisive factor in VR technology is the computer that handles the data. The computer absorbs vast amounts of information to track the positions of the eyes and hands and then converts those positions into the changing geometry of a table or chair as it shifts in thousands of different perceptual angles captured by the human perceiver moving through a virtual environment.

The information intensity of VR allows a special experience called "telepresence." Information can tell us, for instance, what the temperature is on the surface of the moon at this moment, the exact size of a lunar crater, and how many rocks in what configuration are standing in the lunar crater. Because we can obtain and control this kind of data, we can create virtual environments that do more than re-present an actual remote environment. A full VR system can allow us to walk virtually on the moon as we stand on earth.[1]

Think of it this way: the data from the moon is input. It gets put into the probes from satellites, rover vehicles, and various measuring devices. The input goes back to earth as data from the lunar crater. The data becomes information when we understand it sufficiently to know how to make sense of the all blips and beeps and flickering lights. (Visit a telemetry room at NASA and you will glimpse the ooze of primordial data.) The information we have about the moon crater can now become output for making a virtual environment. That is, we can now feed this information into displays that output the color, shading, and shapes of the lunarscape. We can feed the information into amplifiers and speakers that output the sounds of the lunarscape. We might even output the feel of lunar objects into devices that give us the tactile feel or the haptic (grasping) force-feedback of lunar rocks. The data from the actual lunar environment becomes information which in turn gets transmitted into video displays and speakers that allow us to see and hear the environment of the moon. Data ➡ Information.

As we see and hear and feel the lunar landscape, we are virtually on the moon. The key word here, of course, is "virtually." VR technology is the intermediary that enables the "virtually." VR is the loop that converts input to output, that fashions the data into information that can become an experience. When we look at the display, listen to the speakers, and hold the tactile feedback device, we join the loop.

So we are now on earth, looking at the lunar landscape. That is still not a virtual environment. We are not quite yet virtually on the moon. What is left out of this picture is the loop that connects my eyes to what I am looking at and my ears to what I am hearing. In a real environment, my perception is a process of continually relocating my sense organs in such a way as to perceive what I need to see. My looking is a continual looking for something. My hearing is a gradual listening to something—or, sometimes, a deliberate tuning out so I don't have to listen to something. The alert attention I give governs my perceptions of the world.

When I look at a video display like a television set or movie screen, I am seeing video but the video doesn't see me. That is, the glance of my eyes does not affect the television screen. The camera director seeks to captivate me with the moving pictures, and the directors, screen writers, and actors all try to enthrall me with a story line and music controlled by the audio engineers who use microphones and

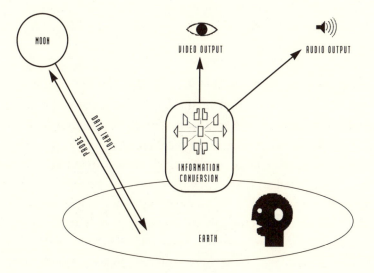

Figure 1.2   The VR Data Loop

editing equipment. The movie theater manager darkens the surrounding world and seats me in rows before a giant display where the one-way visual transmission cuts down the interaction I normally enjoy with the real environment where I play a role. These techniques regulate the normal ecology of my perceptual life by imposing constraints. Just as every living being plays a role in an ecology of the natural environment, so too my seeing and hearing plays a role in the ecology of the perceptual environment. Many VR researchers have expressed a debt to the psychologist James J. Gibson, who applied an ecological approach to visual perception.[2]

To establish a virtual environment, we need a system that outputs the data we receive from the moon, but that system must also be able to detect where my senses are pointing. It must display the information that corresponds to where I am looking and listening. In other words, VR simulates the situation in which I come to know things by paying close attention to the information that surrounds me. VR simulates the situation in which I can make discoveries of my own. Only when I can explore the given world with my perception do we have the sequence: Data ➡ Information ➡ Knowledge. (A series which does not necessarily advance to the next step, which is Wisdom or good decisions.)

Sticking with our moon example, we can now picture a system that takes data, converts it to information, and makes possible direct knowledge.

Now you can see why we need such powerful computers. The VR system must convert data both ways. It must tell us what's out there, and at the same time it must tell the data probes where we are pointing our eyes and ears. The system must continually update the displays to show us what's happening out there, and it must take into account where we move our eyes and where we turn our head to position our ears for this or that sound. Not only must the pictures reflect what we look for, but the sounds must emerge from audio spaces where they would emerge if we were actually present in the lunar landscape. This smart system must take into account the turn of our head to see as it feeds us the sounds from the appropriate direction relative to the lunarscape. To top it off, the system must perform all this work as events happen! Only a real-time simulator would allow us to feel we are—virtually—present in the lunar environment. This virtual presence is the *telepresence* mentioned earlier, and in engineering circles, the term "telepresence" often implies a capability for remote causation: someone can experience how things are being affected at a remote site through robotic tools, as if those things were actually within reach. The engineering meaning of telepresence usually implies the use of robots, whether simple mechanical instruments or complex machines with a certain degree of artificial intelligence.

Real environments in the primary world do not present themselves for our amusement nor can they be switched on and off like the situations in movies or television shows. Real environments are anything-goes and messy. They have no pause, no fast forward, and—most important—no rewind. Our actions can affect what happens next. So anything that simulates a real environment must have something of that spontaneous, improvised feel of real environments. The word used to describe this aspect of VR is "interactivity," meaning that the displays react to our actions just as we react to the displays. This endless acting and reacting is interactivity, activity "inter" or between two sources of action. I see, for instance, two rocks in the virtual crater. I

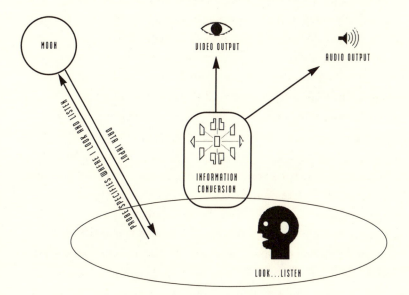

Figure 1.3   The VR Experience

pick up the smaller one and place it on top the larger. It stays poised in precarious balance. I test gravity by striking the rock with my wired glove. The virtual rock wobbles, then floats to the ground. The rock I saw with my eyes was a simulation, a computer-generated image, just as the wobbling motion was a result of an animation program that makes the rock move frame-by-frame as in a movie. Still, the rock's gravity behavior came from real data about the lunar surface, and the way the rock fell followed the patterns of lunar physics.

Telepresence

When a VR system succeeds in creating the interactive feedback loop between our perceptions and the real environment, then we have full telepresence. The term "telepresence" comes from the Greek word tête, meaning remote, and presence, a complex notion that we understand intuitively but that takes effort to unpack. We experience a low-grade telepresence when we hold a real-time conversation with someone on the telephone (Greek tête + phonê = "remote voice"). The telephone achieves limited telepresence because the "bandwidth" (amount of information) remains limited to voice, so that we are blind to gestures, facial expression, and other expressive features. Insofar as we can be with someone on the telephone, we are telepresent in the same artificial space. When we travel abroad, we appreciate the telephone as a way of bridging the geographical gap between ourselves and our loved ones. We can be present—in a way—to those who want or need to be with us. The telephone produces a thin band of telepresence.

Telephonic telepresence expands if we add a modem and plug a computer into the phone line so it can reach the Internet. The thin band of telepresence increases as two or more people use Internet conferencing software to see, hear, and write to one another without time delays anywhere on the globe. The desktop computer's microphone and camera combine with the keyboard and onscreen "white board" to set up a virtual conference room. People can talk, look at one another, share drawings and charts, and even share software programs. They can all, for instance, discuss and edit the same document at the same time from remote locations even though they might not share the same document software. An Internet conference expands telepresence beyond the old Bell telephone, but it still falls short of the telepresence demanded by VR in the strong sense. Aware of our remote physical distance, we enjoy a common virtual space, but we still find ourselves sitting outside a shared virtual world, looking at a computer screen. We look at the shared world through a screen.

The computer screen in similar to television—vision at a distance. We see what is happening remotely in real time, but the patch of vision we see depends not on our own bodily movements—where we move our head and eyes, where we walk—but rather on where the director chooses to point the camera. Television keeps us out of the feedback loop. We see and hear what happens at a distance, but we ourselves are kept at a distance.

Telepresence has a wide range of meanings, and on the high end of the telepresence scale is teleoperation. When we operate machinery like the lunar rover and feel to some extent that we are "there" on the moon, then telepresence includes teleoperation. The moon example we are using could easily become high-grade telepresence if the system gave us a set of remote controls so we could steer a lunar vehicle. We could then look, steer, and see where the vehicle is cruising in the crater. If the vehicle was mounted with a swivel camera that sends the pictures back to us, then we would see what the vehicle "sees." We would feel to some extent that we are inside or on top the vehicle that we are driving. Under the right circumstances, we might feel we are present on the moon, cruising the lunar surface.

Teleoperators are used to achieve effects on remote objects, such as the robotic arms used by nuclear waste engineers who dispose of radiated waste materials without themselves physically approaching the materials. Deep-ocean divers use teleoperators to explore ship wreckage at depths no human body can tolerate. While VR hooked up with robotic devices is a powerful combination and shows telepresence in a you-are-there mode, telepresence itself need not include teleoperation. As was mentioned, we can join others for an Internet teleconference and share a common work space, but the shared space appears not as a primary, real-world place but as a simulated, stipulated place. And the place appears through a screen in weak 2-D (two dimensional), or 3-D rendered 2-D (onscreen) virtuality.

VR adds more bandwidth when it supports the mechanical power of teleoperators, but teleoperation is not necessary for virtual reality. Our moon example illustrates the magic of telepresence because the moon stands in the sky as a remote, usually unreachable part of our daily landscape. But what if the virtual landscape we reach through our audio and video systems does not in fact exist anywhere in the primary world? What if we use computer graphics and sound samples to design an exotic information landscape? What if we meet one another in a completely artificial world? What if we set up a VR system to simulate not the moon but a loony tune? The system can reproduce whatever data we input. If the input calls for the parameters of Roger Rabbit's Toontown, then it is Toontown that we enter in our VR system. If we construct creatures with a certain degree of intelligent behavior, we can then put them in the shared computerized space and cultivate them as artificial pets. What we see and hear will not reproduce a remote landscape but an imaginary landscape or imagescape. We will be telepresent not in a physically distant place but in a physically novel place. If the contours of the images convey the import of certain information, then we visit a landscape of data or infoscape. Because such artificial places can be designed and shared between people, we can be telepresent to one another in a virtual environment. This environment will allow telepresence in an artificial reality.

The VR that simulates mental data rather than physical space has about it a different flavor than the VR that allows us to explore or control the surface of the moon. Our attention shifts away from controlling the environment and toward sharing the images we think up. We can, of course, still manipulate the pictures we see, and those animated pictures may elicit actions from us, but our focus will be less on causality and more on understanding who dreamed up this environment and why. The non-causal reality turns us slightly away from actuality and towards the suspended artifice of the environment. We might picture this purely artificial telepresence like the diagram in figure 1.4.

Of course, the world of artificial telepresence need not be purely mental or subjectively invented. The telepresent artificial world may

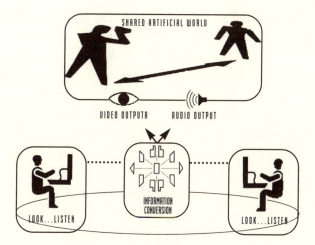

Figure 1.4   Artificial Telepresence

not anchor in anything as "out there" as the moon, but it may still revolve around an entity or construct that is as real as a book or as socially binding as a legal contract. The Internet conference mentioned earlier is a form of telepresence that permits lawyers and insurance adjusters to examine the same documents in realtime over phone lines and to use their fingers to point and rewrite sections of the documents they share in 2-D electronic space. This is an advance over the familiar teleconference because the addition of hand manipulations and revisable documents allows the conference to be more than talk. Agreements based on the changes to an electronic contract can be legally binding. And the electronic space where such agreements occur is sometimes called "cyberspace." The laws governing cyberspace are just beginning to emerge.

By sidestepping the link to the actual world, artificial telepresence — as opposed to teleoperational telepresence — gets things done smoothly in the realm of social contracts, personal communications, and artistic expression. With artificial telepresence, you can introduce further artificial entities, animated agents, who might act autonomously in the virtual world — something you might not want to allow if you were trying to represent an actual physical environment. Obviously, artificial telepresence allows a certain amount of liberty in not having to employ robots, mechanical arms, and real-world probes for temperature, texture, and physical attributes. Connecting to the primary world is costly and requires the engineering science of robotics. As we shall see in the chapter "InfoEcology," the cost of teleoperation decreases with the introduction of new techniques for bringing the real world into the artificial. But teleoperation need not be an integral part of a VR system, since artificial telepresence can be a preliminary phase, say of automobile design and manufacture. Later, teleoperation can be added when factory robots implement what prior social interactions have designed. As we see from advanced mathematics, nearly everything dreamt by the human imagination eventually finds a counterpart in the physical world. While we can distinguish artificial from teleoperational telepresence, we should not be too quick to separate them.

The distinction between artificial telepresence and teleoperational telepresence comes through in the different terms used by various VR research centers. Some laboratories, such as those at the Massachusetts Institute of Technology and at the University of North Carolina, refer to virtual reality as Virtual Environment research. They prefer to speak of VE rather than VR. Military research centers do much the same, preferring to speak of Virtual or Synthetic Environments. Other centers, such as the Human Interface Technology Lab at the University of Washington, frequently speak of Virtual Worlds (VW) research. These different terms reflect varying emphases in the projects. When you focus on planetary exploration, as NASA does, then you want to refer to Virtual Environments. Military projects often train people for real-world missions, sometimes to protect a remote site. These projects emphasize what happens to the simulated environment as much as what happens in the simulated environment.

As mentioned earlier, the term "virtual reality" has come to signify the whole scope of artificial telepresence. When Jaron Lanier first coined the term in the mid-1980s, he did so with a specific emphasis in mind. He founded the company Visual Programming Languages (VPL) to produce communication tools. VPL patented many components of early VR equipment—such as the dataglove, the head-mounted display, and the datasuit—with the purpose of integrating them into what Lanier in 1987 called "a reality-built-for-two or 'RB2.'" The whole point of VR, according to Lanier, is to share imagination, to dwell in graphic and auditory worlds that are mutually expressive. As an avant-garde jazz musician, Lanier wanted to provide tools for freely improvising realities that could express and communicate outside conventional language and symbols. Lanier's emphasis on VR as artificial telepresence helped clarify and expand the scope of the technology.

Before Lanier, Myron Krueger pioneered a similar path. Combining art with computer science in the 1970s, Krueger built room installations that track the body with cameras and then project real-time moving graphics of the participant's gestures against a wall where other projected electronic images relate to the participant's movements. Krueger designs environments that hover between abstract patterns and recognizable representations. Though not invented to reproduce the physical world, Krueger's "artificial reality" applies to business communications. In fact, the application I mentioned earlier—where lawyers and insurance adjusters redact the same documents in realtime over phone lines and use their electronic fingers to point and rewrite sections of the documents shared in 2-D space—was an application invented by Krueger. Myron Krueger's genius was sparked one day as he was experimenting with this form of telepresence which at first glance seems abstract and unfeeling. The monitors at each end of the phone lines showed only an electronic document with two pairs of hands. But one day, as the electronically mediated hands pointed to the same section of the document, one person's hand accidentally crossed and "touched" the other person's hand: the second hand recoiled suddenly as if to acknowledge that the presence of another person in the participatory graphic has its own aura of private space. From that moment, Krueger grasped the profundity of telepresence.

Types of Immersion

The two-dimensional document shared in artificial reality by legal workers brings up the question of another important feature of VR. An essential attribute of any system is the sense of immersion that it produces. Immersion is to VR enthusiasts what high-fidelity stereo is to audiophiles. Immersion is the you-are-there experience you get when listening to an expensive stereo system. Most people don't take the time to get this experience, but audiophiles and music collectors cherish the feeling. You eliminate distractions, relax before a good hi-fi system, and close your eyes. The music washes over you until suddenly, wow!, you are whisked away from the room and hear an invisible orchestra or jazz group playing in front of you. Your ears click in, and the sounds spread out in three-dimensional aural space. The bass player is right over there at your near right, the pianist at your left, and you can hear the drummer standing behind the guitarist. You can follow the line of the melody as the musicians pass it around. The music has some of that three-dimensional imaging that we take for granted in the real world (if, that is, the acoustics are good and we aren't sitting behind a pillar).

Immersion also resembles the deep vision we have with those "Magic Eye" postcards, books, and calendars. I mean the popular 3-D images hidden in the random colored dots generated by computers. These Single Image Random Dot Stereograms were originally developed in the 1960s by Dr. Bella Julesz to study human depth perception. Placing ourselves before such images, preferably during a quiet, meditative time, we can feel ourselves snap into another world. The eyes converge or diverge so as to allow the brain to decode the 3-D information tucked into the repeating patterns printed by the computer program. When deep vision hits, we experience a plunge into another dimension—at least on the level of vision. We see the fish, the space ship, the planetary system, whatever was encoded in the image, and our eyes explore the objects as if looking at entities that are solid and three-dimensional. That is, of course, an illusion, for the pictures are flat and we cannot move our heads around to the other side of the entities we are contemplating. We remain stuck in our perspective.

VR immersion gives the feeling of plunging into another world. The graphics presenting the virtual environment are 3-D graphics. The computer's calculations run fast enough to show the graphic perspective of any side of the objects that we would like to see. The audio of the virtual world instantly repositions the sounds depending on where the user's head is positioned. Sometimes the 3-D graphics go beyond 2-D illusory perspective and include 3-D video displays where the eyes lock into a stereo image, which, unlike the Magic Eye image, allows us to walk around it, stick our heads into it, and perhaps feel its solidity with our hands. Unlike the old-time stereoscope (Remember clicking the wheels of the Viewmaster?), VR goes beyond the single-perspective immersion where we see and can *almost* reach out and touch the image but still remain outsiders looking in. The VR type of immersion makes us full participants in artificial worlds.

Immersion remains a complex and elusive phenomenon. The psychological aspect of immersion seems particularly intractable to rational analysis. While we often recommend an experience to others that seems to us engaging and involving, we find it hard to pinpoint exactly what makes it engaging or involving. Likewise, the psychology of immersion seem relative to individual backgrounds, education, and experiences. One person's adventure is an other's waste of time. A book or movie may immerse you but make your friend yawn. One constant, though, is the drive itself for immersion. As symbol-loving beings, we look to steep ourselves in stories, numbers, and pictures. As far back as Plato and Diotima, philosophers have studied the human drive to enter more deeply into ideas and myths. Humans are essentially immersive beings and love diving into other strange environments—even if those environments lack the oxygen and sunlight we need to survive.

There seem to be various levels of immersion, perhaps even a scale of immersive experiences. But this is tricky ground here because we cannot quantify an experience that has profound ties to human backgrounds and individual psychology. We might, nevertheless, roughly note the wide degrees of involvement that different media deliver in terms of sensory detail and amount of interactivity.

While we do not want to lose sight of the technological component of virtual reality, with its distinctive emphasis on sensory immersion, the fact is that sense perception remains a single but important element in the psychology of immersion. Sense perception belongs to the hardware component of VR. The various ways of achieving immersion, both low and high-tech, catch our attention today as VR makes immersion a central issue. While the makers of movies and books seek immersion by projecting images and weaving narratives,

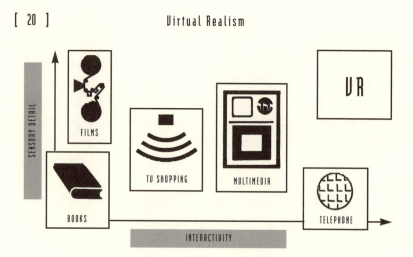

Figure 1.5   The Range of Interactivity

they do not approach immersion so single-mindedly and with such focus on the tools used to immerse the participant. VR has an empirical bias, and until we adapt it smoothly to our primary world, VR will remain merely a technology, a compelling obsession with techniques.

Helmets (HMD)

The empirical bias comes out clearly in the early versions of VR where the viewer wears a head-mounted display. The head-mounted display (HMD) resembles the hood placed over a trained falcon's head so it doesn't fly away. The HMD allows the user no choice but to ignore the distractions of the surroundings. The HMD uses tiny light-weight stereo binoculars to display computer graphics just inches in front of the eyes. The earphones built into the helmet allow the user to hear only the computer-controlled sounds of the virtual environment. By shutting out the primary world, the HMD forces the user to take all sensory input from the virtual world. The HMD allows you a choice of where to look, but the choices are limited to the virtual world. As you move your head, eyes, and ears, the displays and earphones present the appropriate viewpoints—all instantly calculated and recalculated by the computer.

Usually fixed to the HMD is a device that tracks the user's position. This tracker tells the computer where you are moving so that the computer can generate the appropriate graphics and sounds. The sensors measure the "six degrees of freedom," that is, the three dimensions (up-down, back-forward, side-to-side) of the human body, plus the angles at which the body can slant (like the pitch, yaw, and roll of airplanes). The tracker may also measure the relative positions of hands, back, and other body parts. Mobility simulators may also map specific body parts, like a foot or finger, which may be used to indicate where the user wants to move when the virtual terrain allows movement. Body parts may be mapped to non-conventional output. If the finger can make you fly, the eye can control which objects are visible or how much pressure the hands exert. Some VR gear uses a treadmill to measure mobility where the user's actual physical motions need to be trained. If you go on a life-and-death military mission, you will want to have actually moved your feet through the virtual scene you rehearsed. Likewise, baseball batters and Tai Chi players practice their art in VR. They try to move the physical body so as to imprint the desired movements on the neural pathways. Add the HMD and tracking sensors to the VR system, and you get a configuration like the diagram in figure 1.6.

The heightened realism achieved by full immersion has its price. Like the hood of the falcon, the helmet covers the eyes and ears, iso-

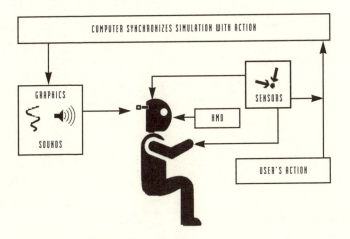

Figure 1.6   Sensory Input and Output

lating the senses. The user is plugged into a system that delivers a concentrated dose of simulation, but the user is also tethered to a wall of machinery. Present-day HMDs weigh heavily on the head when worn five minutes, and become unbearable in an hour. The nycron glove, whose sensors measure finger and hand movements, fits tightly on the hand so that its fiber-optic wires can detect muscle movements, but the hands soon become sweaty and uncomfortable. Today's liquid-crystal displays (LCDs) in mounted helmets deliver such poor resolution that if you saw a real building the way you see a virtual building, you would be legally blind.

An important factor in VR display design is the scope of the field of view. If too narrow, the field of view makes the virtual environment seem remote—like two small television sets placed inches in front of the eyes. Without a minimum 60–80 degrees of lateral scope in the field of view, a head mount usually fails to engage the eyes and brain in the you-are-there experience needed for telepresence. A narrow field of view places the images at a psychological remove, making you feel you are looking at the things out there rather than feeling surrounded by a world furnished with things that are engaging. The remoteness seems to vanish momentarily during certain operations, like the hands that meet and react over Myron Krueger's electronic document. But in general, the field of view requires width and resolution to switch the brain to a point of presence. Off-the-shelf available equipment today fails on both accounts, in that the field of view is too narrow and the display resolution is poor, but the hardware under development will eventually correct both problems.

The problem of how best to connect the senses to the simulation is a stubborn one, what engineers call a "human factors" problem, which will go away only with considerable advances in hardware. Some researchers are experimenting with low-level lasers that circumvent the LCD display by projecting directly onto the eye's retina. Some believe that the HMD will in ten years become as lightweight as a pair of sunglasses, with wireless transmission to free up the user. No one is really serious about the neural plug that allows users to "jack in" directly to the brain or plug a human nervous system into the computer input/output. Scientists just do not know enough about the brain and nervous system to even begin experimenting in a responsible way. If it's dangerous to stand close to a high-energy magnetic field for a long period of time, how much more dangerous must it be to plug the brain into an electric current? Science fiction suggests otherwise, however, and cutting-edge researchers will doubtless push forward with their cutting. On the safe side, some medical researchers are finding ways to read the body's own energy emissions so that position trackers might do their work without burdening the arms with clothing.

VR with head-mounted display is often referred to as "full-immersion" VR, because of the hooded-falcon factor. Sensory isolation does not of itself, though, achieve what researchers call "presence." Presence is that locked-in experience, similar to the hi-fi enthusiast's "wow" we noticed earlier. Presence is the you-are-there feeling. Crucial to presence is the involvement of the participant, and crucial to involvement is the interactivity available to the participant. Interactivity means more than being able to reach out and move the lunar vehicle or lean on the handlebars to turn the bicycle down the virtual roadway.

Our full presence in the world comes not only from manipulating things but also from recognizing and being recognized by other people in the world. Our involvement increases dramatically when we feel that we are, in fact, in a drama (the word *drama* in ancient Greek originally meant action or deed). Drama here does not mean Aristotle's classic structure of plot with a beginning, middle, and end. Rather, drama broadens to include dramatic situations where someone—an agent in our world who recognizes us as an agent in the world—watches what we do and responds to our actions. In a Toontown world, for instance, I might appear to others as an animated figure having the physical features and appearance that the system delivers according to the stipulations of myself and the others. The system, in other words, is a network. Several agents are meeting as virtual agents in the same virtual space.

Networks and Simulators

Networked computers can enhance the feeling of presence. Interactivity goes beyond interacting with things to become collaboration or conflict with others. Some of the most successful pioneering work in networked VR comes, understandably, from military applications. How do you practice running tanks over farmlands or exchanging machine-gun fire on a hilly terrain? Rehearsal in the physical world carries a high price tag. To minimize environmental and personnel costs, the military in NATO developed SIMNET, a networked simulation of tanks rolling over a virtual terrain. Teams of tank personnel, each in their own metal mock-up, view other (virtual) tanks through the scopes. The virtual tanks seen on the animated terrain represent the maneuvering of other teams hooked up to the network and seated in their own tank mock-ups at distant locations. The team members learn to work together just as if they were actually present in real combat. The simulated guns fire, rocking the physical mock-ups with not-completely-devastating explosions. Teams emerge from the mock-ups afterwards sweating profusely from excitement and fear. In this way, NATO forces in Germany and the United States have been practicing for years on the same virtual training ground. Such a remote system is known as a distributed interactive simulation or "DIS" because the same virtual landscape must be spread out in realtime over a worldwide computer system.

The team of soldiers practicing in SIMNET tanks exist in the limited virtual reality of simulators. The military use simulators to train soldiers and pilots, and these physical simulators have had a strong influence on the development of virtual reality. Many of the VR pioneers, like Ivan Sutherland and Thomas Furness, researched simulators for the military. The HMD took shape from the heads-up-display (HUD) used by military pilots. As the heads-up display becomes increasingly electronic, it merges with simulators. The cockpit shrinks to electronic displays that the pilot can put on the head like a helmet.

Simulators are used to increase the competence of experienced pilots with new aircraft and to expose them to conditions of adverse weather and equipment failure. Many commercial pilots today upgrade their licenses by spending a certain number of hours in a flight simulator before they take off with their first load of passengers in a specific aircraft.

Flight simulators are devices that provide a controlled environment in which a trainee can experience conditions approximating those of actual flight. The true flight simulator is a metal room on a motion platform that contains a replica of an aircraft's cockpit. It simulates with astonishing precision an aircraft's rolling, pitching, and yawing motions. A computer coordinates the instrument readings, and the flight controls can adjust for the inputs that control the position of the simulator, the aircraft's characteristics, and information about the terrain over which the aircraft is supposed to be flying. Video displays simulate conditions outside the cockpit. The motion platform of a good simulation can even create vection, which is the pull on the viscera that you feel with air turbulence or in fast elevators. Similarly, the SIMNET tanks mechanically shake and rock with the sound of explosions when they are hit by a virtual enemy tank.

A flight simulator for training pilots carries a high cost in gear and discomfort, but the costs are quickly justified. It is better to train pilots in full-gear simulators than have them burn up actual flight time in expensive aircraft. The simulators can provide more variety and challenge than routine flight hours. The military pilots in the 1993 Gulf War used computer simulations for mission rehearsal and thereby reduced the risk to their lives. Most had flown over virtual desert sands repeatedly before making the actual runs—and their simulations used recent satellite data to create a vision of the actual terrain. Ship pilots likewise learn to navigate treacherous waters through computer-based simulators, and nuclear power plant crews practice emergency responses in the same way.

With such specific aims, these training simulators do not require total im-mersion. Nor do they allow more interaction than would be expected of those who remain in the role of pilot. The flight simulator provides only those aspects of VR that are relevant to the task at hand. The pilot need not have the capability to lift a finger to fly through the virtual cockpit to observe the virtual plane from a 200-foot perch above the fuselage. Nor does the navigator need to be able to lift the ship from ocean to clouds. Interactivity can be limited to those situations imposed by the performance of an actual aircraft or ship. Free will stays under the finger of those who set up the task and test for training accuracy. The SIMNET teams sit locked to their tasks as they coordinate tank controls and communication with other team members.

As the VR paradigm spreads, more and more training situations call for simulators. We will soon take our driving exams in simulators, and many jobs that require physical skill will test us and improve our performance through simulation. But the team of soldiers in the simulated tank or the pilot in the metal room on mechanical arms remain restricted to complex but rather narrow tasks such as flying an airplane or fighting other tanks. As such, then, a simulation is less than virtual reality in the strong sense of the term.

The CAVE

One contending alternative to the helmet is known as "The Cave" or CAVE (CAVE Automatic Virtual Environment). Its name refers to the famous "Myth of the Cave" in Plato's Republic. This VR room, or "VROOM" as it is called, does away with helmets and gloves. Instead, like the cave in Plato's myth, it contains graphics projected onto the walls of a small room. The user dons stereo-synchronized glasses and uses a light-weight navigation wand to maneuver. Researchers Thomas DeFanti, Daniel Sandin, and Carolina Cruz-Neira developed the CAVE at the Electronic Visualization Laboratory at the University of Illinois at Chicago, and the CAVE had its premiere at the 1992 computer graphics convention SIGGRAPH '92. Early work on the CAVE was connected with the art installations of Myron Krueger. The CAVE mode of VR inspired the "Holodeck" in television's *Star Trek: The Next Generation* which is a highly fictional variant of CAVE hardware.

The CAVE is a surround-screen, surround-sound, projection-based system. It immerses the participants by projecting 3-D computer graphics into a ten-foot square cube composed of display screens that completely surround the viewers. It tracks head and hand movements to produce the correct stereo perspective and to isolate the position and orientation of a 3-D input device held by one of the viewers. A sound system provides audio feedback. The viewer explores the virtual world by moving around inside the cube and grabbing objects with a three-button, wand-like device. Instead of wearing helmets to experience a virtual world, CAVE dwellers put on lightweight stereo glasses and walk around inside the CAVE as they interact with virtual objects. Multiple viewers can share the same virtual experience and can easily carry on conversations inside the CAVE, enabling researchers to exchange discoveries and ideas. One user is the active viewer, controlling the stereo projection reference point, while the rest of the users are passive viewers. The CAVE was designed from the beginning to be a useful tool for scientific visualization. Its goal was to help scientists achieve discoveries faster by expanding the resolution, color, and flicker-free qualities of high-end workstations. Most importantly, the CAVE couples with remote data sources, supercomputers, and scientific instruments via high-speed networks. To fill its graphic walls, the CAVE requires enormous computing power when compared to present-day desktop machines and computer workstations. Companies in Detroit have built large VR theaters that apply the CAVE to automobile design.

The consumer electronics market already offers total-surround home entertainment systems that have a primitive resemblance to the CAVE. The CAVE helps us understand where the television market, with its increasingly immersive hardware, is headed. In recent years, television news and talk shows have increased interactivity through call-in shows and through feedback from the Internet. In the main, though, television pours out unilateral, non-interactive content, while the CAVE allows people to explore and interact. Astronomers walk through projections of galaxies, and physicists experience Einstein's equations. The modular database libraries in the CAVE that range from astronomy and physics to weather pattern analysis distinguish it from total-surround broadcasting as we know it in the 1990s.

The CAVE and the HMD are the two main doors to virtual reality today, at least in the strong sense of the term. These two prototypes of total immersion, sometimes called "goggles & gloves VR" and "teleporter room VR," are separate entrances into virtual reality. They both offer strong sensory immersion and the experience of telepresence. The power of these prototypes lends a meaning to all the satellite applications of virtual reality. Not every application of VR, however, demands the same amount of immersion. Some hardware delivers a lesser degree of immersion while still providing useful telepresence. Once we omit teleoperation, the cost/complexity factor of a VR system parallels the degree of sensory immersion we want to achieve. As we have seen, sensory devices by themselves do not equate to full immersion. VR depends ultimately on activating the inherent telepresence capacity of human beings. While telepresence never equates to unaided imagination, there is something within the human being, a central point from which we stretch outside ourselves, that makes the technology work. Total sensory immersion depends in the long run upon our ability to enter into what our senses receive. In the short view, however, we can classify several stepping stones that lead up to the two main doors of virtual reality.

Three Stepping Stones to VR

Each of these stepping stones stops short of full immersion, but each step contributes something to the range of VR options. Each step offers a different degree of complexity and a different apparatus to do a specific job through telepresence. Each step shows another side of the human ability to become telepresent in different ways and to different degrees.

Our brief introduction to the stronger tools of VR concludes by mentioning three other limited modes of virtual reality:

- The BOOM

- Desktop VR

- VRML

The BOOM is a "binocular omni-oriented monitor." As the acronym suggests, the BOOM hangs a monitor from a long flexible metal arm so the user can maneuver it into any position. The monitor itself resembles a small periscope, with two large glass lenses into which the user peers. The maneuvering action is smooth rather than rough like a periscope because the lightweight BOOM swivels in any direction horizontally or vertically, and the user can move it effortlessly to any height or angle. Instead of seeing the outside world, however, the monitor displays a 3-D stereoscopic virtual environment. The BOOM has the feel of a mobile window onto any corner of an artificial world. The monitor box discloses any corner or perspective of the virtual world. The BOOM allows the viewer to stand while turning and panning or it attaches nicely to a computer workstation where it permits seated access to 3-D worlds when appropriate. Engineers using CAD (computer-aided design) programs use the BOOM for modeling aircraft wings under construction, for example, which would otherwise remain hidden by the flat dimensions of a blueprint or would be obscured by the non-physical geometry of wire-frame models. A Boeing engineer can, for example, stick her head into the computerized model to see what clearances the mechanics will have when they maintain the aircraft. The recent Boeing 777 was the first aircraft to go directly from the computerized model to actual production without passing through the costly phase of physical mock-ups.

A step below the BOOM is the widely used VR mode known as "Desktop VR" or "Window on a World (WOW)," or simply "Fish-Tank VR." This weak mode of virtual reality puts 3-D graphics on a computer monitor and creates a stereo effect through the use of shutter glasses. The glasses pick up infrared emissions from the monitor so the left-eye sees one image, then alternates with the right-eye which sees another image. Each eye synchronizes with its corresponding stereo image. Similar to the red/green glasses that use color filters for providing different static pictures for each eye, shutter-glass images use the rapid-fire computer display to convey to the brain two different moving images which the brain then fuses into one scene. The binocular disparity based on the human eyes' left/right diverging angles on the world provides the cues that make us feel we are in a place where our bodies can move forward/backward, up/down, left/right. This binocular fusion results in depth information that seems normal to the human eye—as opposed to the way fish or deer see because their eyes are positioned on both sides of their heads. The result of the shutter glasses is a 3-D world on a square monitor screen. Such systems can also track the head position and use the motion parallax effect. This means that closer objects appear to move faster than distant objects as the user navigates through the virtual scene. Such computer graphics go beyond the cues of static optical perspectives and activate dimensional cues that our bodies normally use in the physical world. Several users can view the same screen while a special mouse with a multiple-motion ball allows the user to steer through the virtual scene, including up-down, right-left tracking when the ball is lifted or lowered.

Arcade games use graphics on square screens to give a first-person perspective to their action. The first-person perspective enhances the psychological immersion. Classic adventure games like *Castle Wolfenstein, Doom, Duke Nukem,* and *Descent* use first-person movement to draw the user into a psychological tunnel that combines narrow interactivity (shoot-'em-up) with a highly linear geography (castles and labyrinths). A more sophisticated task psychology (exploration and riddles) enhances the psychological immersion of interactive games like *Myst.* A variety of graphics techniques pull in the user and engage the telepresent imagination. Obviously, 3-D graphics help, as well as the traditional 2-D depth cues like interposition, shading, brightness, size scaling, texture gradients, and all the tricks of linear perspective since the Renaissance. Many of the popular adventure games on computer engage the telepresent imagination even though they run on flat, 2-D monitors without the tracking of shutter glasses. The graphics invite the eye to come in, and the movements of the hands on the mouse or joystick affect the action on screen, transporting the player to the world of adventure.

Still, the fish-tank world continually runs up against the limits of the small screen. It is true that we can stare long enough at the monitor of a desktop computer until our focus becomes so intense that we begin to see it as if through a window on a world of data, but such a focus cannot draw on the full intuitive knowledge we carry as incarnate beings. Our bodies carry knowledge accumulated through years of unconscious experiment. The child experiments with sand castles, spilled milk, and mud pies. Every moment of silent exploration builds a tacit understanding of physical space and its complex object relations. Desktop VR draws to a very limited extent on this intuitive understanding. To draw fully on body knowledge, we need full immersion. Fish-tank VR loses its spell every time we turn our heads away from the monitor. This 3-D world remains out there, in front of us, on screen. If the head turns left or right, or we look up at the ceiling, the immersion vanishes and we are no longer present in the virtual world on the desktop. Some situations may benefit from this double exposure, and research on augmenting primary reality through computer overlays has many applications.

The final stepping stone before the two main entrances to virtual reality is VRML. This developing computer language supports 3-D graphics on the Internet. VRML is a cousin to HTML, which stands for "Hyper Text Markup Language." Using HTML, individuals create their own "home pages" and businesses create their "web sites" for the World Wide Web, a way to browse through global information on the Internet. Any personal computer in the world can connect to the Internet and access hypertext (click-and-go) documents and images on the Net. Current Internet images range from scanned home photographs to video animation with audio hot links. The newest cousin to HTML is VRML, "Virtual Reality Modeling Language." Like HTML, VRML generates images, but the VRML images are three-dimensional and interactive. With the right software, any computer user can call up the images and enjoy the illusion of entering a virtual environment through the desktop.

What raises VRML above the typical fish-tank VR is its network connection. As mentioned earlier in discussing simulators and SIM-NET, the felt quotient of immersion rises with the addition of other people to the interaction. Telepresence increases with mutual human presence. When I log onto Worlds Chat (trademark of Worlds, Inc.), for instance, on the Internet, I first visit the gallery of avatars to select how I will appear when I enter the virtual world. I may choose to appear as a penguin. Others have already assembled in their own chosen avatars. When I then enter the virtual world, others may greet me and acknowledge my avatar. Another penguin-clad user greets me with "Nice suit, Fishy," and the greeting affirms our being there together. I can chat with others, and the interaction supports the realization that I exist in this artificial world, which is also a social world similar in certain ways to the one where I grew up. Nevertheless, this window on the artificial world still keeps us outside looking into the virtual world since we perceive first of all a window and not the virtual things and people existing in that world. One glance up, or to the right or left, and we are again outside the limited frame of that particular world. VRML helps us step towards, but not yet, inside virtual reality in the strongest sense.

The limits to virtual experience have their benefit. As the Internet continues to expand its audio and animation capacity, for instance, we will have many choices. We may want to connect with video and audio on occasions, and at other times we will prefer the limited bandwidth of the telephone. We may want to blend some video still shots with audio, or use photographs, or any number of options. Limiting our telepresence can also prove convenient when, for instance, we prefer to be heard rather than seen. Each application of telepresence calls for its own amount and specific type of immersion. If you are training bicyclists to take virtual curves at high speed, you might indeed want them to sit on steel fixtures so their legs can pedal and their arms maneuver. If you set up a virtual flight controller to oversee airline runways with an unobstructed view in any direction and from any height (with the video and audio fed by earth and satellite cameras), you might want the user to feel physically unchallenged, comfortable for hours, and no more bodily involved than a person who scoots a swivel chair across a smooth floor. The task at hand determines what kind and how much immersion to put in the virtual world. There is more to immersion than helmets and gloves.

All the variants of virtual reality we have examined in this brief tour center around the "I"s of immersion, interactivity, and information intensity. These three components of experience continue to spread through contemporary media culture as satellites radiating from the central light of virtual reality technology. The stress of these components on traditional culture is considerable. We go a long way toward alleviating that stress when we attain some clarity about the central source of the stress. Understanding the strong sense of virtual reality is the first step towards being realistic about virtual reality.

Figure 3.1 View of *The Virtual Dervish* by Marcos Novak, 1994–95, courtesy of Marcos Novak.

Figure 3.2 View of *The Virtual Dervish* by Marcos Novak, 1994–95, courtesy of Marcos Novak.

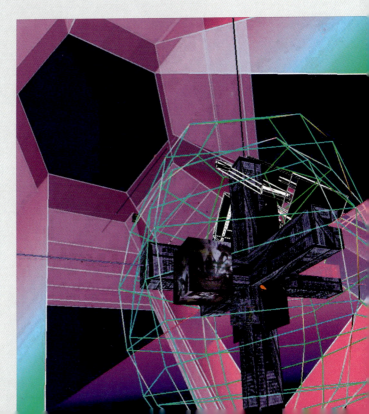

Figure 3.3 *Topological Slide* by Michael Scorggins and Stewart Dickenson 1994–95, courtesy of Michael Scroggins.

Figure 3.4 (above) *Topological Slide* by Michael Scorggins and Stewart Dickenson 1994–95, courtesy of Michael Scroggins.

Figure 3.5 (right) *Placeholder* by Brenda Laurel and Rachel Strickland, 1994–95, courtesy of Brenda Laurel.

Figure 3.6 Unembodied Fish from *PlaceHolder* by Brenda Laurel and Rachel Strickland, 1994–95, courtesy of Brenda Laurel.

Figure 3.7 Embodied Spider (foreground) with Snake (on left) from *PlaceHolder* by Brenda Laurel and Rachel Strickland, 1994–95.

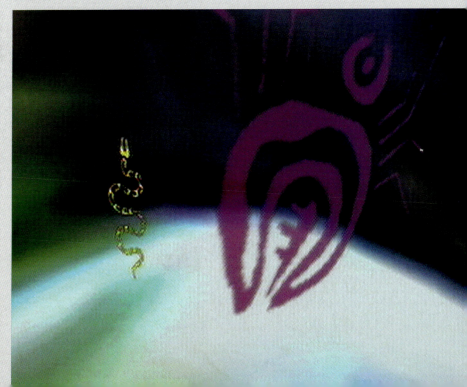

Figure 4.4 Photo of the Interactive Installation "Elective Affinities" by Sara Roberts, 1995, photo credit: Ira Schrank.

Figures 4.5 & 4.6 Photo of Interactive Exhibit "Portrait One" by Luc Courchesne, 1990, photo credit: Bertrand Carriere.

(above) Photo of Interactive Exhibit "Family Portrait" by Luc Courchesne, 1993, courtesy of Luc
ne.

(below) Photo of Interactive Exhibit "Hall of Shadows" by Luc Courchesne, 1996, photo credit: Ric
blay.

Figure 4.11 (above) Two-Dimensional Silkscreen "Bridge at Remagen" by John Massey, 1985, courtesy of John Massey.

Figure 4.12 (left) Photo of "Virtual Reality Simulator," 1992, by Robert Wedemeyer (Security Viewers, Seashells, Leather, Wood), courtesy of Robert Wedemeyer.

s 5.1 to 5.4 A mosaic
ges from the virtual
-building process.
grammetry photo (top);
ame CAD (right);
added to the model in
); final textured virtual-
version (bottom).
courtesy of TRW.

Figures 6.1 to 6.4
Images from
"OSMOSE" by Char
Davies. © 1995
OSMOSE author Char
Davies, © SOFTIMAGE
INC. All rights reserved.
Concept and direction
by Char Davies, graphics
by Georges Mauro, cus-
tom VR software devel-
opment by John
Harrison, musical com-
position and program-
ming by Dorta
Blaszczak. roduced by
SOFTIMAGE.

2

Virtual Realism

His words hovered in my mind for months, then boomeranged with painful irony. What he said over lunch held the future in a horrible way that neither of us could grasp at the time. His words foreshadowed a tragedy that would injure him and implicate our schizophrenic culture. At the time, the prophetic words were innocent of the shadowy terrorist the FBI calls "the Unabomber."

Lunch was at a Sheraton Hotel on the second day of a national conference on virtual reality held in Washington, D.C., December 1–2, 1992. I had organized the conference for the Education Foundation of the Data Processing Management Association, and Professor David Gelernter was the keynote speaker. I had been looking forward to talking with him, and lunch seemed a perfect opportunity. The Yale computer scientist had invented the Linda programming language and had also written eloquently about the human side of computing. I knew him not only as a writer but also as a friendly reader of my books. I looked forward to an exchange of ideas.

Our conversation moved from pleasantries to questions about how to humanize the computer. Several of David Gelernter's sentences imprinted themselves on my memory and later played back to me in ways I could not—would not—have imagined: "We are on a social collision course," he warned. "One portion of our population is building computer systems—the software cathedrals of this era—while another portion grows increasingly alienated from computers. This situation holds the greatest danger of a cultural collision." Here was a premonition about the cyberspace backlash.

Seven months later, on June 24, 1993, David Gelernter opened a
mail package on the fifth floor of the Watson computer science
building at Yale, and the package blew up in his face. The office was
in flames, and David barely escaped. He staggered to the campus
clinic, arriving just in time to save his life. The permanent injuries
he suffered from the mail bomb included a partially blinded right
eye, damage in one ear, and a maimed right hand.

Two years later, on April 24, 1995, a letter to Gelernter from the
Unabomber taunted: "If you'd had any brains you would have realized that there are a lot of people out there who resent bitterly the
way techno-nerds like you are changing the world and you wouldn't
have been dumb enough to open an unexpected package from an
unknown source." Here was the low-blow attack on techno-nerds, the
in-your-face and personal malevolence that announced a culture collision. The social train wreck was no longer around a distant corner
of the future.

On September 19, 1995, the *Washington Post* caved in to the Unabomber's threats by publishing his 56-page, 35,000-word manifesto
entitled "Industrial Society and Its Future." The newspaper sold out
early the same day. By evening, I could not find a single copy of the
Washington Post with the 8-page manifesto insert. The next morning,
I went online to the Internet and downloaded the entire 200-kilobyte
text of the manifesto from the World Wide Web site which the FBI
had put out concerning the Unabomber. On the Internet, no one can
kill you with a mail bomb—at least, not yet. Desperate to be published, the Unabomber now had his own "home page," complete with
wanted sketches and maps pinpointing the series of explosions, all in
high-tech format, thanks to the FBI. I did a text search of the manifesto and found the word "computer" frequently used in conjunction
with "control" and "technology." The serial bomber blamed technology, especially computers, for several things, including: the invasion
of privacy, genetic engineering, and "environmental degradation
through excessive economic growth."

The Unabomber Manifesto borrows from the school of social critics who follow Jacques Ellul. Ellul's *Technological Society*, a bible in
the 1960s, demonized an all-pervasive technology monster lurking

beneath the "technological-industrial system." The Unabomber Manifesto draws heavily on this line of thinking but goes further by linking technology with computers. The killer critic sees computers as instruments of control to oppress human beings either by putting them out of work or by altering how they work. The Manifesto states:

> It is certain that technology is creating for human beings a new physical and social environment radically different from the spectrum of environments to which natural selection has adapted the human race physically and psychologically. If man does not adjust to thi00s new environment by being artificially re-engineered, then he will be adapted to it through a long and painful process of natural selection. The former is far more likely that the latter.

The dilemma posed by the Unabomber Manifesto appears in the work of other alarmist critics. Many people in fact share the Unabomber's view without harboring the same pathological desperation. The no-win dilemma they see is either to permit evolution to wreck millions of lives or to use technology to forcibly re-engineer the population. Either artificial engineering or laissez-faire evolution seem the sole options: Either manipulate humans to fit technology, or watch technology bulldoze the population until only the techno-humanoids are left standing. The Ellul school of criticism posits a monolithic steamroller "technology" that flattens every human activity. Recent members of this school, like Jean Baudrillard, nationalize that alien Leviathan and call it "Americanization." They fear the ghostly "representations of representations" that inject Disney-like simulacra into every facet of cultural life, emptying active content by exploiting images.

We not need look outside the United States to find Luddite theory. Since the publication of the Unabomber Manifesto, many American policy writers have felt the need to distance themselves from the Unabomber because they in fact oppose the same technology monster attacked by the Manifesto and they share some critical sources. While agreeing with the Unabomber's ideas, they understandably want to distance themselves from terrorist practice. The number of such critics grew in the early 1990s when information technology extended into all areas of life, spawning the multimedia industry and virtual reality companies. Computer networks like the Internet came into general use in the early 1990s, and economic forecasts indicated that the computerized infrastructure was transforming the national economy as well as the American culture. Not surprisingly, critics took note.

The Cyberspace Backlash

Not long after the arrival of cyberspace came the cyberspace backlash. A cultural pendulum swings back and forth to feed sensation-hungry media. The media feeds on the overstatements thrown out by wide mood swings. A trend climbs in six months from obscurity to one of the Five Big Things of the month. The media's editorial strategy guarantees backlash: simplify an issue; then exaggerate what was simplified. Cyberspace was no exception, and the swing against cyberspace was inevitable.

The backlash runs from those who are frustrated by the frequent need to upgrade software to those who experience Alvin and Heidi Toffler's "future shock" as a personal, existential jolt. While the Tofflers preach "global trends" from an economist's overview, the individual suffers painful personal changes in the work and marketplaces. Waves of future shock may be intriguing to futurist policy makers, but those same waves look scary in the eyes of someone scanning the horizon from a plastic board adrift in the Ocean. The big picture of evolutionary trends often overwhelms and silences the personal pain of living people. These people will eventually find their voices in a backlash against the confident soothsayers in business suits.

A streak of the Unabomber's Luddite passion weaves through the cyberspace backlash. The titles of several books published between 1993 to 1995 give a glimpse of the breadth of the backlash. Among the books you find: *Resisting the Virtual Life* by James Brook and Iain Boal, *Rebels Against the Future: The Luddites and Their War on the Industrial Revolution* by Kirkpatrick Sale, *Media Virus* by Douglas Rushkoff, *Data Trash* by Arthur Kroker and Michael Weinstein, *Silicon Snake Oil: Second Thoughts on the Information Highway* by Clifford Stoll, *The Age of Missing Information* by Bill McKibben, *The Gutenberg Elegies* by Sven Birkerts, *War of the*

Worlds: Cyberspace and the High-Tech Assault on Reality by Mark Slouka, and *The Future Does Not Compute* by Steve Talbot. Obviously, these books show infinitely more grace than the Unabomber's crude, coercive manifestos, but they all reject, to varying degrees, the movement of life into electronic environments.

These critics tend toward what I call "naïve realism." Many of them take reality to be immediate experience, and they see computer systems as alien intruders on the terrain of unmediated experience. The elaborate data systems we are developing still exist outside our primary sensory world. The systems do not belong to reality but constitute instead, in the eyes of the naïve realist, a suppression of reality. The suppression comes through "the media" businesses that collect, edit, and broadcast packaged experience. The media infiltrate and distort non-mediated experience until immediate experience is compromised. Computers accelerate the process of data gathering, and further threaten, in their eyes, the purity of immediate experience. Computer networks add unnecessary frills to the real world while draining life blood from the real world. Reality, they assert, is the physical world we perceive with our bodily senses, the world we see directly with our own eyes, smell with our noses, hear with our ears, taste with our tongues, and touch with our own hands. From the standpoint of this perceived world, the computer is at best a tool, at worst a distracting mirage. The mountains, rivers, and great earth beneath our feet existed before any computers, and the naïve realist sees the computer as an alien entity in God's pristine world. The computer, say the naïve realists, should remain a mere tool. It is a subordinate device that can distract us from the primary world. We can and should, if the computer enervates us, pull the plug or even destroy the computer.

The naïve realist struggles with many fears. There is fear of abandoning local community values as we move into a cyberspace of global communities. There is fear of diminishing physical closeness and mutual interdependence as electronic networks mediate more and more activities. There is fear of crushing the spirit by replacing human movement with smart objects and robot machines. There is fear of losing the autonomy of our private bodies as we depend increasingly on chip-based implants. There is fear of compromising integrity of mind as we habitually plug into networks. There is fear that our own nature is slipping away as genetics transforms organic life into manageable strings of information. There is fear of the sweeping changes in the workplace and in public life as we have know it. There is fear of the empty desolation of human absence that comes with increased telepresence. There is fear that it will be the same power elite who "moved atoms" as they pursued a science without conscience who will now "move bits." By voicing such fears, the naïve realist sounds an alarm that contrasts sharply with the idealistic good cheer of futurists like Alvin and Heidi Toffler.

Idealists vs. Naïve Realists

Futurists like Toffler describe a culture shaken by future shock. But their shock comes in macro-economic waves, not in personal and existential distress. In this sense, futurists like Toffler are idealists. Idealists take the measure of individuals by placing them in the larger context of economics or politics to which the individuals belong. The Tofflers look to the economically and politically global, not to the individual or existential. Their big idea absorbs individuals. Like the other "digerati" celebrated by *Wired* magazine, Toffler welcomes the digital revolution and you had better join or be crushed by the wheels of history.

Such idealism goes back to the early pioneers of computing. Rationalists like Leibniz and Descartes, the seventeenth-century philosophers, pushed computation and mathematical physics ahead of ethics and feelings. Their faith in progress relied on the reduction of thinking to systems of rational logic. So large was their optimism that they easily became targets for Voltaire who caricatured Leibniz in the character Professor Pangloss in the novel Candide. Pangloss's tortured young student Candide meditates: "My Master said, 'There is a sweetness in every woe.' It must be so. It must be so." The idealist points to evolutionary gains for the species and glosses over the personal sufferings of individuals. Idealists are optimists, or, on bad days, they are happy worriers. The optimist says, "This is the best of all possible worlds, and even the pain is a necessary component." In the eyes of naïve realists, the idealist is selling snake oil.

The cyberspace backlash strikes at futurist flimflam as much as it reacts to felt changes. Postmodern theory, with glib talk of "cyborgs," "software cities," and "virtual communities," provokes its opponents by flashing a brand of intellectually sophisticated terror. Postmodern rhetoric, lacking a compassionate basis in shared experience and common practices, was out to frighten the insecure and to train commandos who attack common sense. After all, language since Saussure is basically a code or system, not a living event for which we are each responsible. Since Saussure, the communicative power of language, its ability to build community, became an object of derision to sophisticated theoreticians. A certain jaded idealism enjoys poking common sense in the eye with hot purple hair, revolutionary verbiage, and cyberpunk affectations. A cyber-vocabulary promotes confusion as a fashion statement. Wave the banner of confusion, however, and you provoke a return to basics. Naïveté then seems a blessing. Yet the dialectical story does not end so simply, because the futurist vision is not without cogency. What the futurist sees is precisely what brings others fright.

Nerds in the Noosphere

The futurist sees the planet converging. Computer networks foster virtual communities that cut across geographical and time zones. Virtual community seems a cure-all for isolated people who complain about their isolation. Locked in metal boxes on urban freeways, a population enjoys socializing with fellow humans through computer networks. Shopping, learning, and business are not far away once we enhance our telepresence abilities. The prospect seems so exciting that you see the phrase "virtual communities" mentioned in the same breath with McLuhan's "global village" or Teilhard's "Omega Point."

Pierre Teilhard de Chardin, the French Jesuit paleontologist, envisioned the convergence of humans into a single massive "noosphere" or "mind sphere" (Ionian Greek "noos" = mind). This giant network would surround earth to control the planet's resources and shepherd a world unified by Love. Teilhard's catholic vision ranged from evolutionary physics to world religion (though his views received more suspicion than support from the Vatican orthodoxy). He saw in the physical world an inner drive for all substance to converge into increasingly complex units. Material atoms merge to create higher-level units. Matter eventually converges to form organisms. The convergence of organic life in turn produces higher level complexity. The complex units establish a new qualitative dimension where consciousness emerges. On the conscious level, the mind—and the networking of minds—gives birth to a new stage of spirit. As in Hegel's nineteenth-century philosophy, Teilhard sees the birth of spirit as the inner meaning or cosmic purpose of the entire preceding evolution. Convergence toward greater complexity, even on the sub-atomic material level, exemplifies the principle of Love (agapic rather than erotic love). Only later, with the dawn of intelligence, does Love come into full consciousness and self-awareness. For Teilhard, this is the Christ principle that guides the universe: "In the beginning was the Logos." Only at its culminating point does history reveal its full meaning as the mental sphere becomes dominant. Teilhardians see ultimate convergence as the Omega or End-Point of time, the equivalent of the Final Coming of Christ.

Teilhard, like Karl Marx before him, absorbed much about evolutionary dynamics from the father of German Idealism, George-Friedrich Hegel (1770-1831). Hegel applied the Christian notion of Divine Providence to the recorded events of civilized history to show a rational progression. Hegel's elaborate encyclopedias and multi-volume histories of Western civilization affirmed a hidden evolutionary will driving purposely towards a single culmination. The fulfillment of history, according to Hegel, was a harmony of unity in diversity, a oneness which later interpreters described as a "classless society" (Karl Marx) or as "social Progress" (the St. Louis Hegelians). Hegel's genius was to see a divine Idea unfold in the material world of historical events—even to the point of squeezing all recorded history into a Procrustean logic of progress. The famous "Dialectic" changed from its original meaning of logical conversation to its new meaning of social movements and improvements. The motor that powered the movement of history was a series of internal civil wars, each bringing the entire society a little closer to perfection. The culmination of all revolutions, for Hegel, produced Western constitutional democracies where the individual and the individual's rights are recognized by the collective society. Just what this heavenly harmony looked like in practice appeared differently to the various brands of Hegel's idealism. While Karl Marx's brand came dressed in the worker's garb of political economy, Teilhard's brand blended synthetic physics with Christian communitarianism. It is especially the communitariansim that attracts network idealists.

Community seems a by-product of the development of machines. At first machines functioned as stand-alone tools under supervision by a single human operator. Then machines increasingly functioned in an ensemble. While the first machines were isolated work tools, they soon became parts of a larger assembly, with railroads, fuel distribution, and highway systems being the obvious examples. The spread of the machine as an assemblage reached into the sphere of human society with radio networks and television networks and now satellite networks. The linked machines plug into the networks with the computer as the controller switch. The result is a networked grid encompassing the earth and giving humans access to nature. Control over nature comes through a combination of human and machine networks guided by computers.

The network idealist builds collective bee-hives. The idealist sees the next century as an enormous communitarian buzz. The worldwide networks that cover the planet will form a global bee-hive where civilization shakes off individual controls and electronic life steps out on its own. In that networked world, information runs free through the planetary nervous system, and intellectual property vanishes as a concept. Individuals give and take freely. Compensation is automated for the heavenly, disembodied life. Electronic angels distribute credit. Private territory and material possessions no longer divide people. Digital mediation does away with the battle of the books, and proprietary ideas give way to free exchange and barter. Cooperative intelligence vanquishes private minds. Extropian idealists (who define themselves as the enemies of entropy) encourage members to put their deceased bodies on ice until scientists can one day either revive the repaired body or upload the brain-encased mind into silicon chips. The Teilhardian Internet is optimism gone ballistic.

Realists are less impressed. They are uneasy with the idealists who celebrate an electronic collective. I know people in rural communities who hear wishful thinking in the phrase "virtual community." It sticks in their craw. For many, real community means a difficult, never-resolved struggle. It is a sharing that cannot be virtual because its reality arises from the public places that people share physically—not the artificial configuration you choose but the spaces that fate allots, complete with the idiosyncrasies of local weather and a mixed bag of family, neighbors, and neighborhoods. For many, the "as-if community" lacks the rough interdependence of life shared. And here is where the naïve realist draws the line. The direct, unmediated space we perceive with our senses creates the spaces where we mature physically, morally, and socially. Even if modern life shrinks public space by building freeways, and even if the "collective mind" still offers interaction through computers, the traditional meeting places still allowed social bonds to be built on patience and time spent together. This is the bottom line for realists.

It is no surprise, then, for realists when they hear that the Internet Liberation Front is bringing down the Internet's Pipeline for six hours, when Anti-Semitic hate groups pop up on Prodigy, when *Wired* magazine gets letter-bombed, or when Neo-Nazis work their way into the German Thule Network. The utopian *communitas* exists as an imagined community, as the Mystical Body. Real community exists where people throw their lot together and stand in face-to-face ethical proximity. Computer hardware may eventually allow us to transport our cyberbodies, but we are just learning to appreciate the tradeoffs between primary and virtual identities. Put the New Jerusalem on hold until we phone security.

Virtual Realism

Both naïve realism and network idealism belong to the cyberspace backlash. They are two sides of the same coin, binary brothers. One launches forth with unreserved optimism; the other lashes back with a cry to ground ourselves outside technology. Hegel would have appreciated their mutual opposition while betting on an eventual synthesis. Unfortunately, no synthesis is in sight. A collision may be imminent. We are looking at an opposition of primal forces, as basic as love and death. One critic, in fact, recently used these very terms in attacking a passage in my previous book, *The Metaphysics of Virtual Reality*. The critic, Gabriel Brahm, edited a collection entitled *Prosthetic Territories: Politics and Hypertechnologies*, in which he wrote:

> Michael Heim is correct when he states that 'We love the way computers reduce complexity and ambiguity, capturing things in a digital network, clothing them in beaming colors, and girding them with precise geometrical structures. . . . We are enamored of the possibility of controlling all human knowledge. . . . We feel augmented and empowered . . . This is Eros.' But Heim is incorrect in his evaluation of this drive to capture and control. One might respond that this, if anything, is Thanatos. The desire for rational calculated control of a predictable total environment in digital form truly has more to do with the death drive than with the love of life.[3]

I agree with Mr. Brahm that computer simulations belong as much to the death wish (Thanatos) as to Eros. Ancient Greek mythology considered Eros and Thanatos to be twins. Passion and morbidity, Eros and Thanatos deeply intertwine. When Eros draws us to marry someone outside ourselves, someone powerfully attractive, we give up more and more of ourselves, even to the point of extinction and self-immolation. This is true of our relationship to computers. We see something of ourselves in computers. We embrace the perfection that satisfies one side of our rational nature. What I called "the paradoxical terrain of cyberspace" (in *Metaphysics*) is an infoscape containing ecstatic heights as well as abysmal fissures. *The Metaphysics of Virtual Reality* cites a lover in William Gibson's novel who possesses all the computerized information about his beloved, but for him the mystery of the being of his beloved has vanished. The beloved has become dead numbers, and ceased to be living mystery, because she has been digitized. If we want to survive well, we must understand this dual nature of our passion. We have to live with it. We must balance the idealist's enthusiasm for computerized life with the need to ground ourselves more deeply in the felt earth affirmed by the realist as our primary reality. This uneasy balance I call "virtual realism."

Virtual realism walks a tight rope. The delicate balancing act sways between the idealism of unstoppable Progress and the Luddite resistance to virtual life. The Luddite falls out of sync with the powerful human energies promoting rationality for three centuries and now blossoming into the next century. The Idealist falls for the progress of tools without content, of productivity without satisfaction, of ethereal connections without corporeal discipline. Both inclinations—naïve realism or futurist idealism—belong to the current of our time. This long thin rope stretches across the chasm of change and permits no return. Indifferent standstill is even more dangerous. The challenge is not to end the oscillation between idealism and realism but to find the path that goes through them. It is not a synthesis in the Hegelian sense of a result achieved through logic. Rather, virtual realism is an existential process of criticism, practice, and conscious communication.

What is the path of virtual realism? Virtual realism parts with realism pure and simple. Realism often means lowered expectations. "Being realistic" often implies reducing or compromising ideals. Historically, in fact, realism often follows periods of high idealism. The pendulum swings back because it had swung so high in the first place. No movement of history begins, however, without an initial affirmation, without a first postulate affirming that it has cleared the mist and found reality. Realism begins as a sober criticism of overblown, highflown ideals. Yet at the core of realism is an affirmation of what is real, reliable, functional. Today we must be realistic about virtual reality, untiringly suspicious of the airy idealism and commercialism surrounding it, and we must keep an eye on the weeds of fiction and fantasy that threaten to stifle the blossom. At the same time, we have to affirm those entities that VR presents as our culture begins to inhabit cyberspace. Virtual entities are indeed real, functional, and even central to life in coming eras. Part of work and leisure life will transpire in virtual environments. So it is important to find a balance that swings neither to the idealistic blue sky where primary reality disappears, nor to the mundane indifference that sees in VR just another tool, something that can be picked up or put down at will. The balancing act requires a view of life as a mixed bag, as a series of tradeoffs that we must first discern and then evaluate. Balancing means walking a pragmatic path of involvement and critical perception.

In *Electric Language* (1987), I developed a theory of cultural tradeoffs as they happen during ontological shifts. There I described in detail the tradeoffs between the computerized and the traditional way of doing things. In *Electric Language*, this meant the specific tradeoffs between electronic and printed texts. The method used was phenomenology, a way of describing the different ways in which we read and write, specifically to contrast reading and writing with computers and with traditional books. Such descriptions highlight the psychic frameworks of two very different ways of reading and writing —not from the viewpoint of the economic, social, and legal products of the written word. The tradeoffs described in *Electric Language* belong to what I called "the ontological shift." The ontological shift was not a reference to the supposed shift from "managing atoms to managing bits." Our practical life using symbols never did move in the element of atoms, for atoms are scientific abstractions. The abstractions of science drawn from the atomic level have had an enormous impact on history, but that impact came not from a change at the core of culture but from the pressure that bore down on the surface of politics, warfare, and the production of energy. Culture only slowly took into account the atomic age. Atoms are abstractions, just as bits and bytes are abstractions. But while bits and bytes abstract from a computational process, they touch information, and information reaches to the core of culture.

The ontological shift described in *Electric Language* occurs in what I called "the tectonic plates of culture," the unnoticed cultural element that supports—at different times in different ways—the symbols of language. No longer papyrus or paper, the new element is digital information. The element belongs to the psychic framework of life, not to the abstractions of physics or the sciences. The symbol element is where much of practical culture transpires. It is where we store our memory, where we record our history, and where the sacred things are preserved. Most important to virtual realism is the sense of history behind the ontological shift. We need the large perspective on cultural change and the way symbolic elements mutate in history. The big picture is crucial for virtual realism, for only from that broad perspective can we envision the tradeoffs that occur in historical drift. This is not the place to go further into these notions. An interested reader can find in the first three chapters of *Electric Language* one approach to that larger history with its ontological shifts.

An important component of virtual realism is what I call "technalysis." Technalysis — as the term suggests — is the analysis of technologies, and the analysis proceeds from a critical but practical standpoint. It is a critical strategy for describing specific technologies, a style of thinking appropriate for walking the fissures of a culture in transition. Whether right or wrong in its conclusions, each attempt at technalysis brings to language the human encounter with specific technologies. Detailed analysis of specific technologies has significant advantages over the wholesale rejection of technology found in writers from Ellul and Baudrillard to the Unabomber. The wholesale suspicion of technology as a monstrous Leviathan supposes that we can extricate ourselves sufficiently from automobiles, telephones, and computers in order to arrive at a negative assessment and eventual disengagement. This suspicion directs its gaze at a monster whose features must remain vague and remote. Fear of the giant technology monster blinds the critic from seeing detail in daily life as we install technologies and as we install ourselves into technological environments. Blind to details, such critics close off the possibility that their analysis might contribute something of value to the concrete planning of future systems. Instead, they maintain a posture of hostility — a posture which spends considerable effort for no constructive dividend. The advantage of technalysis — the detailed phenomenology of specific technologies — resides in its working alongside "human factors" engineering, which, however remote from its participants, places the human being at the center of technology.

Virtual realism meets destiny without being blind to the losses of progress. It strives to enrich the unfolding future from a personal standpoint by referring to moments when we have been at our best. As we look beyond alphabetic writing, increasingly away from symbolic processes and towards virtualized processes, our path must be one of virtual realism. Some signposts along this path are listed below.

- **Be clear about what virtual reality is in the strong sense** (see "VR 101") and virtual realities in the loose, popular sense. The strong meaning implies full sensory immersion—not keyboards and monitors. The keyboard and the monitor are relics of typewriters and television sets. The screen, the keyboard, the joystick, and the trackball are a far cry from immersive technologies. We associate them with "virtuality" only in the weakest popular sense. By maintaining a stronger meaning in our vocabulary, we permit a dialogue with information systems engineers who are developing full-sensory systems. Sloppy semantics leads to false panic, confusion, and a breakdown of communication between the engineering and the non-engineering communities. At the same time, careful criticism can carry the energies of both extremes through a middle path. If a middle way does emerge, then we will have earned the new word "technalysis," a word that means the informed public criticism of technologies before they become the invisible furniture of daily life.

- Acknowledge the new layer of reality and the complex relationship with computers it brings about. **Avoid glib exaggerations such as "Now we're cyborgs," or "Everything's virtual reality."** Look to the reality shift as an increased power to envision ourselves inhabiting artificial worlds, but do not obscure the gap between primary and virtual realities. Primary reality never consisted of atoms but always included the felt awareness of ourselves as bodily energies.

- **Refuse to fear an all-pervasive technology monster.** Computers can indeed become control instruments to oppress human beings, but it is up to us to adapt them critically to our human world. Adapting information systems to enhance planetary life is InfoEcology. InfoEcology softens the cyberspace backlash by clarifying transitional techniques where virtual relates to real worlds.

- We no longer need to believe we are re-presenting the real world of nature. **Virtual worlds do not re-present the primary world.** They are not realistic in the sense of photo-realism. Each virtual world is a functional whole that can parallel, not re-present or absorb the primary world we inhabit. Denouncing artificial worlds as distractions from the real world is just as off-balance as wanting to dissolve the primary world into cyberspace.

- Realism in virtuality refers not to photo-realistic illusions or representations. Reality also means a pragmatic functioning in which work and play fashion new kinds of entities. **VR transubstantiates but does not imitate life.** Art and artistic design show us how to experiment with novel entities and with constructed worlds. VR technology is about entering worlds and environments, and worlds arise from humans adapting things through pragmatic functioning.

- Current hardware and software permit us to glimpse the virtual world, but we stand only at the doorstep of virtual reality. We should therefore **bracket the current attacks on "virtual life" and "virtual communities."** Much contemporary vocabulary anticipates a technology whose true impact remains unclear. The shared language can knit a feedback loop between engineers and lay persons as long as the words are guided by clear perceptions. We must be wary of the language used to sell technology and not confuse it with the vocabulary of critical feedback.

- By 2015, virtual reality will deliver functional realities where the hardware and software recede into the background and the tasks of virtual life become foreground. Until then, VR remains a "technology" in the sense of something that doesn't quite work yet, that remains unassimilated and unready for prime time. **Now is the time for constructive criticism, while the electronic layer of reality remains largely in prototype on the drawing boards.**

- **Realism in VR results from pragmatic habitation, livability, and dwelling,** much more than from scientific calculation. The social transition to cyberspace is, therefore, as important as the engineering research. A virtual world can achieve a functional isomorphism with a primary world—it does not have to re-present the primary but only to foster a similar livability.

- We need to watch closely how cyberspace intersects geo-physical space. InfoEcology—the study of how information systems can be fitted to enhance of life—becomes a top priority. Observe closely those **spots where high-end VR touches earth-centered applications** (see the chapter "InfoEcology" for one example).

- It's not realistic to say, "Okay, we're cyborgs and we can remake ourselves any way we want; we can change identities, genders, etc." Where idealism overreaches, pragmatism can intervene and help. VR can help us **look closely at the bio-psychic imbalances created by computer technology.** With its simulations and varied input/output devices, VR can help us critically examine the stress that pervades our culture. Virtual reality can integrate the individual whose neuro-physiology has been torn apart by violence, anxiety, and incessant shock. Neither idealistic nor realistic, virtual realism points to a path of pragmatic healing.

These are the ten steps through the narrow gate of Virtual Realism. They are signposts that deliberately emphasize clarity about names and concepts. The right name illuminates and enlightens, as we learn from *Genesis*. Getting the right name goes beyond utility. It touches ethics and civic life, as Confucius taught in the ancient "rectification of names." The right words help us harmonize with things. If language terrifies one part of the populace and over-stimulates another, then we have not found the right words. If our language sinks below the clear understanding of things, then we lose the bonds that bring us to speak the same language. Mutual silence is the seed of hatred and the father of violence. Fiction and fantasy can foster communication about technology, but it can also reduce communication. Beware of fictional language that obscures rather than facilitates the discussion of technology.

Measure your understanding of these ten signposts of Virtual Realism by testing yourself against Bill Gates. The chairman of Microsoft appeared in an interview conducted by David Frost which first aired on public broadcasting in November, 1995. Frost cited a passage from *The Metaphysics of Virtual Reality* where I argued that the extended use of VR is likely to alter our sense of reality. Gates responded by pointing out that the most virtual of activities is the activity of reading a book or other printed material. If reading doesn't make the average person withdraw from the world and other people, Gates argued, then the new media won't either. Stop for a moment and consider Gates's response. Measure it against the ten signposts above. Ask yourself what will most likely happen if software designers and their managers do not understand the semantic steps leading from VR 101 through the narrow gate of Virtual Realism. What does this understanding bode for the culture that produced the Unabomber?

Because the new reality layer brings an ontological shift, we have been thrown, every one of us, into the roles of reality theorists and metaphysicians. To help us find balanced words, we could do worse than listen to the great French critic, Joseph Joubert (1754–1824), who wrote:

> The true science of metaphysics consists not in rendering abstract that which is sensible, but in rendering sensible that which is abstract; apparent that which is hidden; imaginable, if so it may be, that which is only intelligible; and intelligible, finally, that which an ordinary attention fails to seize.[4]

3

The Art of Virtual Reality

The snow hits your windshield without mercy. The car's headlights reveal nothing about the highway. You can only guess where the lanes are, where the shoulder begins, where the exit ramps might be. The blizzard has so iced the road that you crawl along at five miles an hour. Other travelers sit stranded in their cars off the road, lights dimming in the dark.

Hours later, you flop exhausted on the bed. Tension tightens your shoulders and forehead. You close your eyes. On the back of your eyelids, everything appears again in startling detail: the swirling snowflakes, the headlights, the windshield wipers fighting the moisture—all in slow motion this very minute.

> *Modern art objects had aesthetic appeal when the viewer could stand apart from them to appreciate their sensory richness, their expressive emotion, or their provocative attitude. Today, detached contemplation still holds antique charm, as the contemporary scene presents quite different circumstances.*

Flashbacks, a kind of waking nightmare, often belong to your first experiences with virtual reality. Subtract the terror and sore muscles and you get an idea of how I felt after two and a half hours in the exhibit *Dancing as the Virtual Dervish* (Banff, Alberta). Even the next day, my optical nerves held the imprint of the brightly colored

transhuman structures. I could summon them with the slightest
effort—or see them sometimes in unexpected flashes of cyberspace.

> *Art is coming to terms with interactivity, immersion,*
> *and information intensity. Aesthetics—the delighted*
> *play of the senses—cannot preserve its traditional*
> *detachment. The modern museum with its bright*
> *spaces and airy lighting is giving way to darkened*
> *rooms glowing with computer screens and hands-on*
> *buttons.*

For hours, you feel a touch of perceptual nausea, a forewarning of
the relativity sickness called AWS (Alternate World Syndrome) in my
book *The Metaphysics of Virtual Reality*. Everything seems brighter,
even slightly illusory. Reality afterwards seems hidden underneath a
thin film of appearance. Your perceptions seem to float over a darker,
unknowable truth. The world vibrates with the finest of tensions, as if
something big were imminent, as if you were about to break through
the film of illusion.

> *The word "art" became controversial when craft and*
> *workmanship donned blue jeans to stand in the mod-*
> *ern factory's assembly lines. Left to its own, art bred*
> *individualists with flare, abstract pattern makers, and*
> *aesthetics. Now, designers are working in teams again,*
> *with at least one member programming the computers.*

AWS is an acute form of body amnesia which can become chronic
AWD (Alternate World Disorder). Frequent virtuality can lead to rup-
tures of the kinesthetic from the visual senses of self-identity, a complaint
we already know from simulator sickness and from high-stress, techno-
centered lifestyles. Carpal Tunnel Syndrome is just the tip of this particular iceberg. AWS mixes images and expectations from an alternate
world so as to distort our perceptions of the current world, making us
prone to errors in mismatched contexts. The virtual world obtrudes
upon our activities in the primary world, and vice versa. The responses
ingrained in the one world step out of sync with the other. AWS shows
the human being merging, yet still out of phase, with the machine.

> *"Art and Virtual Environments" was a 3-year research*
> *project at the Banff Center for the Arts, in Alberta,*
> *Canada, which concluded with a conference May*
> *22–24, 1994. Commissioned to write about the virtual*
> *worlds at Banff, I spent six hours in head-mounted dis-*
> *plays, and my comments focused primarily on two art*
> *works: the* **Virtual Dervish** *by Marcos Novak, and*
> **PlaceHolder** *by Brenda Laurel and Rachel Strickland.*

The lag between worlds is not the same as the lag between the
head-mounted displays (HMD) and the user's eye movement. The
HMD lag comes from a timing defect which computer hardware
development will eventually remedy. The AWS lag occurs between
the virtual body and the biological body. The lag comes not from
asynchronous interruptions within the virtual experience but from the
sequential switching between worlds. A conflict of attention, not
unlike jet lag, arises between the cyberbody and the biobody. A world,
in the deepest sense, is a holistic context of involvement based on the
focal attention of the world's inhabitants. We feel a switch between
worlds when we visit a foreign country, though the foreign world is
cultural, not virtual. When a user identifies with a world, it then
becomes an existential reality—even if only a virtual reality.

AWS occurs when the virtual world later obtrudes on the user's
experience of the actual world, or vice versa. AWS is simulator sickness
writ large. Researchers who compare VR with military simulators
remain pessimistic about the widespread use of VR. Many pilots cannot
use simulators, and those who do train in simulators are grounded for
days afterwards. Simulator experience counts toward upgrading a pilot's
license to more powerful aircraft, but the hazards of simulator sickness
exclude a large portion of pilots from upgrading their licenses in this
way. Drawing on their studies of simulators, many military researchers
believe that the population at large cannot regularly spend hours in virtual environments without suffering serious side effects.

AWS is technology sickness, a lag between the natural and artificial
environments. The lag exposes an ontological rift where the felt world
swings out of kilter. Experienced users become accustomed to hopping

over the rift. Dr. Stephen Ellis, a scientist at NASA/Ames and at the University of California- Berkeley School of Optics, says that his work in VR often has him unconsciously gesturing in the primary world in ways that function in the virtual world. He points a finger half expecting to fly (as his cyberbody does under the conventions of the virtual world). His biobody needs to re-calibrate to the primary world.

AWS is not an avoidable industrial hazard like radiation overexposure but comes rather from the immersion intrinsic to virtual world systems. Immersion is the key feature of VR systems. Virtual reality in general immerses the user in the entities and events of the computer-generated world, and the immersion retrains the user's autonomic nervous system. The human learns to respond smoothly to the virtual environment, but the frequent re-adaptation to the technology affects the psyche as the virtual world injects its hallucinatory afterimages into the primary world.

The move from one world to another has familiar precedents. Exiting a movie theater resembles somewhat the exit from a virtual world. After hours immersed in screen adventures, you emerge from the dark to blinding bright daylight. The sensory shock brings with it a residual emotional tone aroused by the film. Everyday familiar objects, a car in the parking lot or someone standing at the theater doorway, now take on a paranormal feeling, depending on whether the movie was a tearful romance or a horror flick. Similarly, someone leaving a VR system needs time to adjust. The user invariably freezes for a minute to take in the surroundings. Typical gestures are to pat the body and affirm the return to primary presence. Because VR reaches more deeply than film into the participant's sensory sockets, the landing back in the primary world takes that much longer than the return from movies. Re-orientation takes time until the participant can walk away safely, and it takes even longer before everyday feeling tone returns. The virtual body lingers in the afterimages because the virtual world had been the background for its previous scene of first-person action, not merely the voyeuristic object of fantasy. The newly formed neural pathways need to be configured while the primary body resumes its involvement in the actual, non-virtual world.

> *The comparison of VR with drug-induced hallucinations*
> *can be misleading. Computer interaction requires the*
> *utmost presence of mind to react quickly and build the*
> *imaginative links that make virtual worlds function. The*
> *random effects of drugs can side-track the software that*
> *engages a person in a virtual world.*

But AWS has its bright side. The only reason we have to worry about AWS or AWD is because of the awesome imprinting power of VR. The virtual environment pulls its users with a power unlike that of any other medium—unless we include the religious rituals and sacred dramas that once provided the context for art works. The fascination of VR recalls the linguistic root of the word "fascination," which comes from the Latin (*fascinare*) and refers to someone's gaze being drawn repeatedly toward the dancing flames of a fire. From the viewpoint of human evolution, VR stands on a footing with the invention of fire. But to induce fascination requires more than the technology of helmets or projection rooms. It also requires a subtle blending of content with the techniques we are just discovering. VR immersion must immerse the psyche as well as the senses if it is to fascinate.

A spectacle is a one-shot deal that everybody wants to see—at least once. Entertainment, on the other hand, calls for repetition, but repetition becomes cloying if it does not nourish. But to fascinate for the long haul, that is the task of art. The art of virtual reality holds the promise of a fascination akin to the flickering shapes projected on the cave walls of the Pleistocene Era 500,000 years ago.

The *Virtual Dervish* at Banff makes a very special contribution to the art of virtual reality. It uses some unique strategies to enhance the sense of immersion. One of these strategies constitutes an important discovery about the nature of virtual environments, a principle that can be applied to any virtual environment. I call it the drift factor or the disorientation principle. Marcos Novak has introduced a systematic relativity into the *Dervish*. He designed the *Dervish* in such a way that the user's interaction with the virtual entities remains relative to random drift.

An example of drift works in this manner: The user signals with the glove to take up a certain position toward the structures of the virtual world, and no sooner has the user established a certain position, than the user and the virtual structures invisibly shift, causing a continuous random drift. The drift remains subliminal and goes largely unnoticed by the user on a conscious level. Once someone points out the drift, however, it becomes obvious. Until then, the user simply feels an unnamed sense of being lost. The user must continually change positions in order to maintain a stable relationship to the structures of cyberspace. As long as the drift goes unnoticed, the user feels the need to get grounded, to constantly re-adjust. The *Dervish* makes you tread water, which means you must stay alert moment to moment. Being lost deepens the sense of immersion, and the sense of continual re-orientation heightens the engagement with the structures in the virtual world.

The drift principle becomes clearer when we look at the origin of the term "dervish." In Islam, a dervish or *darwish* is a member of a religious order of mendicants whose mystical practices include rituals of singing and dancing. These mystics spin themselves in circles (hence the cliché "whirling dervishes") to attain an ecstatic pitch of mental and physical energy. The Mevlana Dervishes in Konya, Turkey, for instance, dance to mirror a cosmic order. The dance leader, wearing a black gown and white turban, stands in the middle of the group. The other dancers, wearing white gowns and dark turbans, spin individually while moving forward along a curved trajectory with the dance leader at the center of the group. This pattern embodies, according to the founder Jelladin Rumi, the planets spinning on their own axes while rotating around the sun. The winding dance mirrors the cosmic spiral that brings the universe into being. When the body becomes the universe, the movements harmonize not only the universe, but the inner self of the dancer. The inward side of the centrifugal dance places the human heart at the center.

> *VR makes going to an art exhibit a completely immersive experience, one that involves more than just looking at art objects. Art here penetrates surface perceptions and throws the mind into a mood akin to*

philosophy—without, however, relying on concepts or explanations. The relativity factor built into VR means that you practice, on a subconscious level, the search for balance. You continually re-discover your center, your balance point, and you constantly adjust your orientation from that center. No keyboard relics of typewriters or television-like monitors in VR! The hunchback computer user glued to a monitor gives way to the radiant body spiraling between heaven and earth. If you hold to the center while immersed in technical systems, you unconsciously affirm the middle way of virtual realism.

Human beings come into their own when they face the basic insecurity of human existence. Philosophers have long noticed this: Plato shows us a Socrates who is always questioning, and Ortega y Gasset insists that we are most human when we feel our lives are shipwrecked. Existing as a human being comes with a built-in sense of disorientation, because humans transcend the sureness of the instincts that guide the animals. The Taoist sage Lao Tzu says that life is a great river that is constantly new. It was running long before we were born, and its exact configuration—the particular currents, the way it flows around rocks, the shape of its banks—is unique at any given moment. The great river of Tao is always flowing, and we can swim in it again and again, touch it, explore it, and drink it anew, but we cannot freeze or hold it. Instead, we must remain ever alert to its movements. The river changes, and we must become wanderers meandering along its banks. As we wander, we must keep our balance at every step of the way. We must center ourselves, because we can find no center outside ourselves. Our lostness forces us to look to the kingdom within, the still center of the cosmos that remains quiet during the confusion of outer storms. The *Virtual Dervish*, like Lao Tzu, Socrates, and y Gasset, looks to the wanderer and pilgrim as a model for life.

The fact that humans transcend instinct is both bane and boon. *Dancing As the Virtual Dervish* heightens our attention and shows VR to be a more powerful tool for engaging and transfixing perception than previous tools. Flight simulators do not engage the senses so aggressively. Drug-induced hallucination enslaves us to perceptions without preserving our basic lostness. One important difference, however, is that the high-pitched awareness in the *Virtual Dervish* comes through technology, not through self-disciplined movements. Technological trance induction does not equate to meditative practice. Meditation enhances the awareness of the subtle shifts in the river of life, and silent meditation allows for the higher, upper body system to re-integrate with the lower nervous systems. Meditation can momentarily neutralize the pull of de-centering evolution which extends and stresses the upper-body nervous system. As it stands today, technology rarely acknowledges the fragile web of energies in the internal human body. Technology works more like human strip-mining than like yoga practice. It pulls the upper-body ever further into the tunnel of technology and offers nothing to restore the resulting imbalance. This difference between traditional meditative healing and technological extension becomes important when we see *Virtual Dervish* in the context of the more general imbalance in the art of virtual reality (which I save for my conclusion).

Dancing with the *Virtual Dervish* snaps us into a different state of attention, and it does so not only because of the intrinsic disorientation built into the user's relationship to the structures in the virtual world. The things the dervish sees in cyberspace also enhance the sense of immersion. The virtual objects themselves, those cyberspace structures I am about to describe, create the discrepancy between virtual and primary realities. When you dance with the dervishes, you encounter structures that refuse to fit the usual categories of human experience.

Level Zero

You step through snowflakes under a starry sky as you approach the Jeanne & Peter Lougheed Building at the Banff Center. It is midnight and you descend one red stairwell after another, down to Level Zero. All is quiet here except for the hum of the smart heating system that warms the buildings of the artists colony this cold March night. You walk past the aluminum and green-colored metal vents on the walls and ceilings as you approach the helmet dangling from the ceiling like a sword of Damocles. The sword, you hope, will turn into the Buddha sword that cuts away the veil of illusion to reveal the truth of VR. You throw the switch to start the Silicon Graphics Onyx Computer running the RealityEngine2 graphics system, the MIDI system, and the Polhemus tracking transmitters. You clip the orientation tracker to your belt and slide under the helmet.

Suddenly, you have landed in someone else's dream. Or is it your own? The dream world strikes you as familiar but startlingly novel. Here is a different world, one suggested more by the revved-up prose style of William Gibson than by any two-dimensional videos. Here is Gibson's cyberspace, the "liquid architecture" described in the writing of Marcos Novak. More like music than solid structures, the gigantic contrapuntal shapes recall the Kyrie of Anton Bruckner's Second Mass: Himalayan solitudes, the mountainous plateaus of Tibet, software landscapes of the spirit, algorithmic metaphors for silent awe in the face of the unattainable, lofty and splendid in their icy sublimity. The structures assault and then elude you, as you float in and out of their vastness. At first, you hardly notice how you are being trained to continually re-adjust your position, but later you realize that your orientation drifts as you take in the surrounding landscape. Even when you are lost and need once again to grasp one of the giant navigation bars that offer some guidance through cyberspace, you still have to keep moving simply to grasp the navigator. You are living in the ever-changing relativity where nothing stays permanently in place. Like the Heraclitean stream, nothing here stays the same —not even you in your position of looking at the changing stream.

Vast, blue-white, alluring structures float in black outer space. You approach the blue-and-white lattices of one of the structures and you climb inside. Now you are totally encompassed by a vast structure, half warehouse, half mountain. You survey the inner distances in an effort to grasp "where" you are, and you tingle with what Immanuel Kant called "the mathematical sublime," the feeling of the sublime that arises when the human senses cannot synthesize the rich information that surrounds and invites them, as in Kant's example: the starry sky. The dimensions of the blue-white structure elude you with their warping curves, and as you try to grasp where you are, your senses are at a loss to hold together all the parts of the building in a single shape.

You climb and explore the convolutions of the lattice structure. Occasionally, you catch sight of a flock of flying cubes, or of giant colored pyramids spinning by and blinking with the eye of Horus. The Eye of Horus appeared originally in ancient Egyptian magic and more recently on the U.S. dollar bill, in the movie Handmaid's Tale, and in the adventures of modern magicians like Aleister Crowley, the "Magician of the Golden Dawn." Crowley conducted a series of initiatory experiments in which he conjured "Aethyrs" or "Aires" or "Spirits." In a solitary meadow, Crowley would hold up a wooden cross decorated with a large golden topaz. The stone served to concentrate his vision. Relaxing his physical body through deep breathing, Crowley projected in his imagination an inner surrogate self, an "astral self," that he allowed to journey through imaginary landscapes. In his vision, Crowley perceived the magical symbol of the eye in the triangle, which is the eye of Horus.

> *Magicians have long mapped the universe onto the imagination. The dark rotunda of the Paleolithic caves at Lascaux show images of a wounded animal and a prostrate shaman. The Pre-Socratic Anaximander fashioned the first globe and map of the universe. Giordano Bruno (burned at the stake in 1600 A.D.) pioneered Renaissance science by mapping the Copernican cosmos to complex visual models. Today, in the cavernous arcades of shopping malls, young pilgrims manipulate electronic images of themselves in the guises of Immortal Combatants and Lords of the Universe.*

You approach one of the pyramids and try to climb it, and you find yourself penetrating through it and suddenly emerging in another universe. Here you approach a huge structure, this time a pink-white cube. Softer lines extend from the cube. Inside the cube, you find oddly shaped, gnarled objects. They are mottled red and blue against a dark background. After several minutes climbing the objects, you discover they are somehow connected. More exploration and you recognize what you think is a gigantic rib cage, and perhaps it is attached to a spine. Only later do you realize you have been mounting an enormous skeleton. You reach the spine and find a heart organ. Then, suddenly, pyramids are floating by, and you see one bearing a photo-like image of a male dancer captured in a pose of movement. Frequently in your exploration, you run up against other pyramids, each with the dancer in a different pose, so life-like, you wonder whether the dancer might not come alive as animation.

> *In one variant of the* **Virtual Dervish,** *Diane Gromala and Yacov Sharir extend the cyberspace patterns into physical performance space. The performance puts the HMD user on stage with dancers who move to wall projections of what appears moment-by-moment in the helmet. The dancers interact with the displayed scenes and, in one variation, affect what the HMD user sees in the helmet.In some live performances, Yacov Sharir displays in his own dancing body the energetic patterns received in the head-mounted display. In this way, the cyberspace skeleton reincarnates itself in the living Tai Chi dance of the primary bodies.*

Each time you see the flock of eye pyramids pass by, you have an opportunity to enter one of them and jump into another universe. Finally, hours later, you find your jump has taken you back to the vast blue-white lattice that first greeted you on your entrance into this dream. You want to know where this lattice exists, what relation it has to other places in the blackness of space. Like an astronaut, you decide you must cut loose and risk all if you are to know where you have been all this time. You must travel to the edge of this universe.

You point and fly slowly toward the edge of the lattice. Then you leave the walls of the structure. Time passes slowly as you fly through the different dimensions of the structure. You are an ant on the side of a cargo freighter. You feel how enormous the structures are. Once you shove off the final wall, you point away from it, further out, out, . . .

where? Time passes and passes. You need to know what these structures look like, from a distance, from a place where they do not dwarf or contain you. Still, you do not turn around, not yet. You wait until you can catch them all in a single view. Finally, you feel yourself at the edge of the black universe, or at least as far as time will allow you to go. Slowly, you turn around. For the first time you see them from a distance—and you are alarmed!

The blue structure appears forbidding and alien, like a semiorganic beast. It looks oddly inhuman, lacking all the warmth you had come to feel for it, all the intimacy you felt as you crawled over its lattices one after another along its warm blue hue, inspecting and even fondling its strong lines. Now you see it for the first time in distant perspective and you feel the transhuman nature of your experience. And there too is the white ethereal cube, the center of this universe, and the surrounding heavenly pinkish white cotton now looks cold and geometrical in space.

Transhuman Structures

What is a transhuman structure? It is one designed by human beings, by software engineers, but because of its mathematical nature, and because of its implementation in computer-generated worlds, a transhuman structure stretches its human users beyond their current humanness, beyond what humans today take a self to be. Merging with computerized entities requires an extension of our humanity—certainly beyond current humanity. The demand for such an extension is nothing new, though each demand in our evolution appears novel in its specific requirements. Since the discovery of fire, the human race has allowed artists to brandish illuminated images before the species, images that, when visualized, effect biochemical changes in the human race. As we imagine, so we become.

The traditional guides to the use of images are the alchemical magician, the shaman, the archetypal psychologist. All these encourage us to give ourselves over to internal images. These images work upon the self which then undergoes an internal, imaginary journey through the images. The alchemical tradition does not encourage us

See Figures 3.1 and 3.2

to "interpret" the images but wants us to allow the images to work us over and to influence us as we wander through them. Our imaginal self should encounter the images on their own terms. To interpret the images—whether they accompany ritual drumming, trances, or dreams—discharges their power by subjecting them to rational understanding. The dream wanderer understands the images by direct experiential contact—not through thinking about them, but by interacting with them. When the active imagination stirs up those scenes that take in more than the subjective experience of the individual, then psychologists like Ira Progoff call them "transpersonal images" because they extend beyond the personal and touch what is universal and mythic.

> *They later tell you, reluctantly, the name of the struc-*
> *ture you viewed from the edge of the universe—*
> *"Mazechamber." You hold onto the name to block*
> *out the irrational awe of the experience. The name*
> *domesticates the experience by clothing the maze with*
> *architectural form. You are told that the center of the*
> *Mazechamber is the hovering heart you saw sur-*
> *rounded by interactive pyramids. The heart acts as a*
> *portal to other worlds. To stay within the heart is to*
> *stand within—and withstand—the vertigo of the*
> *Mazechamber.*

The transhuman structures of cyberspace are virtual images that arise neither from the unconscious, nor the mythic. Transhuman structures are mysterious to us because we usually restrict our experience to what we have already assimilated. As humanists and individualists, we flatter ourselves to think that art is an expression of personal feelings and sentiments, of preferences and free choices, unfettered by the sciences of mathematics and cosmology. Prior art forms, such as medieval and Asian art, were not like ours, humanized and freely expressive. Nor did they appeal to familiar archetypes. The transhuman shatters the comfort of our domesticated finite concepts. The transhuman structures of cyberspace combine the assumptions of our computerized culture with the artistic skills of "spacemakers," (Randy

Walser) or shapers of "liquid architecture" (Marcos Novak). Exemplary of the transhuman, the images in the *Virtual Dervish* do not fit into the personal or social ego but challenge human identity.

Certain installations smooth the edges of the transhuman, without, however, removing it completely. Perry Hoberman's *Bar Code Hotel* at Banff, for instance, shortens the divide between humans and virtual entities by putting the tools for interaction within a shared human workspace. The simplicity of walking around, choosing a labeled bar code, and grabbing a dangling bar code reader creates fun in a multiuser environment. Because the users move in the same physical space and share the same tools, each user can more quickly assimilate and humanize the encounter with strange virtual entities which otherwise might startle a solitary user in a head-mounted-display environment. People quickly learn to scan the bar codes to manipulate the virtual entities. The neighboring workspaces allow the users to learn by joint experiments. In a relatively short time, the newcomer feels comfortable working the entities and feels free to watch others interacting in the virtual environment. The software that produces the environment receives the bar code data from the users' input over a network link and uses the codes to determine the behavior of the hotel environment and the "characters" within it. The software then produces a pair of video images (one for each eye) that are fed to a pair of projectors. Each image is projected through a set of polarising filters that work with the polarised lenses in the viewer's glasses to produce a stereoscopic 3-D image. Though not difficult to engage, *Bar Code Hotel* presents users with sufficiently complex patterns—including patterns of autonomous growth and change in the entities—to unsettle the user's ego confidence.

Consider also the *Topological Slide* by Michael Scroggins and Stewart Dickson. You are standing on a swivel platform and through the helmet you see a stereo space. An enormous mathematical structure surrounds you, something like a complex tunnel or giant concrete culvert where young people might skateboard. As you shift your weight, rock your balance, and point, you sail down the vast slide that unfolds before you. The tunnel wraps around you to become sky, earth, and walls. Here you skate through transhuman structures, in complex disks like the ones Poincaré imagined. But your virtual feet can traverse mathematics and you can explore the structures as you would a new neighborhood. Sliding through topologies can undo our efforts to balance, and the structures we explore will remain just out of mental reach, much as the series of real numbers over 12 remains beyond the grasp of a single direct intuition.

The "rider" on the *Topological Slide* wears a head-mounted stereoscopic display that provides an interactive wide-angle view of a 3-D computer graphics environment generated in real time. The rider stands on a platform that responds to the rider's movements, and translates the leaning and weight shifting movements of the rider into navigational commands that control the graphics environment. At the same time, a Polhemus sensor tracks the rider's head movements and translates them into control signals that allow the rider to look around the 3-D space at will, as she rides the topology. The result is that the rider experiences a vivid sense of motion and the ability to surf a surreal ocean of geometry. The computer-generated 3-D environment consists of a model of a complex topological surface. Riders are "bound" to this surface, and they are free to traverse the surface by leaning in the direction they wish to move. The degree of lean in a given direction determines the sliding speed.

A topological surface selected for exploration is derived from a mathematical formula. Sample surfaces include an *enneper*, a disk folded in so that it intersects itself, and a *trinoid*. In addition to the visceral experience of surfing and sliding in a fantastic environment, *Topological Slide* provides an enlightening spatial or sculptural experience that conveys an intuitive understanding of topological concepts.

Current culture is understandably reluctant to encounter transhuman structures. By definition, culture absorbs, assimilates, and humanizes. Ron Kuivila's playful commentary in *Virtual Reality on $5 A Day* pokes fun at the quick and easy assimilation of transhuman structures. Kuivila shows us "helmet critters" swimming in schools like fish in a pop-culture feeding frenzy. The helmet piranhas fluctuate to a sound track laced with hip advertising lingo. The parody shows us the head-mounted display floating in the massive visor of popular culture where VR is itself "virtual" and not real.

Kuivila's exhibit reflexively discharges horizontal VR into vertical VR so as to reflexively discharge the encrusted barnacles of the all-too-easy assimilation of hyperbole and misplaced expectations.

The drive for instant assimilation overlooks the cultural archeology of VR. Not only does VR go back to precedents like Plato's Cave and Leibniz's logic of possible worlds, but it also builds on military flight simulators and art installations in the 1960s. The art of the 1960s experimented with many of the elements: interactive happenings, installations, computer graphics. All of these appeared prominently in early experiments that are still legendary. (See Douglas Davis' 1973 classic *Art and the Future: A History-Prophecy of the Collaboration Between Science, Technology and Art*.) But what divides the VR era so sharply from all previous art eras is the rendering of phenomena into data. The digital revolution means that we read the entire material world as data. Sights, sounds, sensations, all become grist for computation. The data storage and retrieval hardware give us a palette so powerful and different that it distinguishes our era. Never before have we been able to skateboard through mathematical constructs or climb over exo-cosmic topologies.

To highlight our historical destiny, Michael Naimark draws on the charm of the turn-of-the-century *See Banff in a Kinetoscope*. Crafting a wooden cabinet with an old-fashioned look, Naimark offers a series of 3-D scenes out of tourist Banff, all in flickering photography that suggests the look and feel of early 1900's photography. We hand-crank the large brass handle to make the pictures stutter into cinema, and we feel the same Schaulust our ancestors felt as they clicked their stereoscopes or tended their fires in the caves. Naimark gives us a time machine (in 3-D space) which all the more highlights our current digitized world that so removes us from our predecessors.

Whatever we may do with VR, we base ourselves on the digital premise. However overwhelming the data world becomes, it will continue to grow. Whatever we launch from here on out will have something transhuman about it. Evolution demands we stretch. The older forms of art and entertainment are riddled with holes that cry out for interaction and immersion. Print and television now invite us to go online. The older forms lack the power to synthesize the inchoate ocean of data. We see today in the World Wide Web of the Internet one of those "legacy systems" that not only incorporates previous software but also rapidly absorbs the culture of commercial advertising, museum tourism, and audio/video telephony. Soon enough, the Web will break the chains of Internet protocols and push into virtual environments, as we see already in the impulse of VRML (Virtual Reality Modeling Language) and other 3-D computing platforms.

The art of virtual reality shatters the modern aesthetics where we sit back as passive spectators or jaded listeners or bored manipulators. The transhuman aspects of VR can approximate something that shamans, mystics, magicians, and alchemists sought to communicate. They invoked the transhuman. At its best, virtual reality becomes vertical reality.

Vertical Reality

Up, slowly higher, upwards, you feel the bus tugging itself in rhythmic jerks from Calgary into the Canadian Rocky Mountains. The hum and movement of the bus sent you dozing, but now your eyes open to the mountain landscape rising around you. Thin white waterfalls streak the dark rocks in the late afternoon. You feel the air thinning and the growing excitement of the ascent.

> *A bus advertisement spells out the sense of place: "Our Reality Is Vertical: Make It Your Reality," runs the motto of the Canmore Climbing & Skiing Company. "Live on the Vertical Edge: You, Us, the Mountains. It's Real. It 's Fun. It's Living. We are the Company that understands how reality becomes vertical. Step-by-step. This could be you: free climb, boogie, dyno, float, layback, shred, flash, fresh tracks, centered, long drop, jam. Safe climbing includes: knots, ropes, relays, rappels, equipment. Safe skiing includes: transceivers, complete turns, avalanche forecasts. They both include: balance, visualization, concentration, efficient movement, respect of the mountain environment and of your own limits."*

If you need visualization skills to ski the mountains, this is the right place. The mountains are here, and so are the visualizations. The Banff Center left behind the horizontal hoopla of entertainment by supporting a series of art and virtual environment projects that would permanently extend the tools we have for seeing and hearing. These virtual environments aim high, even to the zenith. They measure the significance of virtual reality. Art in the mountains reclaims its primal task to transform the biochemistry of the species. As we visualize, so we become. The vision aims, the energy flows, the physical body follows.

In fostering creative impulses, the Banff Center stands aloof from the horizontal marketplace. It conditions us for the fluidity of any marketplace. In its grandeur, the Center stands like nature, like the national parks where we climb to strengthen our skills as survivors. The time is ripe for rare environments in a rarefied atmosphere. Up we go!

> *The ad copy sends you dozing again, and in your reverie you hear many voices that have marked this high place. You sense the imprints left by the many visitors and voices that over the years left their mark on the Banff Center for the Arts. A piano solo ripples the trees, and rocks recall string quartets. The vertical peaks lift to upper regions of space, where explorers provide feedback for their society. Like a shaman down from the mountain, addressing the tribe in oblique stories, the artist engages the imagination, keeps kneading the mind in free space, making it pliable, so that human identity can change and achieve balance in the twisting currents of the great river of life.*

"Each place on earth has a *genius loci*, a guardian spirit characteristic of that place," say Brenda Laurel and Rachel Strickland. "In *Place-Holder*, we try to capture that sense of an actual place." The experimenters of *PlaceHolder* bring us down to earth, to this earth, and not to some extraterrestrial cyberspace of the mind. Yet—and here comes the transhuman element—the experiment begins with an elusive, nonempirical "spirit of place." When the human being synthesizes the sensory elements of a situation, and when that synthesis includes the human pragmatics and functions of the situation, then we have a whole that is more than the sum of its empirical parts. Then we are dealing with spirit, with the spirit of a place. Michael Naimark, a collaborator on *PlaceHolder*, who made the camera-based 3-D computer models, speaks of the "sanctity of place." *PlaceHolder* aspires to the realm of spirit. We ascend once again, but we ascend in order to go down more deeply into the earth. "The way up," said Heraclitus, "and the way down are one and the same." This is vertical reality.

We need stretching both ways. The Virtual Dervish draws us upwards to an ethereal, magical cyberspace, while PlaceHolder brings us downwards to the earthly habitation we tend to ignore. Place-Holder helps us meditate on earthly existence, outfitting us with the virtual bodies and virtual senses of critters like Snake, Crow, Spider, and Fish. Both VR prototypes do more than induce an "altered state of consciousness"—as if consciousness could exist in a drunken vacuum. They take us somewhere important, somewhere that changes our outlook on the primary world.

PlaceHolder advances VR by targeting the look and feel of a situation. Instead of the usual cartoon-like polygons, PlaceHolder uses for its background landscape a mixture of animation and 3-D models based on documentary-style camera work. Parts of the surrounding world were photo- realistically blended into the electronic environment. The geography of *PlaceHolder* took inspiration from three action locations in the Banff National Park in Alberta, Canada—a cave, a waterfall in Johnston Canyon, and a formation of hoodoos overlooking the Bow River. These physical places were woven into the fabric of the virtual environment—not so much as re-presentations of the physical world but more to suggest a functional bond with the earth. The highly visual emphasis is balanced by the audio voice recordings planted in the scene or made on the spot by visitors to the virtual world. Sound recordings of waterfalls and wildlife add further definition to the scene. The digital basis of the worlds allows several geographically remote scenes to appear juxtaposed in the visitor's experience, further helping to concentrate the feeling of place

See Figures 3.5 and 3.6, and 3.7

as the Banff National Park. Tracking pods hedge the helmeted players where they move, and the hedge of real-world stones and grasses
buffers them nicely by blending actual nature props with the virtual
landscape.

PlaceHolder challenges the dominance of the visual sense by relying heavily on sound recordings to create the ambiance of places.
Waterfalls, wildlife calls, and the place markers of the animal critters
shape the feeling of place. The title *PlaceHolder* suggests another
important function of sound. Most electronic environments—unlike
human existential environments—remain indifferent to human presence. Fully human environments are reciprocal affairs, where a person leaves a mark—for good or ill—and where a person in turn
becomes forever marked by having lived in that environment. Electronic environments seem uninhabited until they can register someone's presence as a permanent feature. The sense of place, for
instance, on the World Wide Web quickly wears thin or is non-exis-
tent as users hop on hyperlinks from place to place. The web site is
less virtual place than drafty wind tunnel. To the strongly kinesthetic
aspect of virtual reality, *PlaceHolder* adds the recorded marker that
hangs in place as a momento to someone's presence. Like the pic-
tograms, graffiti, or trail signs left behind by travelers, these placehold-
ers remind future visitors with recorded animation and sound that a
creature was here before and felt some belonging to the spot. Unlike
the many artificial worlds being built today on the Internet—including elaborate cybertowns with "virtual" apartments—the *PlaceHolder*
reinforces the sense of place with ambient 3-D sound and kinesthetic
appropriation.

> *Hoodoos is the plural of hoodoo, which in West African*
> *means bad luck, and is a cognate to the word "voodoo"*
> *or "vodoun." In geology, "hoodoo" means a column of*
> *eccentrically shaped rocks. The word refers to places*
> *with spirit, spooky or otherwise, places with their own*
> *charm, spell, fetish, or curse. Such places stake out an*
> *interface between memory and physical location. With-*
> *out its own lingering spirit, a merely physical or elec-*
> *tronic location fails to engage the psyche.*

Like the *Dervish*, the *PlaceHolder* project reveals a hybrid variant of the two formerly separate streams of VR: the VPL-style head-mounted display and the Kruegeresque projection room as developed by the Electronic Visualization Laboratory's CAVE at the University of Illinois at Chicago and by Pattie Maes' ALIVE at the Massachusetts Institute of Technology. With *PlaceHolder*, a goddess and her attendants stand outside the helmeted players, initiating and coordinating the players. The goddess and her attendants help the participants navigate and assist by injecting a dramatic narrative. In the goddess's eyes, the players are helmeted bodies seen in the third-person while the players are at the same time interacting as fully immersed participants in a shared virtual world. The status of the goddess and her attendants was one of the more hotly controversial aspects of the experiment, as some immersed players wanted to reject all pressures felt from outside the interactive world(s). Again, the metaphysical question of how a single unifying perspective can cover multiple worlds while still preserving their individual freedom—a question first posed by Leibniz—came to the fore.

The full power of *PlaceHolder* appears only in its merger of inside/outside points-of-view. The person who puts on a helmet to enter *PlaceHolder* begins by choosing a "smart costume." The costume clothes the participant in one of four spirit animals whose iconography goes back to Paleolithic times. Spider, Snake, Fish, and Crow are not mere symbols. The participants change not only their outer appearance when wearing the critter costumes. They also assume certain first-person features of the primary animal world. In the virtual world, the creature costumes confer first-person perceptual properties appropriate to that animal, as well as the appropriate locomotion and vocal abilities. The person who assumes the character of Snake actually experiences the limits of reptile perspective and sees a visual world actually colored and reduced to that specific ocular system. At the same time, becoming Snake allows the person to enjoy the motility of that creature. Fish sees the world differently from Spider and Crow. By assuming first-person features of that animal world, the participant emulates the shaman's power to identify with the critter world. Traditionally, the shaman goes to the mountains, meditates and dreams, and leaves the body when guided by an animal spirit that empowers the shaman with superhuman vision.

In *PlaceHolder*, not only does the first-person perspective change. The human body likewise adapts to its modified sensory apparatus. If you stand outside the virtual world of *PlaceHolder*, you can watch helmeted people flap their arms like wings, caw with their voices like crows, and bend over to dive like birds from the sky. You see the human body fully engaged in a virtual world. They belong to a world that has the functional equivalent of animal flight, animal sight, animal movement. These bodies are not just going through the motions; they are responding to events in their perceptual fields. Such a harmony of internal and external is rarely achieved, and this particular experiment has ancestors in the Taoist health exercises known as the "Five Animals Movements," which appear on pottery painted centuries ago and which still claim thousands of practitioners.

But we should not kid ourselves. Our VR shamanism functions vertically as a technological variant of shamanism, not as traditional or even New Age shamanism. Shamanism arose in oral cultures around the world throughout history and continues to arise. The contexts and the goals of technological culture differ from traditional shamanism. It is not that technology smothers every cultural activity, but that every cultural activity gets modified by in its specific technological configuration. As instances of VR, both *PlaceHolder* and *Dancing with the Virtual Dervish* are triumphs of the union of art and technology. The limited nature of this triumph ran through another project at Banff created by a Native American who expressed the greatest reservations about bringing his cultural heritage within the purview of virtual reality. Lawrence Paul Yuxweluptun had many personal doubts before finishing his art work for the virtual environments projects. In the end, he displayed his work not in the wires and lenses of the head-mounted displays or in the projection room. Instead, he created a small wooden scope built into a wall where the viewer had to sit on a wooden stool and put forehead to viewer and earphones to ears in order to enter the virtual world. No head trackers followed the viewer's gaze. Lawrence Paul takes us into a virtual Indian longhouse, the traditional large log building in which ceremonies are performed in his tribe. His art work *Inherent Rights, Inherent Vision* makes us hear dogs bark and wolves howl as we move hesitantly and cautiously into the sanctuary of Native American shamanism. The long road to the lodge, the mystery of the drums and fires, the sounds of the night and the animals all keep us at a distance us even while we are there. Spirits float through the house, including the half-human and half-eagle Transformation Spirit. The spirits appear drawn in the stylized fashion known as Northwest Coast Native Canadian "freestyle." Lawrence Paul's own personal struggle shines through as he reluctantly set his Native American shamanism within contemporary technology. While each people has the right to its own vision, each people's vision brings with it a unique set of responsibilities.

At the concluding panel on virtual environments at the Banff Center, the discussion turned to the dangers of appropriating cultural symbols with information technology. The inherent rights and the inherent vision of a people become increasingly difficult to preserve and respect as all cultural symbols become grist for the systems of information. Information levels all input to transmissible bits. The flow of information may be a boon to communication on a global scale, but its impact on the local and the private is still open to assessment. During the closing panel discussion, one elderly Native American leader by the name of Little Bear made a direct and heart-felt appeal. Little Bear said: "Young people often come to me and ask to learn the way of the shaman. They look to the shaman for answers about how to improve the world. What I tell them is: Go find your own leaders. Ask your own teachers to show you the way. You must rely on their wisdom. They will show you the way."

We are just beginning to understand the responsibilities that come with VR. The art of virtual reality takes us deeper — not into nature but into technology. The vision remains technological through and through. Our shamanistic pipers dance us further into computers, simulations, and the ontological layer of cyberspace. *PlaceHolder* refers explicitly to earthly places, and it stirs our self-understanding as creatures of earth. The *Dervish* shatters the comfortable perceptual apparatus of our individual egos, and it may even loosen the frozen network of our social selves. But every form of VR expresses a technological destiny, our merger with computers and information systems. The ideas behind the merger began three hundred years ago, and we should not now pave over the ambiguity of that destiny by picturing ourselves playing Native Americans in a liquid cyberspace. Our scenes are play-acting, and our architecture stands on bits and bytes. Computer technology for vertical reality is no exception to the drive that aggressively renders reality digital and sometimes even strives to re-present reality.

VR is not simply a revival of something archaic, but a brand new emergence of an old human propensity. While we can learn from our predecessors and neighbors who use visualization, many of our questions are indeed new. Ultimately, they are questions we alone will have to answer, questions which reverberate in dissonant phrases like "Nature and Cyberspace."

4

Interactive Design: Tunnel or Spiral

Interactivity pounds at the doors of all broadcast media. Newspapers publish daily reports about cyberspace, then invite readers to subscribe to their online news services. Television programs encourage on-air feedback via email. Movies and popular television shows maintain viewer newsgroups and offer World Wide Web sites with click-on audio and video. As the era of one-way messages fades, the tone of unilateral broadcasting sinks to the trashy low-end of media culture. Quality switches from the TV remote controls to the computer console. Programming ceases to be unilateral when interactivity arrives.

Digital switching is, of course, under the hood of interactivity. The computer establishes a reciprocal relationship between sender and receiver, viewer and producer. Because computers handle high-speed transmission to-and-fro, the separating line between sender and receiver, viewer and producer, begins to blur. The digital switch converts text, sounds, and video to transmissible bits. And bits produce incoherent fragments that are hardly distinguishable from cultural noise. The blast of information shatters what remains of cultural coherence in the wobbling worlds of print and film distribution. The digital era splatters attention spans till the shared sensibility dribbles into fragmentary, disintegrative de-construction.

Interactivity signals a process of reconstruction. The digital Humpty-Dumpty needs mending. Reconstruction is a process of designing wholes, virtual worlds, that are both received and actively assembled—full, rich experiential places fit for human habitation.

From the bits of the digital era arises the holism of virtual design. Virtual design means building worlds from digital fragments, engineering usable software environments from disparate information sources. Worlds are not simply re-packaged fragments. Nor do virtual worlds re-present the primary physical world. What emerges are new functional wholes, habitats that emulate the engagement of real worlds.

Software engineering and software architecture support these virtual worlds, but artists with traditional skills must play a pivotal role in their construction. Virtual architecture must go well beyond wireframe models set in clean Cartesian coordinates. Polygons in Renaissance perspective are only the first steps of interactive design. Worlds require mood-tuned scenarios that draw on traditional artistic insights. Virtual design can take cues from musicians who have explored the edges of digital design, the power of the body in interactive performance, and a host of possible ways to achieve and interweave affective scenarios.

Virtual world design faces the crossroads: the tunnel and the spiral. The tunnel sucks us further into technology as a forward-thrusting, fovea-centered, obsessive fixation. The spiral moves us into virtual worlds that return us to ourselves, repeatedly deepening the awareness we enjoy as primary bodies. Technology can string us out to become peripherals of our machines, or it can add another layer to the ever-deepening return to enriched, enhanced existence. The tunnel and the spiral appear today in entertainment arcades and in the installation art of gallery exhibits. A future integrity beckons in the interactive design that combines computer-enhanced perception with the gift of self-perception.

Fragmentation

Plumes of black smoke streak over the rooftops. You can see the smoke trailing for miles eastwards from the Pacific Ocean high over the city of Redondo Beach. A Mozart piano concerto floats brightly on the car radio as you look through the windshield for the source of the smoke trail. Along Pacific Coast Highway, Mozart rattles the keyboard, sparkling and elegant. Now you catch sight of the fire. The Pier of Redondo Beach is burning! It is November 1989, and I am sitting in my car, watching the creosote-wrapped pylons go up in smoke, along with businesses and restaurants, all the while enjoying the counterpoint of the Allegro from Piano Concerto #22, K. 482. The Allegro shows how happy an allegro can be. The piano states a brief melody, then repeats it in playful variations, sometimes adding a twist of sadness to mock the dominant mood, but always speeding up again until quiet joy becomes wild glee, as I watch part of the beach city burn. What is the meaning of this split between aesthetic reaction and real-world vision through the windshield?

We are fragmented, split—as well as empowered—by the marriage of technology and art. Art, in the modern period, became aesthetics. Prior to the Renaissance, art functioned within a world and expressed that world. Art was held by a context of commitments to a commonly held iconography and symbology. Art at that time was not aesthetic but veridical; it pointed to basic truths and helped build a world. Since the Renaissance, art freed itself from the clutches of the various worlds and became increasingly aesthetic, or what Immanuel Kant called "a disinterested play of the senses." *Aisthesis* in Greek means what the senses perceive, the sensations of what you see and feel and touch—as opposed to the entities that you intend as you see, feel, and touch. Perception by itself is passive, but using the senses, as James Gibson's psychology reminds us, is active.[5] Your active seeing originates the sense precepts of what you see, feel, and touch. Intention guides attention, and from attention comes sense perception. But art as aesthetics has disengaged the senses from the intentionality that builds worlds, so that art could become aesthetics, a free-floating play of the senses. Plugged into technology, art finally becomes a fragmented collage without coherence. The lovely tune on the car radio lacks the coherence of context. It is a piece of another world in a world going up in smoke.

Modern aesthetics tore the art work from its world, storing art in museums or laying it at the feet of connoisseurs. The arts separated into fine and applied, into fractured disciplines of music, literature, theater, and visual arts. By concentrating on sense perception, art freed itself for a future link to technology. Art as pure art atomized the senses so that technology could amplify and enhance each of the senses in turn. Now headphones and home VCRs carry out the logical development of aesthetics. Contemporary music, as Glenn Gould demonstrated, revolves around captured recordings. The concert hall is wired and scheduled according to recording contracts. Theater and visual design are no longer innocent of celluloid and cameras. Modern aesthetics fragments the senses, and technology amplifies the fragmentation. Electronics further closes the doors on the physical public spaces where artists and musicians once worked. When the musical body rebels against closed doors, as in rock concerts or in contemporary raves, we notice how disembodied and how isolating our digital culture has become.

The Isolation of Glenn Gould

Neighbors walk past my front yard in Redondo Beach as I weed the garden. They push baby carriages, bounce basketballs, and sometimes they see me look up from my ice plants to say hello, but they do not hear me. Nearly every one of them wears headphones plugged into a portable Walkman. Their favorite recorded music creates a private curtain that veils my voice from their world. So I smile, wave discreetly, and try not to break their trance. Other residents speed by in automobiles rigged for sound, wrapping themselves in music or talk radio, seeing me on their visual periphery while absorbed in symphonies or Motown sounds. Unlike vision, sound is an environmental envelope. The ear takes in all directions at once and electronic audio places the body inside a sonic bubble. Sound modifies the habitat, and today many individuals create their own sound space.

Hours later, seated near an arrival gate at LAX, I reflect on artificial environments as I plug my Etymotic SR-4 earphones directly into my ear canals. The soft rubber instantly deletes the sound of rushing traffic and overhead jets. Isolation earphones in place, I write on my portable computer, listening to Bach piano music projected into 3-D audio space by a battery-powered portable HeadRoom amplifier made in Bozeman, Montana. The finely imaged music throbs through my skull as if my nerves were connected to the microphone pickups at the Thirtieth Street Studio in New York City in June of 1955. In the past, music performance had a social aspect. People listened collectively, in groups, at concerts or salons. The occasion was as important as the music. Attention turned as much to the performer as to the composer's work. Now my telepresent body sprouts ears that are accustomed to a vast range of recorded music, from Jim Morrison's *The Doors* to Glenn Gould playing Bach's *Goldberg Variations*. I look up, and the orchestra I hear is invisible, while the passers-by remain deaf to the powerful rhythms and melodies I enjoy at the moment.

It was Glenn Gould, the Canadian pianist (1932–1982), who foresaw the day when we would each become digital deities. Gould saw over the horizon to an era when electronics would discover the land of interactive design. The future listener, in Gould's vision, would not be a passive listener in a concert hall. Nor would great performers any longer give their best years to jet travel and motel rooms. In "The Prospects of Recording" (1966), Gould argued that "the function of the concert hall as we know it today will be entirely taken over by electronic media a century hence."[6] In the age of recordings, Gould observed, listeners identify music with "clarity, immediacy, and almost tactile proximity." Recordings have established a standard of aural aesthetics that live performances cannot meet, so that the social circumstance of live performances seems to diminish the musical experience—especially if the experience includes parking and crowded auditoriums. Gould rejected Aristotle's notion of art as powerful theater, art as emotional release or catharsis. Instead, Gould advocated a Platonic art that should be experienced in contemplative serenity away from the applause of the mob. Art should go directly mind to mind, heart to heart, without the intermediary of theater or social hoopla. Recordings make this possible in ways that even the intimate salon cannot.

Although musical experience no longer revolves around a social ritual, portable electronics has made music a pervasive element in life outside concert halls. Recording technology permits listeners to fashion their own musical experience and to blend music with daily life. The music that pervades social life—through the thousands of recordings on the market and through countless radio and television broadcasts—can only arise within a controlled studio environment. Today's concert halls are built to enhance the recording of live performances.

Musical performance directs music to the microphone—sometimes even when the performance occurs in concert halls wired for sound. You hear a facsimile of music when you are put on hold on the telephone, and Musak haunts the shopping malls. Electronics sticks music in your ear. Because we are so frequently exposed to an enormous range of world music as a cultural background, we are now prepared to become interactive with digital sound, as selectors and mixers and even editors who do more than buy recordings. The immense background of recorded music against which we live our lives not only makes art belong to daily life but the cultural backdrop teaches us the whole range of rhythms and styles of music so that we can make creative choices to shape our own sonic space. The digital age pushes art further online.

Though he died just before the dawn of the digital era, Glenn Gould placed his career as a piano virtuoso in the service of the idea that music was migrating from live performances. He believed the theatrical style of on-stage performers playing to live audiences was to be superseded by recorded sound that could be selected, manipulated, and re-arranged by private participants in the musical event. Gould, who had become famous throughout Canada by age twenty and made a sensational American debut in 1955, left the concert stage in 1964 after nine years of superstardom. At age thirty-one, Gould announced that he was withdrawing from live performances and would henceforth make only recordings. His final concert in Los Angeles on April 10, 1964 was a unique event in music history. Gould, who had been awarded the highest possible praise—laudatory reviews and sold-out concerts worldwide—simply walked away. He devoted his days to recorded performances until he died of a stroke in October, 1982, ten days after his fiftieth birthday.

Phonograph recordings allowed Gould to perfect his studio performances much like a film maker who uses editing, splicing, and other post-production techniques. Gould also saved himself from what he called "the tremendous conservatism" that overtakes any artist pressured to perform the same music again and again, until it becomes difficult, if not impossible, to move on.[7] Like the overworked professor delivering the same lectures year after year, the live performer often suffers a death sentence as an artist who had something to say. Recordings allow music to remain fresh for the performer and still reach the millions who enjoy private auditions. The universal feelings of Beethoven's triumph, Bruckner's ecstasy, or Haydn's cool suavity fill millions of ears and allow individuals to design their daily sonic spaces.

One of the most famous recordings ever made was Glenn Gould's 1955 recording of Johann Sebastian Bach's *Goldberg Variations*. The solo piano piece created a sensation in its day on long-playing vinyl, and it remains one of the best recordings ever made. Much of the ballyhoo at the time centered on Gould's apparent eccentricities—the creaky, beat-up piano stool, the pocketfuls of pills and remedies he carried everywhere, the scarves and sweaters he wore in sweltering weather. What remains of his sound production is remarkable. Besides the technically phenomenal playing, Glenn Gould delivered exultant virtuosity with swaggering rhythmic verve and dazzling runs. Memorable through Gould's whole archive of recordings is the vocal hum he adds to his playing like a signature. From his earliest recordings, Gould's background vocalizing signaled the performer's desire to get lost in the music, to forget audience, to achieve ecstasy rather than communication, to bask in a divine playfulness like a child on the floor in a quiet room, alone with toys. Communing with the music in silence, unaware of outer circumstances, not playing to the audience, Gould's solitude mirrors the digital listener's communion with the Platonic heaven of music for the sake of music. Outside the bounds of social roles, with no concern for applause, the performer shapes what the user receives in a gift of intimacy. The day his recordings are broken down into digital building blocks and reassembled, Glenn Gould's true audience will share his private ecstasy. Gould believed that the future of music lay in a collaboration between performer and listener bridged by interactive technologies. A Platonist by inclination, Gould wanted to draw listeners into a meeting of minds by turning away from the physical theater of the body.

The suppression of the human body for the sake of digital interactivity stands out as a flaw in Gould's superhuman Platonism. Even his good friends and colleagues spotted the flaw in Gould's philosophy. Yehudi Menuhin, violin virtuoso and Yoga enthusiast, appears in the film "Thirty-Two Short Films about Glenn Gould" (directed by Francois Girard with a screenplay by Girard and Don McKellar), where he says about Gould:

> Like all people who try to rationalize their position and do what they want at any cost and then seek some sort of universal justification—Glenn Gould fell into a trap. Gould's trap was that he dwelt a little too much on the morality of his decision. Obviously, from a purist's point of view, he had an argument. Audiences are made up of people who have seats that allow them to see somewhat better or hear somewhat better. At times, in the large churches, there are audience members who sit behind a pillar and see nothing. Sometimes the acoustics at a live concert are exaggerated, or we hear too much or too little of something or the volume is too loud, or the reverberation hurts the ears. Gould did have a point, it's not always ideal . . . *but that's part of life.* To me, that is a vital element of living. Personally, I think Glenn Gould's life seemed a bit too artificial. But like I said, that's because I'm not of his stature, creatively. I could not create my own life and lead it to the exclusion of the rest of the world, doing nothing but applying myself to the physical and intellectual work, trying to avoid every current of air behind the protection of a scarf, unable to bear the thought of someone touching my shoulders. And yet, at the same time, he loved to go to the fishing villages, in the wide expanses that Canada has to offer: he liked that. He liked nature. He liked the fishermen a lot more than he liked audiences in New York.

Menuhin defended his friend in the last analysis, but his first observation points to the exiled body that stands forlorn outside every Platonic utopia. Gould, says Menuhin, was that exception whose absolute creativity demands refuge from the crowd of humanity. But music, as Menuhin sees it, emerges from humanity, not from Gould's ethereal, Platonic mental ecstasy. The humus in the word humanity refers us etymologically back to the earth, and our upright bodily posture stretches between heaven and earth. I have seen Yehudi Menuhin in live concerts where he conducted a small chamber orchestra with his violin dipping and waving, and with his body swaying like a tree rooted in the earth, channeling music as a cosmic flow. Menuhin's body becomes the music, becomes the dance. The schools Menuhin established for training young musicians include yoga practice in their curricula. In Menuhin's view, the body belongs essentially to the humanity of music. Will our interactive digital devices pull us increasingly out of touch with the subtleties of live communication? Is our interactive intimacy with music doomed to pointing, clicking, and pushing buttons?

The question is not which devices we choose, but, more fundamentally, our lifestyle. When the SONY Walkman appeared on the market, it did so without the support of advance studies of the market for the product.[8] The product designers had no market data to suggest that such a product would be successful or even that there was an existing market for it. The designers conceived the product, a small tape recorder that did not record but only played back, based on their understanding of the 1980s lifestyle, values, and activities. The designers saw the trend toward a new kind of music listening based on acoustical privacy and solitary recreation. The designers brought to the market a product that later seemed a brilliant answer to needs that no one had yet identified. They understood how music belongs to lifestyle, to the underlying understanding of what it means to exist in the contemporary world. Gould's solitary integration of music in the 1960s became a hit in the mass market of the 1980s and 90s. As music goes increasingly digital, we can expect to see Gould's ideal listener welcome the computerized home delivery of music. Listerners will become users, people who actively edit, splice, and re-work their private soundspace.

When teaching seminars at the Art Center for Design in Pasadena, I often show screens of the World Wide Web displayed from computer through an overhead projector on the big screen of an auditorium. A large audience can then look at the screen and discuss the same interactive designs. This approach, however, quickly reveals the intrinsic solitude of interactivity. After discussing several screens, it becomes apparent to everyone in the room that only *one person* is fully engaged with interactive viewing—the one who makes the choices about where to click and which screen should come next. Only the person taking the narrow path of decisions enjoys the full interactive experience of digital media; the other people in the room who do not make the decisions are essentially onlookers. If the whole viewing audience is asked to agree where to go next, the experience bogs down and attention turns away from the screen. Usually, the people merely watching the interaction get to think about what is happening, but they do not partake of the experience in the same way that the solitary user does. The intimacy of the screen gets lost in the crowd. Essentially, interactivity implies solitude, at least with current digital technology. The split in philosophy between Glenn Gould and Yehudi Menuhin, between solitude and humanity, appears at the crossroads of the digital era.

The Dancing Body of Jim Morrison

The counterpoint to Glenn Gould's ethereal, de-materialized, Platonic intimacy with canned music is another North American musician who celebrated the body in revolt. Put on a recording by *The Doors* and try to sit still. It's not easy. The music lights a fire under your feet and shamelessly flashes its ecstatic purpose: Get up and dance! The legendary lead singer of *The Doors*, Jim Morrison, was an avowed convert to the anti-Platonic philosophy of Friedrich Nietzsche. Shunning the austere control of Gould's polyphonic Bach, Jim Morrison played shaman for thousands of American youth in the 1960s who invited the immanent rhythms of rock & roll into their awakening flesh. Not the private listener but the live group happening in concert halls became the revelatory shrine where Jim Morrison reincarnated Dionysos, the outlaw god who inspires revelry, anarchy, and bodily abandon. Morrison's tomb in Pere-Lachaise cemetery in Paris (1943–1971) displays layer upon layer of graffiti from the hands of hundreds of pilgrims who still feel drawn to that inspired madness.

One of the few popular performers to work from an intellectual heritage, Morrison drew not only from his early reading of Nietzsche, but also from the poet Arthur Rimbaud, the theater director Antonin Artaud, the Jungian analyst Erich Neumann, and the artist William Blake. The Morrison heritage was the well-established Romantic critique of the intellect as an isolated, disembodied rationality. Like the intellectual ancestors he chose, Morrison sought redemption from rationality which he understood to be nihilistic calculation. In its modern form, rationality defines its world as a set of dispassionately controllable objects, and this calculating rationality answers to nothing. The cool, passive intellect develops a science to control phenomena, but its

science lacks wisdom, because reason has defined itself as a non-partici-
pant in the world it manages. The dispassionate intellect develops
media that feed on voyeurism. To oppose this system and revitalize
experience, Morrison sung his Orphic poetry to provoke passion and to
create a theater that affirms the body. He created events where the content of communication became pure participation.

Morrison criticized the passivity of the eye-centered culture that
reads the world from a distance and that holds back participation and
downplays passion:

> We are content with what is "given" us. We no longer have "dancers," the possessed. The
> cleavage of men into actor and spectators is the central fact of our time. We have become
> obsessed with celebrities who live for us and whom we punish. We have been metamorphosed
> from a mad body dancing on hillsides to a pair of eyes staring in the dark. If all the radios and
> televisions were deprived of their sources of power, all books and paintings burned tomorrow,
> all shows and cinemas closed, all the arts of vicarious existence. . . . [9]

Like Glenn Gould, Jim Morrison heard a call to break the mold
of performer/passive spectators. Unlike Gould's Platonic approach,
Morrison sparked cathartic release, an Aristotelian catharsis that
invites dionysiac dance. Morrison sought interactivity not by sending
the audience into digital solitude but by liquefying the line between
performer and audience. He combined live beatnik poetry, radical
theater, and psychedelic synesthesia. "Doors" refers to the poet
William Blake's motto, "If the doors of perception were cleansed, we
would see things as they are: infinite." Aldous Huxley's book *The
Doors of Perception*, popularized Blake's argument in the 1960s.
Huxley brought Blake's argument to bear on drugs, mysticism, and
literature as tools for de-programming the culturally induced unifor-
mity of perception. Morrison—along with Ray Manzarek, Robby
Krieger, and John Densmore—put music to the task by creating *The
Doors*, a Rock phenomenon in 1960s culture. Though *The Doors*
used amplifiers and recordings to spread the cathartic experience,
their recordings fed off the legend of the live concerts.

Morrison drew on Antonin Artaud's theater of cruelty ("I call for a
theater in which the actors are like victims burning at the stake, sig-
naling through the flames") and the Artaud-inspired off-Broadway

"Living Theater" of Julian Beck and Judith Malina. *The Doors* concerts—especially as Morrison's acclaim grew—combined tribal ritual,
political action, and psychotherapy. The rock concert became a vehicle for experimental theater. Artaud's vision of ecstatic social breakthrough ran through *The Doors*. For Morrison, the breakthrough went
beyond personal liberation to encompass the treatment of a more general psycho-social malady:

> More or less, we're all afflicted with the psychology of the voyeur. Not in a strictly
> clinical or criminal sense, but in our whole physical and emotional stance before the
> world. Whenever we seek to break this spell of passivity, our actions are cruel and awk-
> ward and generally obscene, like an invalid who has forgotten how to walk. [10]

After the long dominance of passive attitudes, the move to interactivity feels not only like a breaththough but also a stumbling convales-
cence. The first taste of interactivity seems chaotically promising, but
as yet unsatisfying. Just as the first photographers shot classical paintings and the first filmmakers froze live theater performances, so too
interactive artists will remain in the awkward hold of more passive art
forms until the art builds its own genre.

The primal model Morrison drew on for his rock poetry was the
shaman. Shamanism throughout the world, according to Mircea Eli-
ade, is a technique of ecstasy. The shaman may have a particular magical specialty (such as control over fire, wind or magical flight), but
common to all shamans is the ability to enter into a trance, contact
other realms, and then return with healing knowledge for the tribe.
The trance is an ecstatic state (literally: *ek-stasis* or "standing outside
oneself") in which the soul of the shaman leaves the body to contact
greater vision (ascend to the heavens) or to fight the demons (descend
to the underworld). The shaman struggles for vision and subjugates
fearsome demons. Often the shaman adopts an animal spirit for guidance and power. For the shaman, as for the rock singer, the trance par-
ticipates in the life of the tribe for which the shaman dances. As the
tribe in turn listens to the shaman, they participate in a deeper understanding of their own flights and terrors. To this end, Morrison adopted
the "Lizard King" persona in his lyrics and performances.[11] Participants in the lizard world sought a Rimbaud-like insanity.

In one of his Lizard King songs, "Celebration of the Lizard," Morrison invites the audience to a play a "little game" in which his hearers crawl inside their brains to play the game of "go insane." The game invites them to first close their eyes, forget their names, forget the world, and join him in erecting "a different steeple." (The European steeple functions as a symbol for centralized order.) The shaman leads the way by closing his eyes to reassure the audience "I'm right here, I'm going too." The explicit goal of the game is to release control together until "we're breaking through." Finding a location deep inside the brain means that the psychic traveler finds a place where there is no pain, a place where the rain falls gently on the town around the psychic steeple. The town stands on a hillside that holds underneath it a psychic labyrinth.In that labyrinthine lair shine fossils from the past, draughts of cool strange air, and the unearthly presence of reptiles. (The reptilian brain, scientists believe, resides at the vestigial core of the human brain from its earliest evolution.) "We're getting out of town, we're going on the run," says the shaman. The pace of the game is run, run, run. The strongest claim of the lizard shaman is that he can "make the earth stop in its tracks."

The shamanic immersion of *The Doors* is far from the immersion of virtual reality. No technology tracks the sensory response of individual users. In fact, the shaman induces a collective trance in which the individual's world—as individual—disappears. Collective trance, described in Nietzsche's first book *The Birth of Tragedy Out of the Spirit of Music*, preceded the Olympian calm and restraint of classical Greek drama. The statuesque posture of classical antiquity was a sucking in of the breath after having reeled under the archaic pain of life's dark chaos. Chaos was the center of the tribal dance where individuality vanishes. The personae of high classical theater descended from the wild antics and travesties of the original dionysian music, but classical theater suppressed its origins under a calm reserve. Thus spoke Nietzsche. And Jim Morrison spun the eternal wheel of the bacchanalia. His stage strategy made unforgettable the kind of interaction that engages full-bodied, passionate presence.

Since Morrison's death, *The Doors* continue to play music, but the music concedes more to technology than to human presence.

In December of 1995, a multimedia laser disc brought the latest incarnation of *The Doors*. By the 1990s, the recording industry in Los Angeles had felt the ontological shift to digital reality, and live work in professional studios has become increasingly rare. Studio work in general has given way to digital solitude. In the past, a studio might employ forty musicians to make music for a Coca-Cola commercial. Today, one musician equipped with a home studio can create nearly the same commercial. Sounds are created on a synthesizer, or sampled from a primary instrument into a digital recorder, or mail-ordered on computer disk, or simply downloaded via the Internet. Roughly 100,000 home studios now compete with the remaining hundred or so recording studios along the Burbank-Hollywood-Los Angeles corridor. For three to five thousand dollars, a musician can set up a professional studio, flip a switch to make a machine sing like a violin or produce the low, brassy sounds of a trombone. Push a button and out comes a steady percussive beat pulsing to whatever rhythm you choose. Home-based studios have grown from a handful in 1980 to one million in 1995, while professional recording studios have shrunk from 10,000 to 1,000 in the same period.[12] The isolated, push-button digital life still waits outside the doors of shared virtual worlds.

Jim Morrison and Glenn Gould belong together as two sides of future interactivity. The rebellious body protests its exile by seeking participation; the mind's inner ear forsakes physical contact and uses technology to merge with other minds. Music has always been the gauge of culture, ever since the ancient Greeks used the word *musiké* to identify what we today call culture. Music ranges over body and spirit. These two 1960s music-prophets affected the history of artistic practice. Though their work remained largely in the domain of pre-digital, unilateral recordings, they dreamt of deeper forms of engagement and interaction. As computer control encourages a different kind of interactivity, and as it demands higher levels of integration, we must heed both these prophets of body and mind. The virtual worlds we construct must not be any less intimate on the mental plane, any less engaging for the physical body.

Reconstruction

Culture evaporates into transmissible bits, fragments increasingly indistinguishable from noise. The information flood sweeps away coherence in the wobbling worlds of print and film. The digital era splatters attention spans until the shared sensibility dribbles into piecemeal, disintegrative de-construction.

Interactivity signals a process of reconstruction. The digital Humpty-Dumpty needs mending. Reconstruction is the process of designing whole, virtual worlds, full, rich experiences that are simultaneously received as they are actively assembled—from the user's viewpoint—as places fit for human habitation. From the fragments of the digital era arises the holism of virtual design. Virtual design means reconstructing worlds from digital fragments, engineering usable software environments from disparate information sources.

Worlds are reconstructed wholes that are both received and actively configured. Worlds are not simply re-packaged fragments or pre-packaged formulas. Virtual worlds do not seek to re-present the primary physical world, nor to borrow integrity by imitation or photo-realism. What emerges from virtual worlds are new functional habitats that emulate the engagement of real worlds. World-making is neither regressive nor representational.

A virtual world establishes a synthetic reality in the strong sense of full sensory immersion—not keyboard, monitor, and mouse. The keyboard and monitor are relics of typewriters and television sets; the mouse is a stopgap tool. A virtual world in the strong sense allows interaction with the user's entire sensory field, creating a 360-degree, 3-D audio and video envelope. Multimedia associated with "virtuality"—in the weak, popular sense—points toward the goal of synthetic worlds while falling short of their wholeness. VRML (Virtual Reality Modeling Language) on the Internet serves as training wheels for the full immersion to come. Immersion must be networked in order to coordinate telepresence. Anyone who believes the arcade game *Castle Wolfenstein* uses virtual reality should go back to "VR 101."

What makes a world? How does a world exist as a world? A world is not a collection of fragments, nor even an amalgam of pieces. It is a felt totality or whole. You cannot make a world by patching together this part and that part and the other, because the wholeness, not so much its particulars, makes the world exist. Nor can we create a world simply by mirroring the primary world. If virtual design pictures the primary world of nature, the illusion might suggest an integral feeling, but soon enough the mirage slips to betray the cracks in the digital environment. A nature-referenced world avoids the active human synthesis, and it also avoids discovering what makes the natural world a world in the first place. The wholeness of the virtual world cannot be borrowed from the already existing physical world.

What makes a world a world? What qualities of interactivity drive full virtual worlds? Besides the sensory and technological components mentioned, we need to invesigate the *internal* components of virtual worlds. What makes their synthetic "worldhood"? Thinkers like Wilhelm Dilthey, Martin Heidegger, and Nelson Goodman sought decades ago to locate the "worldness" of the world.[13] Their definitions of worldhood came from the need of cultural historians to distinguish different epochs of history while still allowing each epoch to maintain its distinctive style, mood, and holistic sense of place. A world in this cultural-historical sense describes a member of a sequence which maintains its integrity as an epoch. While philosophers are only beginning to address the synthetic worlds of computer technology, we can find in these thinkers some clues about the general form of worldhood to help us think about virtual worlds.

Heidegger, for instance, defines worldhood as a "context of relationships" (*Bewandtniszusammenhang*). This definition is formal and abstract, but it suggests that the entities in a world are constituted by their interrelationships. In other words, the woven fabric of usage—the functionality of things—makes them belong together. "World" is a verbal notion, a continual linking of one thing with another: the nail belongs to the hammer, which belongs in turn to the hand, which belongs to the arm, which belongs to the person whose intention it is to get the job done, and so on. The world is not a collection of things but an active usage that relates things to each other, that links them. The parts of the world are nouns that need the action verbs to put them into motion. By themselves, the nouns can never articulate a meaningful world. They need first-person action to bring them to life. Worlds are functional wholes.

Besides function, another aspect of the formal definition of "world" is that it is a *context* or weaving-together of things. World makes a web-like totality. The web gives context to anything that happens within it. World is a total environment or surround space. We often speak of world as an environment for human involvement when we refer to "the world of sports" or "the world of the Otavalo Indians," or "the world of nuclear physics." The world in this singular sense refers to the horizon or totality of all the involvement belonging to a certain context. As we gain experience in a context, we build background knowledge—what Michael Polanyi called "tacit knowledge"—that makes sense out of everything happening to us within that specific context. We need not refer explicitly to this knowledge in a conscious way because much of it, in fact, resides in our bodily skills and sub-conscious savvy. When I learn, for example, to play an instrument, I practice connecting the notes on paper with certain breath and hand movements until I no longer have to think about reading the notes and transferring them to the finger movements. I no longer need reason about the importance of paper notation when I exist in "the world of music." If some day I play the instrument in an orchestra, the value of the sheet music is self-evident in the context of performing with other instrumentalists. The notes on paper have tacit value within that world. My long apprenticeship makes me belong to that world, and the relationships between me, the sheet music, the instrument, and the other players constitute one area of that integral world.

An example from current operating systems points out the difference between functional context and primary-world references. Personal computers today offer work spaces containing folders. The folders on desktop computer displays, whether Apple or Windows, are functionally folders when we use them every day to store work-related information. We make new folders, fill them with memos, reports, and other information. We empty them, move items between them, and throw them away. A folder icon identifies the many functions that the software allows us to perform. Yet these folders do not depict or represent paper folders as they appear in the primary world. They are icons. The electronic folder differs from the physical folder not merely because it lacks the tree-based paper substance. Iconic folders differ from paper folders in so many significant ways, that we might, if hard pressed to explain our language, say that we call them "folders" only in a metaphorical sense. A metaphor bridges two entirely disparate things: "Her cry was a siren." Folders on the software desktop are not *merely* metaphors. The software folders are functionally folders. That is, within the context of computerized work flow, the software folder performs the functions that a paper folder performs—but not in the context of physical paper. To explain this without explaining it, many people simply say, "They are virtual folders," by which they want to point out the as-if, functional quality of the iconic entities. In the context of desktop computing, the folder icon is indeed a folder. While what we use today as a desktop on a computer monitor screen can hardly be said to constitute a world, it is indeed the desktop of future virtual worlds. Someday that desktop will exist in a room that exists in a structure that exists in a neighborhood that exists in a city that exists in one realm of a virtual world.

A world turns on the axis of action. The formal definition of worldhood points to the inward assimilation that must occur through human action if a world is to come into being. Involvement in things, through action, puts those things in a relationship to one another so that a context emerges. The axis as axis is what we call a home. Home is the base, the center, existentially speaking, of any world. When new worlds emerge —we see this in the Internet's spread of "home pages," —everyone first builds a home or point of departure. The home is so familiar that we need not assimilate it. Home is the node from which we link to other places and things. Home is so familiar that we no longer think of home as familiar, unless home feels threatened. Home is the point of action and node of linkage that becomes a thread weaving the multitude of things into a world. The essence of home is familiarity. Besides familiarity, a world in its formal definition must also have sufficient variety and contrast to facilitate action. Home could not be home without a work bench, guests, and a window looking out at the alien aspects of nature.

In noticing the difference between home and the many things "outside," we leave the formal definition of world and its worldhood and turn to the content: the things themselves that get assimilated and belong to the world. How do things belong a world? Of course, the genesis of each world affects how the things emerge and relate to one another, and each world's genesis gives the things in that world a distinctive cast and color. We can get some general notion of what it means to put things in a world by looking again at how a musician absorbs experiences and things into the art work, for virtual worlds are works of art as much as they are feats of engineering.

Virtual worlds usually begin as wire-frame models. The software designer works with polygons and the geometry of Cartesian coordinates. But the structural design is only the beginning of world building. Software architecture must open its doors to inhabitants. It must become interactive. The human interaction side of world design requires art. And one art that especially balances the skeletal grid of Cartesian coordinates is music. Of all traditional arts, music is the most liquid and affect-based. Music flows. As a temporal manifestation, its rhythms appear and disappear. Music is soft. It opens the emotive dimensions filtered out by the hard wire-frames of Cartesian design. While coordinate geometry defines space as extension (Descartes), music shapes space into atmospheric, emotive scenarios. Music has logical structure, especially in the symphonic tradition where patterns of rhythm, melody, and harmony become elaborate. The structural patterns of music share something of the fluid, florescent quality of software as it undulates through electronic environments. The way certain musicians have consciously shaped a world can help us understand how a virtual world incorporates things in such a way as to make them into a world.

World Construction

"To me 'symphony' means constructing a world with all the technical means at one's disposal," wrote Gustav Mahler.[14] Writing in 1895, Mahler had at his disposal the acoustic arsenal of the Late Romantic orchestra, which for his Third Symphony included: 4 flutes, 4 oboes, 5 clarinets, 4 bassoons, 8 horns, 4 trumpets, 4 trombones, a tuba, 2 timpani, 2 glockenspiel, a tambourine, a tam-tam, a triangle, a suspended cymbal and a bass-drum cymbal, a side drum and a bass drum, 2 harps, a section of first and a section of second violins, a viola section, a cello section, a string bass section, a women's choir, an alto solo, several side drums off-stage and a flugel horn, and, finally, a boys' choir with 4 tuned bells. The list mentions only the instruments, without counting the many millions of practice hours needed to master the "technical means." But the technical means and their mastery do not by themselves produce a world in music. The world composed is not a world of technically produced sound. It must make music. The technical must serve world design.

What are the building blocks of Mahler's worlds? At the time Mahler composed, music diverged into two contending camps of composition. One camp built structures of so-called "absolute music." This music worked formal patterns into themes, counter-themes, expositions, and recapitulations, much in the style of Mozart, Beethoven, and Brahms. The other camp, influenced by Wagner and stemming from Hector Berlioz, produced program music, also known as tone poems. This music came attached with literary references and scenes that could be described on paper program notes. Richard Strauss, for instance, wrote orchestral music that literally portrayed scenes from literature, such as Don Quixote's attack on windmills; or from daily life, such as a man reading a newspaper at the breakfast table. Strauss consciously illustrated each theme. Mahler vacillated between the camps of absolute and program music. He would sometimes write down programs for people to read, and then he would quickly withdraw and reject those same programs. His compositions were based on the complex structures and counterpoints of absolute music, but at the same time Mahler brought the inner shape of actual experiences into his symphonies. While he rejected the musical depiction of the usual program music, he added to absolute music the inner shape of his most vivid life experiences. His own biographical experiences took musical form and became the content of his world design. Mahler wrote music as a cinematic collage of his own life experience. His symphonies are musical worlds that parallel and comment upon his personal life world.

Mahler composed film music before the discovery of film. Like

Berlioz before him, Mahler forged a highly visual musical language. He turned the classic style away from circular patterns and shaped it into a changing stream of motifs. The motif or *idée fixe* recurs in the music but it recurs more like a mysterious figure in a dream than like a predictable pattern. Later composers, such as Ralph Vaughan Williams, Dimitri Shostakovich, and John Williams, would write twentieth-century film sound scores that draw on this dramatic style. Mahler's symphonies work with strong scenic elements.[15] Instead of beginning with a picturesque scene to illustrate, however, Mahler begins with an emotional/musical audio scene, each having a distinctive mood and rhythm—not unlike the *leitmotif* technique of Richard Wagner. He then works with these audio scenes to bring them into relationships with one other. The symphony becomes the complex story of how these audio sequences conflict, harmonize, and transform one another. Historically, an audio scene might appear first in a brief song. The scene then goes from a song to part of a song cycle. It may then go into a cantata, and finally enter a symphony. Typical audio scenes from Mahler's experiences:

- The cavalry horns in the military academy across the street from his childhood home

- The hurdy-gurdy man in the street outside the family house where young Gustav ran outdoors once during a quarrel between his parents

- Funeral marches

- Children's games of playing dead (lying still on a table surrounded by flowers and candles)

- The conversation of young lovers in a quiet evening

- Sleigh-bells on a sled jingling through the snowy woods

- Folk dances from Austrian villages and Jewish festivities

- Walks in the woods when nature feels vibrant and friendly

- Sailing on the ocean in a small boat

- Lines from a poem by Nietzsche

- Nursery rhymes and children's fables

All these emotional scenarios become compositional elements in Mahler's worlds. For Mahler, music and visual images intertwine in complex ways. The auditory events create the symphonic universe, but the sounds are tied through visual scenes to existential reference points. The existential references furnish substance and emotional weight to the auditory images. While Mahler's scenarios appear as music and mimic real-world sounds—marches, funeral processions, bugle-fanfares, bird-calls, serenades, dances, or street songs—his own verbal statements about the meaning of the concrete images and emotive contents became a source of confusion. Deryck Cooke notes:

> The trouble is that words tend to produce concrete images that distract from the music's emotional and psychological purpose. Hence, Mahler, asked by a journalist for the meaning' of his Second Symphony, replied: "I believe I have expressed my intention clearly enough in the music. When I conceived it, I was in no way concerned with a detailed program of events, but at most with an emotion." Yet he eventually gave the Second Symphony a program—only to reject it later! But this is understandable: he wanted, he said, to leave the interpretation to the "individual insight of the listener"; finding little insight, he tried to explain in words; finding the words taken literally instead of symbolically, he withdrew them.[16]

A virtual-world builder must likewise eschew literal references. Software entities can indeed weigh in existentially, but they should not be limited by real-world references. In turn, the soft world offers the freedom to shape an interactive scenario in unprecedented ways. The user is likewise free to cooperate in unforeseen ways (cooperate here means literally co-operate, or work together).

Mahler used orchestral means to weave emotive scenarios that fill his symphonic worlds. The technical tool of the orchestra stretches and transforms a series of conventional emotive scenarios until they constitute the composer's world in music:

- A children's nursery tune, "Frère Jacques," turns into a sinister funeral march leading to a ghostly canon that ends with a toy-like fanfare and cheap band music (First Symphony, third movement)

- A sprightly folk dance (*Ländler*) begins stamping and swinging, then balloons out of shape, like Alice in Wonderland, to gargantuan proportions and becomes clattering trumpets and whooping horns while the hearer feels the music receding away "as if a homeless night wanderer looked into a bright window to see well-dressed figures in a ballroom, dancing to music he cannot hear, gyrations that seem strange and senseless, the whole world reflected in a concave mirror, distorted and insane" (Second Symphony, third movement)[17]

- A funeral march slowly loses the dignity of conventional grief and becomes angry, rebellious, and full of bitter despair (Third Symphony, first movement)

- A macabre death dance on a shrieking fiddle fits into a montage of folk dances and heavenly songs (Fourth Symphony, second movement).

These are just a few instances of how Mahler's symphonies make worlds from previous songs, poems, and life images.

Each process of world-making proceeds by composing or decomposing older materials, by identifying repetitions and evolving new patterns, by deleting and supplementing, by organizing and ordering aspects of the world(s) already there. Mahler's collage of conflicting memories and scenarios allows listeners to enter on many levels, because the composer avoided setting down a single literal program or interpretive path while at the same time he anchored the worlds existentially in life experiences and personal struggles. His symphonic worlds preserve the integrity of the individual mind that book culture produced through its textual totalities while still inviting the act of interpretation.

Art traditions like symphonic music, graphic design, and cinema suggest strategies for constructing virtual worlds. Each tradition contributes something to reconstruction. Music, as the example of Mahler's symphonies shows, can contribute a non-sequential montage technique for emotive scenarios that are temporal and auditory to offset the Renaissance visual perspective and Cartesian coordinate systems that tend to dominate graphics-based software. The emphatically 3-D perspective of the older 2-D graphic displays can give way to more profoundly moving interactions. Space, from the standpoint of the system participant, has a temporal framework and an affective tonality inasmuch as space manifests varying distances and tonic relationships. Why should a virtual office not provide each business meeting with its own soundtrack? And why should canned sound tracks not give way to interactive music that is composed by those who dance to the music?

The process of reconstruction will never gain ground as long as world engineers exclude professional artists and as long as artists and designers avoid teaming up with engineers in software development. Art traditions are infinitely richer than "human factors" engineering, and "interface design" is only a baby step towards world building. The challenge to both art and engineering is interactivity. That is the third factor that brings the artist and the engineer together. And both art and engineering stand before a crossroads. World-building must navigate two different types of interactivity.

Two Models of World-Building

Virtual design stands at the crossroads of interactivity. Two models of world-building beckon: the tunnel and the spiral. The tunnel sucks us further into technology. The tunnel molds human perception to push forward, to ignore peripheral awareness, to fixate. The spiral, on the contrary, rotates us in virtual worlds that return us to ourselves, that deepen the wide-angle awareness we have of ourselves as primary bodies. The tunnel teaches us to maintain first-person perspective while the spiral attunes us to others from whom we learn about ourselves. The tunnel feeds us more information. The spiral aspires to wisdom. A virtual world can swallow us until we become the peripherals of our machines. Or a virtual world can add another layer to the ever-deepening return to enriched, enhanced existence.

How are users best immersed in virtual environments? I mean this from a technical-ontological point of view. Should users feel totally immersed? That is, should they forget themselves as they see, hear, and touch the world in much the same way we deal with the primary phenomenological world? (We cannot see our own heads—just part of our noses—in the phenomenological world.) Or should users be allowed and encouraged to see themselves as cyberbodies? Should they be able to see themselves over their own shoulders? Should they be aware of their primary bodies as separate entities outside the graphic environment? Should they be able to see other primary bodies interacting with virtual entities? Or should they suspend physical experience? Should we see the primary bodies of others in virtual worlds, or does telepresence mean that we will never be certain of the society we keep, how much of it is illusory or artificial? Should we make up the avatars that represent us or be given various identity options by the software designers? What makes full-body immersion? What makes psychological immersion?

Two different answers to these many questions split at the crossroads. The tunnel and the spiral appear today in the two types of virtual reality gear we looked at in "VR 101." Both types of gear share the same goal of full sensory immersion. One type is the CAVE and the other is the head-mounted displays of Thomas Furness, Frederick Brooks, and Jaron Lanier. The HMD style is the familiar hardware of helmet and gloves, and the CAVE is a projection room where graphics are projected onto the walls and ceiling.

Here is a brief refresher about the CAVE. The CAVE derives from the early work of Myron Krueger and appears today in the CAVE at the Electronic Visualization Lab of the University of Illinois at Chicago. The CAVE is a surround-screen, surround-sound, system that creates immersion by projecting 3-D computer graphics into a ten foot square cube composed of display screens that completely surround the viewer(s). Head and hand tracking systems produce the correct stereo perspective and isolate the position and orientation of a 3-D input device. A sound system provides audio feedback. The viewer explores the virtual world by moving around inside the cube and grabbing objects with a three-button, wand-like device. Unlike HMD type of VR, the CAVE does not require users to wear helmets. Instead, they wear lightweight stereo glasses and walk around inside the CAVE as they interact with virtual objects. Because of the importance of the physical space or room, the CAVE often goes under the more generic name of VR-room or VROOM. Multiple viewers often share virtual experiences and carry on discussions inside the VROOM. One user is the active viewer, controlling the stereo projection reference point, while the other users are passive viewers.

From a phenomenological viewpoint, the difference between the

CAVE VR and the HMD VR is profound. The HMD brand of VR leans toward what I call Tunnel VR or perception-oriented immersion. The projection or CAVE brand of VR, on the contrary, produces Spiral VR or apperceptive immersion. The VR that tunnels us down a narrow corridor of perceptions differs subtly but profoundly from the VR that spirals us into higher layers of self-perception. Let me explain Tunnel VR and Spiral VR. Then I will clarify what I mean when I say that Tunnel VR is a perceptive immersion, while Spiral VR is an apperceptive immersion.

First, we can distinguish perception from apperception. The term "apperception" arose in the late eighteenth century when Immanuel Kant first brought out the distinction. Perception goes toward entities and registers their color, shape, texture, and other properties. Perceptions have sensory qualities we perceive with our eyes, ears, nose, skin, or kinesthetic sense. Apperception, on the other hand, perceives not only entities but also notices that which accompanies the perception of any entity: our self-activity. (Kant traced apperception back to Descartes, who set down the first axiom of modern philosophy in his *cogito, ergo sum*: "I am thinking, therefore I am real.") With perception we see something. With apperception we notice *that* we are seeing something. Apperception implies a reflectedness, a proprioception, a self-awareness of what we are perceiving or doing. For Kant, this type of perception implies that human beings enjoy a freedom and self-determination in their activities that animals do not. Kant also believed that apperception makes possible a critical attitude toward what we perceive. Once we sense our separation from a stimulus, we can then enjoy the option of responding to it in various ways, or perhaps even choose not to respond at all. Since Kant, we have also learned from philosophers like Wittgenstein and Heidegger that intelligent awareness includes the non-linear, supporting context (*Lebensform* or *Lebenswelt*). Without the total, wide-angle awareness of context, the perceiving tunnel mind gets lost in a labyrinth without a clue on how to return to the supportive center of existence. The apperceptive context injects meaning and value into discrete perceptions.

The concept of "apperception" allows us to highlight the advantage of one type of immersion over the other. In perception-oriented

VR, the head-mounted display shrouds the user's head much like the hood that covers the head of a pet falcon. Such falcon-hood immersion derives from not having a choice about where to look. The falcon grows tame under the hood because the hood temporarily blinds it to the larger world. Likewise, HMD immersion results from the primary body's blackout for the sake of the cyberbody, and a tunnel-like perception of the virtual world is the consequence. The user flies into a virtual environment with maximum immersion, but the intensity of immersion strips away self-awareness. What gets lost is the wide-angle view of the relaxed eye that includes peripheral, all-at-once vision. Another loss is the awareness of other primary bodies. Just as the presence of other people who recognize me as an agent feeds my own sense of presence and freedom, so too does the absence of others diminish my agency. "Other people" in the primary sense are not simulated entities or cartoon avatars. They are people with independent desires, boundaries, and need for self-respect. Their complexity—and their occasional intractability—is what makes human recognition valuable. No simulated entity provides the same kind of recognition that a real person can. Because the falcon effect excludes the primary body, the HMD graphic environment reinforces tunnel vision.

The CAVE or VROOM typically provides experiences beyond the perception of entities. The user enjoys apperceptive experience. Because the user's body is immersed without having to adapt to the system's peripherals (heavy helmet, tight data glove, calibrated earphones), the CAVE immersion does not constrict but rather enhances the user's body. In turn, the projected immersion shows a different phenomenological landscape from perception-oriented systems. The CAVE creates a very different experience by allowing users to acknowledge one another in their primary bodies. The user's embodied activities are seen to be rooted in the physical body, and the existence of the user's primary body is mutually acknowledged. Although peripheral, the acknowledgment nonetheless affects the background atmosphere of the shared experience.

Computer simulations tend to be perceptive immersions. Typically, computer graphics represent entities. The world and its entities come ready-made from the hands of designers or commerical

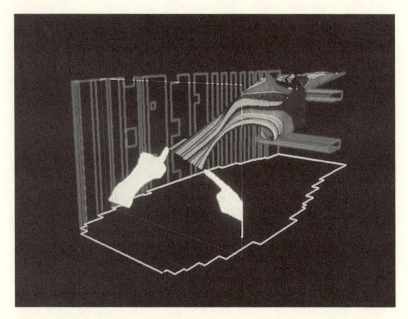

Figure 4.1: Classic interactice enviroment by Myron Krueger. Courtesy of Myron Krueger.

providers. As in the popular arcade games of Nintendo or Sega Genesis, the user develops the skill of navigating and controlling things in the virtual environment provided by the game's designers. The very terms we use to think about the "user" versus the "programmer" indicate the ready-made quality of typical computer simulations. The immersion happens through a suspension of selfhood. From the phenomenological viewpoint, HMD immersion renders entities directly. We see not only what the graphic images refer to, but we identify with them. Like the kid in the shoot-'em-up arcade game, we squint down the tunnel to lose ourselves as characters in the game. In VR, we see virtual entities in the graphics that refer us to things. Like the tame falcon, we are directed by HMD VR primarily toward entities and we are sent into a tunnel-like perceptual field where we encounter the entities.

The CAVE is not a tunnel but a shared place for telepresence. Apperceptive immersion allows us to feel ourselves perceiving the graphic entities. The freedom of bodily movement permits us to remain aware of ourselves alongside computer-generated entities. Apperceptive VR directs us towards experiencing the virtual world rather than toward the entities themselves. To put it simply, HMD VR creates tunnel immersion, while apperceptive VR creates a spiral telepresence that allows us to go out and identify with our cyberbody and the virtual entities it encounters and then return to our kinesthetic and kinetic primary body, and then go out again to the cyberbody and then return to our primary body, all in a deepening reiteration. The spiral of telepresence can work like a vortical helix that ascends upwards, taking us to new dimensions of self-awareness. Instead of *Tron*, we have the *Mandala* system. Instead of *Mortal Kombat* or *Doom*, we have *Myst*.

See Figure 4.1

The CAVE can create a social experience of shared discovery through telepresence. Not by accident was the first commercial version of projection VR named the *Mandala System*. The mandalas of Asian art oscillate between outer perception and inner self-awareness, all in an integrating spiral. The VR *Mandala System*, based on Krueger's earlier *Videoplace* , uses a blue-screen technique to project the individual's shape onto a single graphics wall. The user looks to the single wall to see the projected self toss the graphics ball and catch it. Two people can throw virtual frisbees. Unlike the protagonist of the film *Tron*, we do not entirely lose ourselves in *Mandala* immersion. The immersive environment is not a labyrinth, but it returns us to ourselves. You constantly see yourself in the *Mandala System*, while in the HMD you see yourself only if you come across a graphics mirror in the virtual world. In the realm of CD-ROM design, *Doom* or *Mortal Kombat* may channel intense energy down single paths of identification but the charm of *Myst* is to stun us repeatedly into becoming more aware of our disorientation, of our powers of exploration, of our sense of freedom. Of course, current multimedia CD-ROMs work only by analogy to VR. Present-day CD-ROMs show only the desktop, through-the-window view of a virtual world, and as such they always remain an abridged and diminished form of virtual experience. Nevertheless, the issue of interactivity in multimedia seems also to fall under the critical issue of perception/apperception.

HMD systems allow us to go "through the window" and engage

computerized entities, but apperceptive systems like the CAVE allow us to go further. If we could employ both hardware systems in the same proximate framework, then we could both enter cyberspace and at the same time celebrate the free play of our physical bodies. The difference between perception and apperception VR systems means more than an ergonomic difference, however. The difference goes beyond physical comfort. Users often appreciate the freedom of movement possible with unencumbered VR, and the word "unencumbered" expresses that freedom. But "non-encumbered" remains a merely negative definition, telling us only what this type of interface is not. By apperceptive VR, I suggest a positive definition of one of the crossroads facing VR development.

From the viewpoint of user phenomenology, the difference is one of the experience of the self. One supports a focused self and the other supports a wide-angle awareness. When we are not strapped into a helmet and datasuit, we can move about freely. The freedom of movement goes beyond feeling unshackled. It also means our spontaneity becomes engaged. Just watch for a few minutes the users of projection VR, how they turn and bend and move their bodies. Then contrast this with HMD users. The difference lies not only in the software or the environment rendered. The difference lies also in the hardware-to-human interface.

The creators of the CAVE implicitly grasped this. By referring to Plato's Cave—Thomas DeFanti fondly and frequently makes that reference,—the inventors of the CAVE recognize the human issue. The human issue concerns the freedom embedded in the hardware-to-human interface of VR. Around 425 B.C., Plato wrote, in Book VII of *The Republic*, a story he heard from his teacher, Socrates. Socrates' story of the Cave framed a centuries-old debate about the status of symbols, images, and representations. In Socrates' parable, the people chained to the floor of the Cave enjoy no physical mobility, and their immobilized position helps induce the trance that holds them fixed in its spell. They see shadows cast by artificial creatures ("puppets") held up behind them. The puppets have been created by human beings who want the prisoners to accept the shadows as the only real entities. The Cave consequently becomes a prison rather than an

environment for spontaneous behavior. Plato's Cave is a dungeon, not
to be confused with an art center like the Caves of Lascaux. Similar to
Plato's Cave, the HMD VR can facilitate a higher level of human productivity and an information-rich efficiency—whether for flying aircraft, undergoing training, or holding meetings in a corporate virtual
workspace—but it does so by exacting a human price.

Socrates ends his story by having one of the prisoners escape from
the mythical Cave. Someone unchains the prisoner who then walks
out the dark dungeon and then glimpses for the first time the sunshine and the light of real entities like trees and rocks and flowers. For
Socrates, the sunshine was the sphere of thinking and mental ideas.
As long as the person stays fixed in a purely receptive mode, chained
to indirect perceptions, the mind lives in the dark. By climbing out of
the Cave into the sun of self-thought ideas, the prisoner ascends to
the primary and true vision of things.

A line often quoted from my book *The Metaphysics of Virtual
Reality* states that "Cyberspace is Platonism as a working product."
With its virtual worlds, cyberspace transcends the physical by replacing it with the electronic heaven of ideally organized shapes and
forms. What must be added to this statement is that we need therefore to offset and balance our electronic Platonism if we are to put
this product to good use. To do so, we must revise the Cave
metaphor. Platonic idealism, especially in its hardware installation,
neglects the powerful primal body energies that are central to non-
Western practices like yoga, acupuncture, and Tai Chi. To escape
tunnel VR, we need to heighten our primary world awareness and
then use electronic systems to support the wide-angle awareness that
comes from liberating practices. In a cave, all outer sounds are
smothered by rock and earth, and this makes the sounds of one's
own heartbeat and breath audible. The CAVE has the potential to
bring us closer to the balanced 50-percent-inner / 50-percent-outer
awareness sought by enlightened traditions. From Tunnel VR to Spiral VR, we gain in self-knowledge. The light at the end of the tunnel
is the open air of liberation at the end of the cave. If we neglect the
fresh breeze that Tai Chi can bring into the CAVE—the somatic
focus implied by Tai Chi—we will never achieve the balanced

lifestyle of virtual realism. The CAVE leads us from the tunnel only when the virtual world revitalizes the body that already exists outside electronic systems. Our ultimate liberation—from idealism and crude realism—is to enhance and deepen our awareness of the primary body by directed use of the cyberbody. The centrifugal power of sensor-motor-activated visualization must be matched by the centripetal nervous-somatic inward movement. Only then will technology transfigure the human body rather than disfigure it. Then we will enjoy the spiral dance.

From the perspective of user *somatics*, the difference between apperceptive and perceptive VR is one of the primary body versus the cyberself construct. The term somatics I derive from Thomas Hanna's usage. Hanna defined somatics as the first-person experience of one's own body—as opposed to third-person accounts of one's body from a scientific or medical point of view. Somatic awareness is that line where conscious awareness crosses over into the autonomic nervous system: breathing, balance, and kinesthetic bodily feedback. The more we identify with a cyberself graphic construct, the less primary body somatics we preserve. Human attention is finite. When our attention becomes stretched and overextended, we feel stress. The HMD tunnel may provide the greatest tool for training and for vicarious experience, but it exacts the greatest price on the primary body.

Mediating these two types of VR is the liberating futuristic vision of Myron Krueger:

> An extremely lightweight, head-mounted display fits within traditional eyeglasses. There will be no extension cord connecting the wearer's head to a computer, nor will the wearer be cut off from the surroundings. It will be possible to make eye contact with co-workers and converse normally. Graphics will be displayed as objects in the physical world. Video cameras in the environment and in the glasses will perceive the participant and detect behavior including facial expression. These cameras will not perceive images. Rather they will track the person's features to determine the state of the model the computer has of them that most closely resembles the current pose. This information will be sufficient to make a three-dimensional graphic representation of the participant mimic that person's actions. This state of information can then be transmitted to another location and be used to construct the appropriate three-dimensional view

of the participant for each eye of every viewer in that location. Complementing this virtual reality technology will be a speech recognition capability that can analyze connected speech, identify individual words, and recognize simple commands that are directed at the computer. While the computer may ultimately be able to determine the semantic context of a conversation, intelligent understanding is not necessary for speech technology to change how we interact with computers, particularly in virtual reality. [18]

Such wonderful hardware could enhance somatics. The HMD and the CAVE would merge into a computer-augmented reality that does not entirely remove the perception of the primary world, or at least allows a wide range of options for layering informational graphics over the primary field of view. Combined with the right software, the sedentary body would rise again and the age-old gap between action and knowledge, information and situation would narrow and perhaps even close. The Tunnel would take us to the Cave, then by re-discovering ourselves by dancing in the Cave, we could emerge liberated, with greater well-being, more deeply comfortable in our bodies.

Interactive Installations

Contemporary art installations also teach us about reconstructing the digital. Artists today who install computer media in physical spaces confront the broader task of shaping technology to be livable and attractive. Right now, many people accept the annoying lights, snaking cords, and computer paraphernalia because everyday work conditions demand that they adapt to the machine "interface." But current technology does not merit survival. Obtrusive computers call attention to themselves as consumer goods but do not blend smoothly with the human world. Designers who install computers in art exhibits are facing the task of everyone who strives to integrate computers into a workable and pleasing holistic environment. Until designers work at the most fundamental levels of computing, the task of integrating "the computer" into the physical world space will remain a problem of individual accommodation.

The museum space that once belonged to modern art has been turned inside out. Curators of Modern art preferred clean, empty, light-filled spaces. These were spaces fit for the stylized paintings

of Matisse and Picasso, and for the elegant mobiles of Alexander
Calder. The room was an abstraction, a controlled place remote
from everyday mess. It was a space as clearly framed as the abstract
paintings hanging on the walls. The Pop Art of Warhol, Lichten-
stein, and others put a dent in the serious arrangements of Abstract
Expressionism, but the imagery of comic strips, soup cans, and
Coke bottles still belonged in the same room with those explorations of formal shapes, colors, and lines. In the nineteenth century, the Impressionists had pulled painting out of the stuffy statue-
filled rooms of Academic Classicism by setting up their easels
outdoors. The museum became a place to compare the Impressionists' light-splashed works and to watch the Cubism grow from
the experiments of the later Impressionists like Monet, Cézanne,
and Seurat. Pop Art then appeared alongside the Abstractionists,
displayed in airy, bright, open spaces. With the advent of electronic art, however, the traditional museum has been turned inside
out. For the first time in a century, the ambient lighting and room
arrangements undergo radical change. Current electronic art flips
off the museum lights, shuts the doors, and invites the contempla-
tor to become a doer. The gallery that exhibits electronic installations looks more like a cave than a sidewalk café.

One example of an electronic environment was exhibited in
Spring 1995 at the Art Center College of Design in Pasadena, California. "Hidden in Plane Sight" by Clarence Major exemplifies and
reflects upon the gallery as a new kind of space, a space darkened for
interaction and a space whose traditional framing activity has been
penetrated by the glowing code of cyberspace.

"Hidden in Plane Sight" brings into view the whole context in
which we perceive art works. By plunging our awareness into holistic
design, Clarence Major crosses the line between artist and curator,
designer and environmental engineer. Electronic space sucks in
older works as if they were information packets and yet this space is
soft enough to be bent back on itself to become the subject of its own
presentation. Major's environmental design is an installation of several "rooms" that begins with the viewer stepping through the frame
of one of the paintings hung on a wall, then wraps the participant in

See Figures 4.2 and 4.3

a surround of interactive movies, then continues through curving walls until the viewer stands before an exit monitor showing the explorations that continue in real time inside the previous rooms. The curving of space becomes itself the work of art. The frame gives way to the tunnel and then spirals back to everyday space. Major reminds us that art work in a software environment means building worlds by absorbing previous worlds and by grasping the context in which anything can appear in the worlds. Context becomes content.

Several darkened rooms in the Williamson Gallery at Art Center in the Fall of 1995 held the space for the "Digital Mediations" exhibit where Sara Roberts installed her *Elective Affinities*. The back wall of the room serves as the screen for a film showing a continuous back-drop of highway as though showing the visitor the view through the back window of an automobile cruising through a rural countryside. Stationed on the floor of the room are four interactive platforms, each holding the face of a simulated passenger projected on a half-mirrored pane of glass. Four projected people, two men in front, two women in back, face forward in a simulated automobile. The hum of the car and its interior sounds are heard in the room. Instead of traveling yourself on a simulated roadway, as in the typical arcade game, the situation is reversed: you view the four simulated passengers who appear to be dri-ving down the highway in an automobile. You are the viewer and the lively filmed images appear to do the traveling. It's as though you could enter the interior of a passenger vehicle without being noticed. In fact, the voyeurism here is clairvoyant, because not only can you watch the four travelers and see their gestures and glances without being detected, but you can even overhear their unspoken thoughts if you wish. Approach any of the pods of the half-mirrored images (pro-jectors inside each platform throws the filmed images on the screen), and you can hear the inner voice of the passenger grow steadily audi-ble. You enter the stream of consciousness flowing through any of the travelers if you approach them. The pods are triggered by sensors in the floor that detect your approach.

The easy thrill of voyeurism, however, quickly turns into a more substantial interest. The comments overheard from one character in the car tell you something about that person's relationship to the

See Figure 4.4

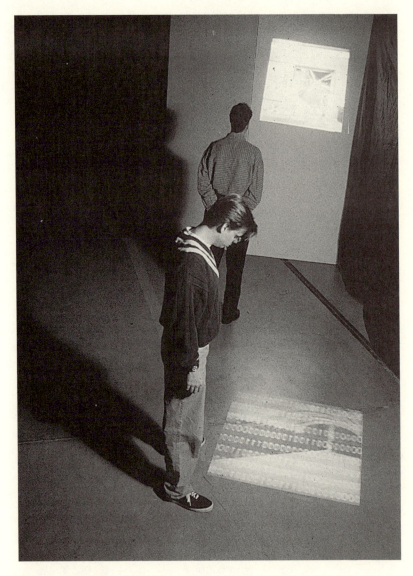

Figure 4.2 Installation "Hidden in Plane Sight" by Clarence Major, 1995.
Photo by Clarence Major.

other characters in the car. You learn that one couple in the car are married and run a business for which the other two passengers work. Infatuations and suspicions smolder among the four. You listen for minutes to the inner monologue as it veers endlessly in ever-different directions. You feel an extraordinary intimacy with these

Figure 4.3 Installation "Hidden in Plane Sight" by Clarence Major, 1995. Photo by Clarence Major.

characters whose private thoughts you can hear as long as you want. The half-mirrored glass that reflects the animated film of the actor's face eliminates the frame-like computer monitor, so you feel intuitively closer to what seems a seated automobile passenger. The filmed facial sequences add a photo-realism that resonates with our deep-seated attachment to the human face, the spark of intimacy ignited by facial expressions. Intimacy and identification grow until finally a curiosity about the other characters arises, and it is time to perceive the passenger from their perspectives.

You break from the pod and approach another passenger pod. A different perspective on the four passengers emerges, though many of the other passengers' daydreams share points in common, which helps you piece together a bit more of the interpersonal world you have entered. Curiosity about other parts of their life stories drives you to another pod, and another. Things get as complex as any nineteenth-century novel. The *pour soi* segues inevitably into the *en soi*, or, to put it in the language of Jean-Paul Sartre's Garcin in *No Exit*, "Hell?—that's other people." Unlike a soap opera or a television talk show, however, the multi-perspective story unravels ever deeper insights into each character and their relationships; the events are less important than the way they are recalled and made present in the situation. The concentration on this one scenario allows you to contemplate the life issues brought up. You discover that the four people are entangled with each other through marriage, business, friendship, and infatuation. Their inner affinities put them together and then pull them apart. Among their secrets are complex attractions and repulsions. The foursome in the car are nearing a pivotal point in their complex relationships.

Twenty minutes in the room, and you feel oddly familiar with Edward, Charlotte, Otto, and Ottilie. A poignant intimacy comes from overhearing thoughts alternate between random small-talk and strikingly personal revelations. Flashes of intuition hit you as you gradually put together a mental-emotional profile all four people. Here is a sample from the audible monologues:

```
Edward: Man is a true narcissus. He makes the whole
    world his mirror. Otto's world is all straight
    lines, perfect circles, following the rules. He
    used to have fun. The rules are taking over,
    though. He sees the world like a plan. Oh, it's
    too bad what happens to people. —That girl needs
```

to be gotten out of the city more often. The way
she stared at those deer! I'll take her to the
beach. Imagine her in a bikini! No, don't imagine her in a bikini. . . . You're driving. Oh,
she would look good!—Driving in, I was shy about
looking back, afraid she'd see me staring. Some
dirty old man leching after her. That's what people might think, I suppose. We need a protected
spot to let this happen, let this little bean
seed get its head out of the ground. Where?

Charlotte: Handed me the flower. He's excited about
finding a dogwood in bloom. Big hands reaching up,
gently cutting off the flower, with his pock-
etknife, not tugging. And then, he wanted to kiss
me. Then?—Funny that he's telling this tale about
the chemically perfect match, perfect union.
Nothing's perfect. We slide along with each
other's faults: my over-sensitivity, his selfish-
ness. Proud of our endurance. This . . . pefec-
tion is almost an insult. What good is it if it
comes easy? It could be that he has noticed a current running between Otto and me. That's weird,
though. I barely noticed it before today. Well,
that's not entirely true. If Edward noticed it,
he would not notice it consciously, but he might
feel it. This little thing with Ottilie could be
his striking back, at me and Otto.

Elective Affinities was based on a novel by the German poet Johann
Wolfgang von Goethe (1749–1832). Goethe's novella, *Wahlver-
wandtschaften*,[19] explored the nature of passionate bonding. Goethe
wrote at the time when chemists first discovered that the bond
between two substances may break when a third substance with a
more complementary molecular makeup approaches the bonded substances. The term "affinity" is still used to describe this chemical phe-

nomenon, and Goethe's novel applied this scientific notion to human affairs. Sara Roberts in turn adapted Goethe's humanistic novel to create a computerized interactive world that blends literature, film, and installation design.

Roberts, explaining her work, tells how she fed into the computer the scripts of intimate monologues revolving around twenty-five different obsessions for each character with twelve different points of interaction among the characters. The complex "thought wheels" she created fill the walls of another room at the exhibit. Actors record the monologues and the computer synchronizes them in cycles according to a matrix of moods based on the following equations:

- self-confidence + tension = manic

- self-confidence + relaxation = sensual & pleasurable

- no self-confidence + tension = worry

- no self-confidence + no tension = depression

Whenever one of the characters looks at another, the look triggers a jump to a different mood among the passengers in the automobile. The characters seem to drive each other. Goethe's humanistic novel of complex emotional intrigue is reincarnated on the computer. Roberts recovers the scientific reference of Goethe's humanistic work by adapting it to the computer. Not physical chemistry, but computer science becomes the transcendental science that helps illumine life's labyrinth. Computing has become the model for complexity, and Roberts evokes the tangled web that Goethe saw in the affairs of the human heart. Goethe's novel has a concluding chapter, but not so Roberts' installation. You leave *Elective Affinities* with no sense of closure, no sense of having exhausted the stories that play on in the virtual passengers' minds.

The half-mirror technique, which projects video of a previously filmed actor onto the screen, has proven a powerful technique in other art works. The technique adds a touch of photo-realism without trying to represent the primary world. It spins an intimate world that evokes the imagination and involves the viewer. Another artist working with this technique has added hypermedia to the stand-alone video characters. Thousands of people first encountered this work at the computer graphics show SIGGRAPH '91 in the Las Vegas Convention Center in 1991.[20] Hundreds lined up in "Tomorrow's Realities" to stand one-at-a-time before Luc Courchesne's *Portrait One*. There they encountered "Marie," a thirty-four-year-old French-speaking Montrealer played by the actress Paule Ducharme. Marie carries on a simulated conversation with a viewer who responds by using a mouse to choose one of a number of possible responses. Marie was an instant success at SIGGRAPH, with crowds standing around to watch as each viewer interacts. The viewer clicks on one of the phrases on the head-level display, and Marie looks up and stares, "Are you talking to me?" Another menu of possible responses pops up, and the viewer clicks on one of the options. Marie responds, and with each response, you see a different video segment that animates the mood and course of the conversation. Sometimes Marie looks you in the eye, and sometimes she sighs and seems bored. If you choose the right responses, you will find the conversation going on and on, to ever increasing depths, engaging some quite personal, and even existential questions. The short conversations leave the viewer with a haunting sense of Marie's presence. My own first thought on leaving the hypermedia portrait was: "I've played with Joseph Weizenbaum's program Eliza that simulates a psychiatrist. That text-only simulator plays to a small part of the human brain, the verbal-conceptual side. Talk to this computer that has video appeal, and you feel an increase in presence of several magnitudes. You feel you are speaking with a friend or psychiatrist who (maybe) understands you. There's something wonderful and scary about the power of video to engage our reality receptors. In this portrait, we are looking at the front end of the computer systems of the future!"

See Figures 4.5, 4.6, 4.7, and 4.8

Recent work by Luc Courchesne expands his hypermedia and also parallels the work of Sara Roberts. Both artists develop interactive computer scenarios that create a sense of intimacy, of human understanding. Both artists direct a crew of actors, photographers, script writers, and computer programmers. Using hypermedia tools, Courchesne adds a further interactive touch by enlisting the visitors'

real-time responses. The viewer's response becomes an integral part of
the conversational event, even though the video portraits are themselves pre-recorded script sequences. The computer's branching capa-
bilities allow the interactive portrait to respond with a complex matrix
of topics. The psychological insight and the drama in the dialogue
cover the limited responses available to the viewer. The limiting artifi-
ciality of the interaction remains beneath the surface so long as the
script delights and instructs. Courchesne's exhibit *Family Portrait*
raises his portraiture to a new level.

Family Portrait appeared at the Power Plant Contemporary
Gallery in Toronto for the Spring 1995 "Press/Enter" exhibit at the
Harbourfront Center. Here the interactive portrait encompasses a
society of networked beings. Each portrait can host one active visitor, but the society of virtual beings can also separate themselves
socially from the visitor or group of visitors. One member of the
family will glance at another and make a remark, sometimes causing
all the family members to break up in laughter, as at some family in-
joke. The visitor can feel rudely excluded for several seconds. Members of the family interact with visitors who approach and click on
the hypertext, just as in Portrait One, but the visitor always feels like
an outsider. On entering the exhibit, four members of the family are
apparently talking with one another, enjoying their shared personal
history. While interacting with the visitor, a family member will
make an obscure reference to family memories, bringing confusion
to the visitor while another family member overhears and comments
on the remembered event. Courchesne works increasingly toward
installations where the visitor chooses whether or not to penetrate
an already programmed social network, much like an immigrant
arriving in a foreign country.

To convey some of the complexity of the background scenario, here
is Courchesne's description of the members of *The Family Portrait*:

Enter a portrait gallery. Norbert is a mathematician and dancer; he is also a friend of
Sebastien, an ethnologist interested in majorettes and rugby teams. Alain is Simone's
son and the former biology professor of Laurence, who specializes in archeobotany and
is looking for work. Thierry and Laurence are close friends, having shared an apartment

in the past. Thierry is a writer and works in a library; this is where he met Marianne, a graduate student in economics. It is through Thierry that Marianne and Laurence met Sebastien, and through Laurence that Marianne and Sebastien met Alain, who also owns a sheep farm in the Alps that is regularly visited by most of these people. Blanche, the author's daughter, first met Norbert in Montreal when he came to participate in a dance festival and stayed in their home. She later got to meet everyone else in Marseille when the author's family spent the summer there in 1992. This edition of the **Family Portrait** is about these people; it documents their life and tells about the process in which the work evolved. The group portrait was recorded in Marseille that summer.[21]

Like Sara Roberts, Luc Courchesne brings literary density to electronic design. In fact, Courchesne has little personal interest in the technology as such. He uses the hypermedia of mouse interaction and HyperCard stacks not because he rejects higher technologies like voice recognition but because he wants to keep developing rich content rather than focus on technologies that are not yet on the shelf. His work links the computer to ancestors in literature and fine-arts portraiture. Courchesne insists that he is not striving for photo-realism as much as psychological realism. He approaches his art as an "imperfect mirror" that does not seek to mirror reality perfectly. Instead, he aims to produce insight and the experience of social truth:

> I use technology to make portraits. A portrait of someone is an account of an encounter between the author and the subject. Painted portraits happened over long periods of time and therefore are more conceptual than photographic portraits. They encapsulate in one single image hours of interaction between the model and the painter. Photography, on the other hand, makes realist portraits. The talent of the portrait photographer is to wait and pick the right moment when the person expresses the density of her being; the subject and the photographer wait for that magic moment in complicity. In my portraits, the entire encounter is recorded, and material is extracted to construct a mechanics of interaction that will allow visitors to conduct their own interviews. As this happens over time, the conversation evolves toward more intimate considerations. The visitor will have to invest time and great care to get to the subject's more secret personality, just as it took time and care for the author to get there.

The mystery that Courchesne builds into his interactive videos does not mirror the sensory impressions of the physical person, though

Figure 4.9 Electronic Installation "Silicon Remembers Carbon" by David Rokeby. Photo by David Rokeby.

the cinematic touch does seem crucial to the interviews. Courchesne's "imperfect mirror" captures the psychological complexity of the individual and society. Without the mysterious attraction of the human face, the "family" would consist of no more than: four aluminum tubes, eight aluminum beams, twenty aluminum panels, four glass sheets, four aluminum pedestals with computers and speakers, four laser disk players, and four video monitors. The power of the glass and metal comes from the world-projecting powers of the human visitor. The point is not to create a Turing test that demonstrates the prowess of engineering. Nor is the point to create illusions or even a striking facsimile of reality. Rather, the point is to employ artifice to explore the mental and emotional mysteries of human contact. This type of interaction expands the visitor's sense of what human relationships are, how they emerge, and how fragile they can be. *Family Portrait* does not try to function as a complete virtual world, but it does show how psychological and literary content adds a winding inner depth to interactive design.

See Figures 4.9 and 4.10

After the human-centered portraiture of Luc Courchesne, it takes your breath away to walk into David Rokeby's *Silicon Remembers Carbon*, also at the Power Plant in 1995. Again, the exhibit room is in total darkness, except for the floor which is flooded with light from above. A large platform over most of floor contains a foot of beach sand. Bright light on the sand illumines the mounds and throws into shadowy relief the footprints you find on a beach. The light from above changes and shifts, bringing out patterns and imposing electronic graphics onto the shimmering sand. You, or one of the other visitors in the room, soon venture onto the sand to add another footprint to the many footprints already there. As soon as you put your weight on the floor, you see the lights change and new patterns undulate across the floor. You experiment, and eventually you are playing with the mix of random and predictable changes in lighting and sand shadows created by your steps. Sometimes the floor slowly changes into a very sharp vision of watery waves washing over the

Figure 4.10 Electronic Installation "Silicon Remembers Carbon" by David Rokeby. Photo by David Rokeby.

sand with a natural ebb and flow supported by appropriate electronic sounds of the sea. Sometimes the waves of light pulse with colors. Sometimes the sandbox becomes a huge electronic sculpture that you might associate with the word "cyberspace," looking like the wash of black-and-white static on a giant television screen tuned to a dead channel. The dark figure of another visitor steps into the sand, and the waves respond with rippling patterns.

What unhinges you in *Silicon Remembers Carbon* is its eerie vision of cyberspace. The environment responds to the slightest shift of weight to physical human presence. But that response does not correspond in size or shape to the normally expected causation. Each step you take sets the environment in motion, but you never know why that specific motion arose or exactly how you caused it. Just the opposite of electronic portraiture, this work exhibits the transhuman aspect of electronic art by invoking the origin of life, the ocean. The ancient Greeks distinguished the sea — the mapped water that sailors knew and navigated — from the Ocean, which is the vast uncharted, thrilling vastness of open water outside known horizons. *Silicon Remembers Carbon* pours the beach back into the computer chip that came from silicon sand, and then that electronic beach allows carbon life-forms in the shape of humans to stumble in and influence that non-human electronic space. The human influence does not function with fully transparent, rational causality. As you walk across the sand, you might catch a glimpse of several shadowy human figures running along the edge of the sandy floor with no evident cause from the visitors in the room. Suddenly, you might notice indistinct figures on an opposite end of the sand scurrying and talking in an unknown language. Most unsettling is the feeling of the continuous liquidity of the light patterns on the sand. Every step or slightest shift of balance effects instantaneous changes in the thin skein of cyberspace. Humans walk on its surface like water spiders skittering on a pond. Heraclitus would have loved to step into this sandbox. Some of us get seasick looking for information on the Internet — even if we often find valuable information there. If the word "cyberspace" conjures up the panorama of a vast non-human territory, then this art lays bare the landscape of cyberspace.

All these darkened rooms with their electronic ghosts signal a shift
to virtual realism, an inversion of modern lifestyles. At the first
encounter, these works seem made of passionless metal and glass
plugged into electricity. But not long after spending time with them
in the darkened room, walking around them, giving yourself to the
interaction, you feel the powerful inner tug of these works, their serious struggle with the meaning of the current transition, the effort to
express this complex historical moment. If you allow these installations to reach down to the place where you live, to that inner discomfort where you feel the effects of media on your mind, to the frequent
doubts about life increasingly caught in the technological grid, to
your struggles to integrate in a sane way the television, computers,
and telephones that populate your life, then these art works can move
you to tears. But the emotional relationship to such art works is complex and confused, like the long, convoluted narrative in Wim Wenders' film *Until the End of the World*. These art works speak to you
about the "media sickness" that burns the brain, of the uncanny feeling that we are "disappearing through the skylight," as O.B. Hardison
put it. As Derrick de Kerckhove says: "There used to be a time when
history was reality, but today reality is in danger of becoming history."

See Figure 4.11

The poignant feelings at this moment of historical transition
were captured by a 1985 silkscreen print hung at the entrance to the
Toronto Power Plant's 1995 *Press/Enter* exhibit. The image *Bridge
at Remagen* by John Massey contains many levels of meaning and
it addresses the various levels of media that are now in transition.
The two-dimensional image holds a drawing of hands done in
three-dimensional perspective. The hands hold a two-dimensional
illusory image, and the image they hold is digitized footage showing a romantic scene from the 1969 Hollywood film *The Bridge at
Remagen* set in World War II Germany and directed by John
Guillermin. The image shows images holding images. The movie
comes down from the big screen and exists now in hands that will
set the movie into another medium. The movie is pulled out of its
element for the time being. At the moment they get passed from
their original element to a more encompassing medium, the
images are most fragile. They must be handled in ways that hide

the fact that they are now growing distant, no longer as involving as they were in their own element. The digitized movie is not the mechanical cinema. A bridge is under way between these media, but it does not yet span the abyss. The moment images are removed from their element, they reveal something about the prior medium that we could not see earlier when we identified with those images on the big screen. The images now seem vulnerable, torn out of their element, desperately in need of new context.

Building a new home for images, besides being scary, is also fun. It is an opportunity for people to come together and experience a confluence of new energies. Most of these installations were built by teams of artists. Usually the team divides the technical and the design work but dovetails both from the beginning of the plan. The technical and the artistic go hand-in-hand. Myron Krueger, the VR pioneer, began his experiments in the 1970s as an installation artist who created interactive environments that appeared first in museums. He traces his computer breakthroughs to the artists of the 1960s who dabbled with involving audiences in a more active way. He was inspired by the Happenings of Allan Kaprow and by the interactive sculptures of James Seawright and Wen-Ying Tsai. These artists, like the contemporary installation artists I mentioned, point to a future where artists see how easily they can acquire technical skills and where software engineers understand how important it is to work with artists from the ground up.

The fun extends to the visitors who enter the electronic installations. The electronic exhibit offers not only interactivity between people and machines but also an opportunity for exchange between people and people. Electronic art almost always invites the visitor to come and play with it. Another person's confirmation is one of the strongest factors in achieving a high degree of presence.

Like the CAVE, an interactive installation widens the spiral of primary presence where people encounter other people encountering technology. This mutual awareness builds a sense of fuller presence. It is the basis for creating worlds and for integrating virtual worlds into the primary world. When I notice others and they notice me, the environment becomes a shared environment. This does not mean

See Figure 4.12

that the CAVE is primarily social, but it does tend to leave the way open for apperception. The environment then supports a richer sense of being present. This principle applies also to online worlds. The stronger my sense that others recognize me as an agent in a virtual environment, the stronger grows my experience of telepresence.

If *Bridge at Remagen* evokes that precarious moment of transition when one medium gets swallowed by another, then Robert Wedemeyer's *Virtual Reality Simulator* invites us to laugh at the ultimate grounding of all media. All of our media rely ultimately on the primal body that tunes in to Earth and Sky. Wedemeyer's *VR Simulator* widens our field of view by re-sensitizing us to context. His simulation of virtual reality widens our view literally because the eye lenses in the goggles consist of two security viewers of the type you see built into front doors where you check who it is that knocks on the door. These lenses allow 3-D depth perception with fish-eye, wide-angle viewing. The earphones are conch seashells, the headband is genuine leather, and the casing is made of solid oak wood. This head-mounted display recalls the wider field of life itself where everything artificial and natural ultimately blends into an integral world. Technology too must contribute directly to that harmony. The *VR Simulator* surely belongs to the gear of the putative Virtual Tai Chi Master who reminds us daily to lift our hands to the sun as we feast on the intimate connection our pulsing bodies have to the cosmic forces that ground and sustain all worlds. This is the head-mounted display that leads us out of the dark tunnel into the spinning sun.

5

InfoEcology

InfoEcology is a hybrid name for a hybrid growth. The word refers to grafting information systems onto planetary health. As a sample of virtual realism, InfoEcology mixes high technology with the pragmatic maintenance of finite creatures. InfoEcology shows how permeable the fences have become between logical systems and survival anxieties. If the fences between fine arts and software engineering are falling, so too are the fences between information systems and planetary activism. The conventional barriers are proving as permeable as the graphic walls of a computerized architectural walkthrough: You push on the wall, and voilà! you are standing on the other side. Walls seem glaringly artificial today, and we acknowledge this with hybrid spellings like InfoEcology.

The term was an offspring, as I recall, from the Amsterdam-based conference called "The Doors of Perception." In January 1995, the planning session for the November 1995 third annual "Doors of Perception" conferences buzzed with the term "Info-Eco." The plan was to bring together information theorists and ecologists from around the world. Ezio Manzini from the Domus Academy in Milan, John Thackara from England and the Netherlands Design Institute, and Willem Velthoven of *Mediamatic Magazine* convened the conference to bring together the "happy" information pioneers with the "worrying" ecologists. The meeting, they hoped, would inject information systems with global purpose. After the planning session, I began using the term in my own way to describe the pragmatics of information systems. Perhaps my usage was characteristically American rather than European. The predominantly European conference in Amsterdam focused its twelve workshops on social organization. They looked, for instance, at how people could cut down on the use of materials and energy by using the Internet to distribute local goods and services. My focus, on the other hand, turned to technological tools as they transform the engineers' approach to ecological disasters on American soil. The Europeans saw InfoEcology as centering on people. The American InfoEcology I describe revolves around technology as a tool for transfiguring disaster.

Our Own Dirty Nuclear Laundry

Stick Planet Earth into a VR system, do a global search-and-replace for toxic waste, delete the garbage and replace it with pristine nature. Oh, and while you're at it, please don't forget to turn on the Telerobotic Coupling Mode, so the real Planet Earth gets cleaned up in the process.

The actual procedure isn't quite so simple, but what I've described comes not from science fiction but from real-world ecology operations. In fact, when I teach seminars on virtual reality in Los Angeles graduate schools, I usually take the students on a field trip to Redondo Beach, California, where they can see with their own eyes a VR system for cleaning up hazardous waste sites. Of course, we don't neglect the flash-and-boom fun trips to entertainment centers like Virtual Worlds in Pasadena—the games *Battletech* and *Red Planet*—but the future of VR on Planet Earth seems deeply tied to sober projects like the one in Redondo Beach at One Space Park Drive, where engineers at TRW Space and Defense Systems are applying virtual worlds to achieve important results for the U.S. Department of Energy.

Unpleasant as they are to think about, we have in this country many dirty chemical processing plants littering the American landscape, the unseemly leftovers of the nuclear arms race. Film documentaries refer to these plants as the "invisible thousand-year legacy of the Cold War." The radioactive contamination in these plants remains invisible to the population, and future generations will have to deal with

the radioactivity in these plants for centuries. The U.S. government
built the plants over a fifty-year period to produce nuclear weapons and
to process the radioactive materials related to nuclear production.

During the Cold War, the U.S. Department of Defense built hundreds of secret buildings to work on radioactive materials for producing atomic bombs. These plants were quick-and-dirty structures
thrown together with war-time expediency. Nobody wondered back
then how we were going to dismantle them, and no one considered
how we might clean them up. Documentation was minimal, and
cost constraints were few. Even in the rare cases where the original
blueprints still exist, most of the buildings have undergone frequent
modifications. Many of the plants are highly contaminated as the
result of fires, spills, and normal operations. Some rooms are so contaminated that no one ever enters them and all operations are performed with telerobots.

Since their construction in the 1940s and 50s, these buildings
haven't conveniently disappeared, though the media now remains relatively silent about them. The U.S. Department of Energy still shoulders the responsibility for overseeing these toxic sites. Far into the next
century, federal engineers will have to deal with the sites by decom-
missioning, decontaminating, and dismantling them. Estimate for the
cleanup of these plants runs around $300 billion and the cleanup is
expected to take 50–75 years.

Sometimes the structures can be modified for other purposes, but
first they must be de-toxified, or torn down permanently. The nuclear
waste products from these plants will remain hazardous for centuries
after the sites are cleared. Dismantling the sites is no trivial task, especially since we have so little accurate information about the structures
or what they contain.

Virtual Reality is playing an increasingly important role in cleaning
up these toxic sites. VR supports planning the operations and also
training the workers to dismantle them with less risk to personal safety.
A virtual walkthrough can reduce human errors and optimize workers'
efficiency in the dangerous conditions of the sites. Efficiency is crucial
because a ten-minute exposure to some "hot" areas can give a worker
an entire year's dosage of radiation (measured in "person rem"), so

every second on the site is a precious commodity. When a plant is shut
down without power and lights, workers can easily fall through holes
in the floor or down deteriorated stairwells. By experiencing the building beforehand through a VR environment, workers can become
familiar with hazards in advance. A worker can absorb subconscious
physical cues and situational orientation so that work in the buildings
goes smoothly.

VR displays also provide augmented blueprints that are rich with
relevant data, such as the levels of radioactivity at a location. The
models of the virtual buildings can be updated in seconds and a precise "blueprint" of every change can be tracked with little effort.
Operations can be planned so that structures are demolished in the
correct order, with optimal cost effectiveness, and with minimal risk
of workers' health. The walkthrough models record the experiences of
the crew as they dismantle the toxic sites.

The Old Way: CAD

Before the introduction of VR, the procedure for dismantling a toxic
site began with manual information gathering. Information about the
buildings was then fed into computers to construct computer-aided
design models (CAD).

Gathering the information was tedious and dangerous. Engineers
in hard hats would first enter the structures carrying clip boards and
tape measures so they could blueprint and inventory each building.
Manual information gathering is a time-consuming and dangerous
task. Special precautions have to be taken to reduce human exposure
to irradiated materials. Though their dangers are mostly invisible,
toxic sites are a mess. The cleanup crews must be on guard against
chemical contamination, radioactivity, and a myriad of physical hazards. At one building, for instance, the engineers had to slam the
entry door several times loudly before entering so the poisonous
snakes would be put on notice. Once they enter a building, the engineers must look for the dark blotches from chemical spills that spot
the cement floors. At one building, engineers had to wear class B
environmental suits (fully covered with respirators), because the roof
had been eroded away by the birds and the floor was contaminated by

bird droppings, which, in high concentrations, can be toxic. At another building, one worker had to give up the pants he was wearing after a full-body scan detected radon gas in his "100% wool" pants, which contained trace amounts of polyester, which in turn attracts radon. Spending time around these sites to collect data requires caution, time, and expertise.

Once the manual collection of information is done, the data goes into a CAD model. Software engineers use the information to draw models to help plan the most cost-effective procedures for dismantling the sites. The CAD models speed up the dismantling process by several times, but traditional CAD graphic models may take months of work to produce. Here the traditional method of data entry by hand remains error prone, and the procedure must be supervised and checked thoroughly. After the data is entered, the software engineers build up a CAD wireframe model and then use graphics rendering to transform the bare geometry of the blueprints into a 3-D model of the physical buildings. The CAD model must offer a rich visualization of the site. Each surface of the model must be manually textured or colored to create a reflection of the 3-D world. This process is time-consuming. The CAD model of a toxic waste site, if it is to become a virtual walkthrough, must also offer an interactive mode. If the dismantling team can walk through the virtual site before dismantling it, and even manipulate virtual objects, then the cleanup crews can proceed more quickly and effectively.

So the logical advance beyond the old CAD approach is to automate the entry of data and, further, to automate the development of objects so that rendering brings about a virtual world with all its furniture. Companies like Alias Research in Toronto have struggled for years with the problem of converting their 2-D simulated renderings into virtual interactive 3-D objects. The problem grows more difficult as virtual-world files need to accomodate a growing variety of software formats and hardware platforms. But the fundamental problem of VR industrial applications has been how to bring real world objects into the virtual worlds with as little reality loss as possible.

"Reality loss" does not means a shortfall of sensory data. It does not mean that a model fails to reproduce every single sensory detail that we receive with our five unaided senses from some putative "objective world." Any "data" the engineer receives will always appear within the context of engineering. No engineering drawing ever reproduces the world pure and simple. A drawing always appears in a working context. A reality loss, then, means that some measurable inaccuracies can be found to lead the project astray despite every effort to produce an accurate model — where accuracy means reliability in the context of use.

A Breakthrough: Photogrammetry + VR

TRW has found a novel solution to the problem of how to put the real world of physical buildings into an accurate virtual model. The solution draws on defense research from the same Cold War that left us the hazardous waste sites. U.S. intelligence agencies developed powerful techniques to gather photo-realistic information about areas of surveillance. Now TRW software engineers have adapted those techniques to solve problems faced by the Department of Energy as it deals with the dismantling of toxic waste sites.

The TRW technique uses photogrammetry (the Greek words *photo gramma metria* mean "accurate drawings from photos"). Photogrammetry goes back to the era of espionage when the spy world found a way to build city maps by stitching together a series of overhead reconnaissance photographs. The spy plane collects the photos, then specially designed software reassembles the photos to make a total overview. The technique even allows users to zoom the view to scale, so that landscapes within the city become visible. From the sky, a spy plane can snap several photographs of a sector of Berlin, and, analysts can later plot a walkthrough operation in one alley located in that specific sector — all in photo-realistic detail.

As part of defense conversion, TRW engineers adapted photogrammetry to automate the construction of virtual worlds for displaying accurate walkthroughs of toxic waste sites. These walk-throughs facilitate faster and more accurate treatment of toxic sites. Photogrammetry was adapted to do close-range work, so that engineers could map the smaller-scale interiors of buildings as well as the outside overviews. To capture the dimensions of the rooms and their objects, the engineer can photograph the site while walking around or standing on a ladder indoors. If the site is heavily contaminated, a telerobot can maneuver the camera. Combined with outdoor photographs, the series of digital photos captures an entire site complete with exteriors and interiors of all the buildings. A special hand-held 35mm photogrammetry camera does the interior shots. (The camera used for photogrammetry has two unique features: Rousseau marks on each of the photographs provide precise guides for calibrating the software reconstruction of angles and objects; the lens has also been calibrated to allow software to correct distortion.)

How Photography Becomes Virtuality

First, the digital photos are put on CD-ROM, so that the special software can massage them. (The photos are 24-bit RGB digital photos, so they require considerable computer storage space. A recent series of 350 photos took 9 gigabytes.) The photogrammetry software maps the objects in the photographs to the virtual image space. The three-dimensional world gets mapped onto the pixel space of the computer display. The modified defense software calculates from any two photographs the exact point in 3-D space where the original objects exist. Features within the photographs, such as doors, furniture, windows, and lights, can be extracted by fitting CAD-like primitives to the photos. Because the modeler works directly on the photos, the objects are always positioned and oriented exactly as they were when the picture was taken. As each object is created, a color or phototexture is applied. TRW's software does this automatically, and the modeler simply chooses a photo or generic texture — which can be brick, wood, color, or even some color sampled directly from the photographs. There is no need for the manual cutting and pasting of textures from the photographs. The software performs the extraction and ortho-rectifies the textures for application to the polygons that constitute the virtual objects. At present, the process is novel and still requires the intervention of an experienced analyst/engineer, so TRW presently provides the service rather than selling the stand-alone package.

The mosaic of Figures 1–4 shows the relative steps in the process. The four images from the Hanford project depict the model building

See Figures 5.1, 5.2, 5.3, 5.4

of virtual realism. The photogrammetry camera shot is in the upper left (note the Rousseau marks left by the special lens). The upper right shows a wire-frame CAD-type rendering of the scene. In the lower left, color has been added to the scene. The final lower-right image shows the textured virtual-world version of the original Hanford site.

The toxic stains in upper-left photo appear on the floor of the plant in the primary world. The textured and colored virtual world (lower right) does not represent the actual site but adds photo-realistic touches that provide cues for later location recognition in the primary world. This functional realism creates a rehearsal scenario for preparing workers for dismantling the targeted site.

The result of the photogrammetry is a photorealistic, dimension-ally-accurate, 3-D model of an existing building—inside and out. The difference between photogrammetry and the traditional method of capturing a structure's geometry cannot be emphasized enough. The tedious process of constructing a 3-D CAD model for each surface of the model, the manual texturing and coloring, all these time-consuming processes are avoided, along with the manual data entry that is so prone to errors. Because the software builds models directly from digital photographs, the model's measurements and dimensions come as close as possible to the building's structure, making the computer model a virtual reality.

Where does the photograph-based building appear? At TRW, the 3-D models appear on Silicon Graphics Onyx Reality Engines which can render the photorealistic worlds in real time. The models derive from the Sense8 World Tool Kit with an X-Motif interface. SGI's twenty-one inch monitors display the graphics, and Crystal Eyes stereoscopic shutter glasses (synchronized to the monitor with infrared flashes) provide desktop virtual reality ("fish tank VR"). A space mouse with six degrees of freedom allows maneuvering, and datagloves can give a more immersive effect. The virtual worlds can be exported to a variety of commercial software formats so the models can work with different applications on different machines running on different platforms.

See Figure 5.5

The phototextures add more than aesthetics to the virtual worlds. Jim Cracraft, who leads the photogrammetry program at TRW, says that a key element of the system is phototextures. "I had been working on a model of a building in Oak Ridge, Tennessee which was to be decontaminated and torn down," Jim says. "For many hours, I moved through this building in the virtual reality environment. I became familiar with every door, column, beam, and window. On one of the exterior walls, there was a metal plate that dripped rust stains down the wall. A few weeks later, I visited the building in person. When I passed one of the walls, I felt a sudden tingle of déjà vu. A metal plate flashed in my mind. So I walked around the wall, and there was the rusty plate! A spooky feeling came over me." For Jim Cracraft, the phototextures add a realism that no generic brick texture can provide. And where people need instant recognition of physical dangers and obstacles, the textures help get the job done. Rehearsals in VR build into the user an alertness to subtle cues of peripheral perception that can later save lives.

Figure 5.5 Desktop VR at TRW. Photo courtesy of TRW.

The official name for the TRW program, according to Dr. Chuck Wuller, who directs the program, is "Characterization Analysis Planning System" (CAPS). CAPS integrates the company-developed photogrammetry, 3-D modeling, computer graphics, and virtual reality programs with commercial CAD, architect/engineering and robotic simulation software. Facility Characterization Services applies to other markets where industrial plants need special attention, such as oil refineries, off-shore platforms, and paper factories. The technique can also be used to build city-scape models for CD-ROM games or for military simulations. "Because it is still relatively expensive," Dr. Wuller says, "photogrammetry is best applied to facilities where access is limited or denied. As the research progresses, however, many of the tasks will be automated by software, which will greatly lower the cost of the procedure."

Another important feature of VR worlds is that they are information intense. Unlike traditional physical models or paper blueprints, the virtual sites consist of digital data, which can in turn link directly to different databases. A virtual reality model can contain any number of pieces of information beneath its 3-D textured surface. Unlike the primary physical world, the data world can provide instant analysis of its mathematical and physical properties. Click on a beam overhead and find out its metallurgical properties, tensile strength, and exactly how high it hangs above the floor.

The database behind a virtual world lowers the cost of real-world cleanups. When the quantities of radioactive waste remain unknown, they drive up cleanup costs. Since the VR model offers accurate lists of materials (what civil engineers call "quantity take-offs"), the virtual world helps answer real-world questions. Engineers need to ask:

- How much number 2 pipe will be removed and how much does it weigh?

- How many waste burial boxes will be required?

- What is the most contaminated object in the building and where is it located?

Besides the alphanumeric data, the VR setup also allows users to "try out" a "hands-on" dismantling operation, such as moving a beam or barrel through a narrow doorway, or testing the supportive strength of a cat walk.

The VR world can deliver the amount of relevant data and the level of visual detail that the job requires. A VR model can size down to the resolution of a screw slot or to the pixel level if sufficient photos are available. Each job will have its own needs and cost constraints, but in principle the VR worlds are like onions that can be peeled layer after layer, depending on what you want to see. CAD allows you to add invisible depths of data to the model. The resolution and level of detail are constrained only by the current system's need for some human intervention in the modeling process. You can zoom in on the model and see the building from any position, even from above through the ceiling, as is shown in Figure 5. This information intensity is, of course, what distinguishes full VR from toys like QuckTime VR which limit themselves to surfaces.

See Figure 5.6

Atomic Bomb Factory, Hanford, WA

See Figure 5.7

To date, TRW has worked on cleanup projects in Oak Ridge, Tennessee, in Fernald, Ohio, and, most recently, in Hanford, Washington. The work at Hanford began in March, 1995, and this work carries special symbolism because of the historic nature of the nuclear plant at Hanford.

The plant at Hanford has the official status of a U.S. Historic Place. The Hanford T Plant produced the plutonium for the first atomic bomb. Plutonium from the Hanford Plant became the fissionable core for the world's first nuclear explosion at the Trinity bomb test in Alamogordo, New Mexico, on July 16, 1945. The Hanford Plant also produced the plutonium core of the weapon dropped over Nagasaki, Japan, on August 9, 1945. Now the same plant that produced atomic bombs is being rebuilt to serve as the decontamination site for other plants at Hanford. The Hanford Plant has been idle for twenty years, and the first phase of its conversion requires that its electrical gallery be retro-fitted so that the building can function as the "de-con station" for the other plants' materials.

Figure 5.6 Ceiling Zoom on Model of TRW Loading Dock.
Photo courtesy of TRW.

To build a VR model of the electrical gallery of the Hanford Plant site, TRW engineers took 350 digital photos (about nine gigabytes) to capture the 800-foot long, thirty-by-thirty-foot building. The engineers used one-third of these photos to construct the functional model.

The TRW virtual-world models also include the feature I referred to as the "Telerobotic Coupling Mode." TRW has a cooperative agreement with Deneb Robotics, a firm in Ann Arbor, Michigan, to create immersion options for "robotic workcells" (a robotics term for virtual worlds). TRW was the first to create phototextured IGRIP robotic workcells, so that a user can manipulate virtual objects which can in turn activate real-world manipulations. At the Hanford T Plant, for example, objects are handled by overhead cranes with operators sitting at video consoles. The virtual model transmits the

Figure 5.7 Model of Ore Hopper in Plant 5 at Fernald, Ohio.
Photo courtesy of TRW.

operator's actions in the virtual world to the overhead mechanisms. In such cases, the software can remember the paths of the operator's actions and can make adjustments for the real-world constraints of the mechanisms. The operator can remain in the loop, can engage some parts of the loop, or the operation can be totally automated.

The Transformation of Engineering

How does the application of virtual reality change engineering? What benefits do engineers expect?

While the engineering applications of VR are new and still developing, Terry Meier of Meier Associates in Kennewick, Washington, has formed a strong opinion after having worked with the TRW crew at the Hanford Plant. "We are looking at a revolution in the engineering field," says Meier, "and this revolution will change the way we do everything, with an impact as big as the impact of CAD machines." Meier says that the photogrammetry-based VR "brings reality into engineering documents. It's not simply the cost savings—which runs roughly 20–50%—but it's the quality of the data that makes this system powerful." Meier observed the whole procedure: a 3-person TRW crew photographed the site for 2 days, then Jim Cracraft spent 2 weeks analyzing and processing the data, then Meier received the virtual-world model of the plant. "Now I have the complete data on the facility," says Meier, "and the data is embedded in the real-world building captured in photogrammetry. I have the reality of the site with a 3-D model which I can zoom into and dynamically pan. I have a model that will be good for the life of the facility."

Reality Captured?

But wait one philosophical minute! The engineer boasts of "capturing the reality of the site." Does this mean that VR photogrammetry shrinks reality to the computer? Is the primary site actually reduced to a representation? Does "capturing reality" mean that we will soon have a VR Turing Test where visitors test whether or not they can distinguish the virtual from the real site? Doesn't the phrase "capturing reality" violate the principle of virtual realism? After all, virtual realism states (citing Chapter Two):

- **Virtual worlds do not re-present the primary world**. They are not realistic in the sense of photo-realism. Each virtual world is a functional whole that parallels, not re-presents or absorbs the primary world we inhabit.

Photogrammetry does indeed apply photorealism to virtual worlds, both for the initial data capture and for some finishing touches of realism. At the same time, however, the engineers do not embrace VR as a full-blown reproduction of the primary building. They do not end up with a completely photo-realistic model even though the model does display certain photo-realistic textures. If the TRW engineers truly sought "to capture the reality" of the Hanford Plant, then these engineers would be suffering from a bad case of virtual idealism. If the reality of the Hanford Plant could be fully contained in the computer data, then we would abandon virtual realism for what I call "data idealism." Data idealism lacks the cautious tone and limiting conditions of virtual realism.

The data idealist believes that perception consists of data input to the senses from the environment. For the data idealist, the more data impressions that go into the senses, the more reality gets to the mind. Reality then becomes a function of data collection. If the senses receive data in a sufficiently rich quantity, then the mind perceives reality, according to the idealist. The more data, the more detail. The more detail, the better the quality of sensory input. The better the sensory input, the more reality the mind apprehends in the visual experience. This is the logic of data idealism. Data idealists hope to capture enough of the idiosyncrasies of experience—like Jim Cracraft's rusty plate—to deliver the full content of reality. The more data the machine can capture, the more reality the user contacts through the machine. For the data idealist, the human body is a data collection machine. The data idealist sees the body as an elaborate input device. Howard Rheingold speaks as a data idealist when he says in his *Virtual Reality*:"Our eyes are stereo input devices; our eyeballs and necks are sophisticated, multiple degree-of-freedom gimbals for moving our stereo sensors," (p. 63).

Because the data idealist believes that human experience consists of sensory input, the idealist believes that machines will eventually capture human experience. When the data rate is high enough, the fidelity will increase, and eventually recording instruments will, in principle, capture all human experience, from every perspective and from every person. One stumbling block for the idealist is the fact that the stream of sensory data pours in second-by-second for each person at an enormous rate. Just turn your head to the left and back again to center and in those two seconds the recordable experience data of your field of view skyrocketed. The dream of the data idealist is to shrink that enormous amount of data to the atomic level so as to squeeze the second-by-second sensory input into a manageable storage space. To this end, the data idealists fantasize data storage on the atomic level. If you postulate such a nanotechnology storage—don't forget to be idealistic!—you can in theory store one human lifetime of experience on a chip the size of a grape. VR researcher and pioneer, Warren Robinett once wrote this idealistic estimate in "Synthetic Experience" published by the MIT Press journal *Presence*, (Vol. I, Number 2, Spring 1992, pp. 229–247):

> The fundamental limit on recorded experience is storage capacity. We can estimate the data rate for human experience by using the standard NTSC video data rate for comparison. A hand-held videotape can currently store an hour's worth of visual and auditory experience.

> In the future, fidelity and therefore data rate will increase for recorded experience, but at the same time storage density will increase. Let us explore the likely changes in these two parameters. NTSC video nominally transmits an image frame of 640 x 480 pixels at a rate of 30 frames per second with the color of each pixel encoded by 8 bits for each of the primary colors red, green, and blue.

> This is roughly 200 million bits per second. To be conservative, we will increase this by a factor of 250 to allow for the greater resolution, field of view, and so forth needed for perfect visual fidelity. Since humans are primarily visual creatures, another factor of 2 should be sufficient to record all the other senses. This gives us a data rate for human experience of 10^{11} bits/second which is probably much more than is needed.

> Current common storage techniques, such as music compact discs can store roughly a 10^9 bits/cm^3. However, we can expect storage density to continue to increase until it hits some sort of physical limit. It should ultimately be possible to encode information in the arrangement of matter on the atomic scale. Assuming a nanotechnological storage device that stores 1 bit for every 1000 atoms gives us a storage density of 10^{20} bits/cm^3. At this density, a lifetime (100 years) of human experience can fit into the volume of a large grape (3 cm^3) and the experiences of all of humanity (10 billion people) for 10,000 years would fit into a cubic mile of nanostorage.

To fit the experiences of all humanity for 10,000 years into a single cubic mile of data storage seems a project of considerable idealism. This is the same idealism that equates reality with bytes and equates being with being digital. Ultimately, such idealists see human beings as servants of machines. Once we think of ourselves as data collection devices, it will not be long and we will think of ourselves as inferior data collectors. Machines can collect data more efficiently, more regularly, and more dispassionately than human beings. In terms of Info-Ecology, such idealists are those who entertain the paradoxical suggestion that to save the planet we should simply eliminate human beings.

We would not be surprised to find data idealism in professors at institutes of technology or in computer science departments. But do the TRW engineers truly believe that the reality of the Hanford Plant is "captured" by photogrammetry VR? No, I think not. We must keep in mind another principle of virtual realism (from Chapter Two) that says:

- Realism in virtuality refers not to photo-realistic illusions or representations. Reality means a pragmatic functioning in which work and play fashion new kinds of entities. **VR does not imitate life but transubstantiates it** through pragmatic functioning.

The engineer is pragmatic. The engineer is not trying to reproduce or even re-present reality inside the VR system. The engineer works in the broad context of the world of toxic clean-up where the goal is to get the job done. For TRW, the job is an ecological job in the primary world. The virtual world used at TRW intersects the engineering world, and the virtual reality of the Hanford Plant appears to the engineers within that pragmatic context, a context limited by the parameters of the job. The TRW engineers do not, for instance, regularly use the head-mounted display. Instead, they use the large desktop monitor around which several users gather. Much of the time they forego the immersion of the shutter glasses. They never think of piling on photorealistic textures to make the model ever "more realistic" or objectively complete. Instead, they reserve the photo touches for key psychological and physical cues that help train workers who will later enter the contaminated buildings. The engineers must indeed put primary world geometry into the virtual world, but the engineering geometry does not exhaust the primary world. Nor can computer space ever contain the full affective topography that inhabits primary places. When Jim Cracraft describes the Hanford project, he invariably begins with the story of the snakes and the slamming doors.

For engineers, it is the job-to-be-done that clears away everything irrelevant. It is the job that creates a context for practice within which the model succeeds or fails. That is the measure of the truth or accuracy of the model. The accurate model is not the model that reproduces the right number of sensory bytes. It is not the accuracy of convincing detail as such that matters. What matters is the accuracy of relevant detail, of revealing particulars. Engineers seek not the accuracy of a mirror that delivers a pure reflection. Engineers seek the accuracy of a map that helps them find their way around so they can do their job. They do not expect to live inside the map—except insofar as the job requires them to build familiar responses into their immediate reactions in anticipation of the times when they will be working on the primary site. They do not intend to compare the virtual with the primary building, but they do want to have as much relevant data as possible at their fingertips when they plan their operations.

Here is where virtual realism supports InfoEcology. Harness information systems for planetary health and you abandon the idealism that computes for the sake of computing. The social connection, so prominent in European InfoEcology, governs American technology less conspicuously. While American engineers once approached their task as a fight with the wilderness, the application of technology today teaches us more about the blind spots in our own awareness and about the ways we can use technology to pre-visualize our real-world actions. Our blind spots have much more to do with mental blinkers than they do with recorded inaccuracies. The self-reflective, pragmatic use of technology undermines the out-and-out warfare against wild nature. The application of VR to real-world tasks transforms VR as much as it transforms the world in which it works.

6

Nature and Cyberspace

In March 1993 at the SCI-ARC School of Architecture in Los Angeles, a student posed a question to Jaron Lanier, the famous entrepreneur of Virtual Reality. "How," the student asked, "will VR enhance architecture." The stocky genius smiled, ran a hand through dangling dreadlocks, and responded enthusiastically: "VR allows us to embellish computer-generated buildings with wonderful enhancements. Users can decorate electronic environments with dazzling colors and sign them with fun designs." Lanier went on to say that the physical dwellings of the future would probably be cheap, dull, unadorned shelters generated by robot factories to put no-frills roofs over the heads of an overpopulated humanity. To compensate for the squalid physical surroundings, VR would provide habitations for interactive personal expression and aesthetic enjoyment. Lanier described a future in which cyberspace offers solace for the loss of natural, livable, environmental space.

Lanier's provocative mix of enthusiasm and pessimism supports many critics who attack cyberspace as a fatal form of escape. Chapter 2 showed us some of the critics who stand on the ground of naïve realism. For them, virtual identities diminish physical identities. If we look, in fact, more closely at the naïve realists, we find an anxiety about the physical ground on which they stand. The firm ground the critics feel themselves standing on actually covers an underlying sinkhole. The nature to which the critics appeal has in recent years been threatened. A large cavity gapes in the human attachment to nature.

Naïve realists want to protect reality from cyberspace, but they are not so sure about how deeply we are still attached to nature. Virtual reality seems to wean us from spontaneous affection toward mother nature where our birthright seems to shrink more every day.

Is VR a consolation for the lost charms of natural things? Isn't such a cyberspace a grand delusion, an electronic Tower of Babel? Is virtual reality an escapist opium for blocking the pain of planetary loss?

Caught in the Net/Web

Many of the metaphors we use today for computers suggest escapism. The "net" and the "web" are metaphors. We can be caught by these metaphors if we're not careful. The poetics of engineering brings us entrapping nets and ensnaring webs. They can trap us into believing that computers constitute a realm apart, an orderly alternative to the messy world we inhabit. The net and web metaphors reflect the artifice of the engineers who build computer systems. Like the chess board, the computer delivers a self-contained system of meaning. While the lives of system engineers do indeed take their meaning largely from computers, the rest of us must shake off the spell of engineering even as we learn enough of its language to manage the computers infiltrating our lives. We must disentangle the webs and the nets in order to make them mesh with the primary world.

The knot turns around the little word "and" in the phrase "nature and cyberspace." How does the connector work? Does the "and" combine, monopolize, absorb, harmonize, contradict, balance, or assimilate? Can we make the connector work? The next century will force each person to learn how to connect—or disconnect—nature and cyberspace. As electronic networks grow in size and power, and as the economy depends increasingly on them, no one will have an alibi. Our descendants will of necessity write their autobiographies in terms of nature and cyberspace. Those stories begin today with those of us who have watched the face of nature change during our lifetimes.

A Child's Sad Eyes

The notion of "nature" once conveyed stability. The spray of water on rocks, the secret forest pathways, even catastrophic storms conveyed permanence. Nature provides a psychic framework whose borders wrapped our lives as a comforting blanket even when we're afflicted by floods and droughts that come with nature's cycles. The psychic framework of nature is now wearing thin, perhaps most rapidly for this generation. Every adult living in the 1990s has stories.

The region where I was born prided itself on being a haven for sport fishing and hunting. The vast woods and plentiful lakes of Wisconsin were home to the first group of conservationists long before anyone had heard of "the environment." In the last twenty years, the largest city in Wisconsin, Milwaukee, grew overcrowded and urbanized, but no event more epitomized the dramatic changes in the region than the 1993 water crisis. For several weeks, the population of Milwaukee had to boil its tap water before drinking it. The septic runoff into Lake Michigan had grown to such a degree that Milwaukee's water resources became poisonous. Bacteria made the water undrinkable. The sense of living under a secure, self-balancing Nature was gone.

I felt venerable Nature shrink to lowercase nature as I grew up in the 1950s and 60s. During those decades, I felt not so much a shock at sudden change as a gradual disaffection with nature. Some of my youth was spent in East Central Wisconsin — Shawano County, to be exact, just 34 miles northwest of Green Bay, Wisconsin. Everyone thought this was God's country, and I thought I lived close to nature. spending summers with my grandparents on the shores of Shawano Lake, in the little resort town of Cecil, Wisconsin, population 536. From the ages of six to twelve, my dreams and waking life were occupied by fish and frogs and ducks. Gradually, however, in the late 1950s and early 1960s, I watched the Shawano Lake I had loved as a boy gradually deteriorate. The fish began dying, the frogs grew scarce, and the whole lake seemed moribund. Shawano Lake was growing repulsive to me, and at the time I had no clues about the source of the changes. Back then, no one spoke about "the environment."

Shawano Lake (pronounced "shaw-no") got its name from the Native Americans who had long ago settled the area. The Shawnee Indians (*shaawanawa* means "those who live in the South") were part of the Algonquian tribes of Canada, especially the people in the

Ottawa River Valley of Ontario and Quebec. "Algonquian," my grand-father reminded us, means "people who live at the place for spear fishing" (*algoomaking*). My grandfather, John Heim, was especially proud of living at the shore of the Lake because one of his ancestors was a half-Indian, half-French Canadian whose married name was Barbara Harmeyer.

My grandfather, who fished and hunted on Shawano Lake for half-a-century, often spoke sadly of how the sky used to grow dark with the wings of wild ducks as they flew in huge numbers over the face of the sun. He recalled how the lake once teemed with healthy fish. Now, he explained, the speed boats with their power motors had cut down the underwater weed beds, the fish could not make their spawning beds in the weeds, and the life cycle of the lake was losing its inner momentum. Though his explanation proved wrong, my grandfather's observations held the poignancy of someone who was feeling a galac-tic shift in the human relationship to nature. An inland lake as big as Shawano —six miles long and three miles wide and fed by the big Wolf River—could absorb the havoc of motor boats. What it could not absorb, however, was the stream of human septic waste that the settlements, including my grandfather's, had been emitting into the lake over the years in ever increasing amounts as the population grew.

Those days, we did not yet know the word "ecology"—even in Wis-consin where the conservation movement had its roots and where the preservation of forests and streams had long been a political priority. Though at that time our understanding of speedboats and vanishing fish was shallow, our sadness ran deep. My attention turned increas-ingly away from the lake and toward the open country and fields. If you could not go fishing as a boy, you went exploring what was left of the forests. Not long after that, the forests also were to become a source of sadness.

Cyberspace vs. Nature

Sadness turned to action. The experience of the loss of nature became a political movement. Clear-eyed practical measures were taken—from regulations protecting the ozone layer to long-range population plan-ning. Yet no amount of action can roll back the tectonic shift in awareness, what some historians call "the disappearance of nature." That shift in awareness underlies the debates about "deep ecology." Rather than argue about specific courses of action to take, perhaps we should first investigate how we perceive and relate to the world.

You can call this debate "Is Nature Obsolete?" or "Has Humanity Defeated Nature?" or, quite simply, "Nature Extinct." The debate first smoldered a century ago when people noticed how the dirt from industrial smoke stacks began darkening the skies and how factories were dominating the landscape. Thinking people began weighing the relative merits of "nature versus culture," and the German philosophers of Romanticism described a war between *Natur* and *Geist*. The debate about nature, with a capital N, began heating up.

At that time, the ancient adversarial relationship of humans to nature flipped. Instead of scratching survival from an overbearing, intimidating, and reluctant nature, human beings felt the tide turn and nature took the role of underdog. The whipped dog of nature became a domesticated pet, and the animal was "seared with trade; bleared, smeared with toil; wearing man's smudge and sharing man's smell," to recall Gerard Manley Hopkins ("God's Grandeur," 1877). Weather became a meteorological prediction represented on television radar maps.

In hot pursuit of nature's secrets, humans had finally attained the scientific knowledge promised by Francis Bacon's dream of a New Atlantis. But soon enough the Technopolis lost some of its steam as the dream turned urban nightmare. Today, the debate continues as we worry about the holes in the planet's atmosphere, as toxic waste seeps into the ground water, and as the global economists seek alternate energy sources to replace fossil fuels. This is the existential context in which human beings first learned to pronounce the words "cyberspace" and "virtual reality."

Nature Made in America

Since the discovery of the New World, Americans have enjoyed a special romance with nature. When not standing in reverence before it, Americans put their sweat into exploiting nature and conquering the land. America gained its identity from returning —in one way or another—to nature. The Founding Fathers of the U.S. Constitution put Nature and Nature's Deity at the basis of human rights, and Nature was there too in the meandering walks of Henry David Thoreau and Ralph Waldo Emerson and the other Transcendentalists of New England and St. Louis. But the romance has grown rocky over the years, and the American marriage to nature has changed both partners. Pure nature seems to have disappeared. The historian and former Librarian of Congress, Daniel Boorstin, noted in *The Republic of Technology*:

> Just as the American's love affair with his land produced pioneering adventures and unceasing excitement in the conquest of the continent, so too his latter-day romance with the Machine produced pioneering adventures—of a new kind. There seemed to have been an end to the exploration of the landed continent —and an end to the traversing of uncharted deserts, the climbing of unscaled mountains. But there were no boundaries to a machine-made world. The New World of Machines was of man's own making. No one could predict where the boundaries might be or what his technology might make possible. To keep the Machine going, the American advanced from horse power to steam power to electrical power to internal-combustion power to nuclear power—to who could guess what."[22]

Guessing the next step has become easy since Boorstin's 1978 challenge. To keep the Machine going, Americans have turned from nuclear power to computer power. Computerized space, cyberspace, offers the next adventure, the unbounded territory we have recently inserted under the New World of Machines. American industry depends more and more on the stream of bits and bytes that makes up the software of information technology. In fact, the electronic infrastructure is about to swallow our previous industrial machines.

In the late 1980s, I began researching a book about the philosophy of space exploration. I interviewed officials at the National Aeronautics and Space Administration in Cape Canaveral, Florida, and at the Johnson Space Center in Houston, Texas. After months of interviewing NASA planners and scientists, I came to a startling conclusion, a conclusion that made me jettison the book I had planned. Like many people, I had mistakenly assumed that the U.S. space program planned to send humans physically to other planets and distant reaches of the solar system. Instead, I found that NASA was designing robots to explore outer space, robots connected by computer to virtual reality systems on earth. Humans on earth could then experience "virtually" what the robot experienced. Humans could see and feel and manipulate things in outer space without traveling to another physical location. Such telepresence costs far less than launching rockets burdened by human life-support systems.

From a philosophical standpoint, cyberspace had absorbed outer space. What was interesting at NASA was not the machines for hauling humans into outer space, but the electronics for transporting humans into electronic space. Nature, it seems, including the farthest reaches of the galaxy, is being captured and bottled in information space. Nature, as we had thought about it in the past, had disappeared.

End of Nature

The electronic absorption of large portions of life—what some call the "virtualization" or de-materialization of life—corroborates the notion of nature's disappearance that haunts environmentalists like Bill McKibben, who wrote:

> Our comforting sense of the permanence of our natural world—our confidence that it will change gradually and imperceptibly, if at all—is the result of a subtly warped perspective. Changes in our world which can affect us can happen in our lifetime—not just changes like wars but bigger and more sweeping events. Without recognizing it, we have already stepped over the threshold of such a change. I believe that we are at the end of nature.[23]

The evidence for this end of nature, to which McKibben and other environmentalists refer, ranges from acid rain to the holes in the ozone layer, from genetic engineering to ecologically induced shifts in weather patterns, from the depletion of fossil fuels to the rise of the oceans. McKibben points to the simple fact of what has already happened: the air around us—"even where it's clean, and smells like spring, and is filled with birds—is significantly changed. We have substantially altered the earth's atmosphere."

The shift we are talking about here is not a change in physical substances or ecological systems—or even in the terrestrial atmosphere.

The change is a shift in the psychic framework by which we view the world. By that I mean the way humans feel when, say, a change in an ecological system alters their background experience and affects their sensibilities. I refer to the affective attitude we have toward the world as much as the world itself. As beings in the world, we inhabit the world as participants—not merely as spectators scientifically observing and then calculating for advantage or disadvantage. The framework of our participation in the world has a look and feel to it, not merely a scientific description. When the world changes ecologically, so does the psychic framework in which we work and love, play and observe. The notion of psychic framework appears not only in my 1987 book *Electric Language*, but also—as I have recently discovered—in some texts from traditional Asian culture.

Nature as a "psychic framework" appears in the description of the Japanese tea ceremony in D.T. Suzuki's lovely book *Zen and Japanese Culture*. Describing the tea ceremony, Suzuki points beyond physical facts to the atmosphere in which gestures, objects, and surroundings cohere:

> The tea-drinking that is known as **cha-no-yu** in Japanese and as "tea ceremony" or "tea cult" in the West is not just drinking tea, but involves all the activities leading to it, all the utensils used in it, the entire atmosphere surrounding the procedure; and, last of all, what is really the most important phase, the frame of mind or spirit which mysteriously grows out of the combination of all these factors.

> The tea-drinking, therefore, is not just drinking tea, but it is the art of cultivating what might be called "psychosphere," or the psychic atmosphere, or the inner field of consciousness. We may say that it is generated within oneself, while sitting in a small semi-dark room with a low ceiling, irregularly constructed, from the handling the tea bowl, which is crudely formed but eloquent with the personality of the maker, and from listening to the sound of boiling water in the iron kettle over a charcoal fire.[24]

What Suzuki describes as a "psychosphere," or "psychic atmosphere," or "inner field of consciousness" is what I mean by a psychic framework. The psychic framework of the tea ceremony is a field of awareness, but it cannot be separated from the technology of utensils, architecture, and decor that affects the participants' state of mind. We should not think of psychic framework as "consciousness" if by consciousness we mean a private subjective state that peers from within to confront a separate world of alien objects. A psychic framework sets the tone that a field of awareness has when it seamlessly flows with a set of furnishings, tools, and physical movements.

The tea ceremony is a technology designed to recapture a lost nature. Anyone acquainted with this ancient art will tell you how artificial and formalized the ceremony is in its every move and gesture. Its highly stylized cultivation aims at a certain kind of experience. The tea ceremony requires a person first to go indoors in order to restore a sense of nature outdoors. Only through the artificial does one regain a lost sense of open harmony with the natural. Our daily struggle for survival pulls us away from experiencing pure, spontaneous nature.

Psychic frameworks shift in cultural life, especially when new tools change our daily practices. Autobiographically, I can describe the end of nature as it appeared to me in the shifts of psychic frameworks over time.

My affection migrated from the lake and forests to works of art, then later to cyberspace. When the lake and forests held my fascinated gaze, I would walk for whole afternoons along the lake shore, watching fish wriggle through weed beds and dart past turtles and frogs on lily pads. For hours I watched the hypnotic waves ripple over pebbles and rocks. I spent mornings hiking in the woods, getting to know the trees and bushes, throwing stones at crows and blackbirds. I climbed fruit trees and disturbed angry hornets' nests. "All the sun long it was running, it was lovely, the hay/ Fields high as the house, the tunes from the chimneys, it was air/ And playing, lovely and watery/ And fire green as grass...." as Dylan Thomas wrote in Fern Hill.[25]

As the lake and woods receded in power, I turned to an inward but similar aesthetic experience. I listened for hours to music, especially classical music. The texture of the music evoked the texture of the lake and woods. My morning walks went through symphonic orchestras and my afternoons were spent in the thickets of string quartets. I learned to play the cello and explored music from the performer's side. There was always adventure in music, always surprising vistas and breathtaking grandeur. The pastoral sounds of Beethoven, Bruckner, Sibelius, and Haydn revealed the serenity of landscapes and the moods of the weather.

In time, though, the psychic framework of my life shifted again. In 1983, I became computerized. At first, the computer looked like a tool that would simply facilitate the tasks to be done. Many of us believed we would gain the time that was freed by relegating tasks to the computer. What a mirage! While some toil has been removed from repetitive tasks, computers have come to occupy a central role and demand more time. They are more than tools, more than handy time-savers. The personal computer became a central, all-absorbing component of daily life. It became a "second nature," a "second skin" in our work, whether we were architects or zoologists. The computer began to filter our memories, our communications, and even the organizing and planning of our lives. Much of our time now transpires in cyberspace in one way or another. Only gradually did I begin to realize that for me cyberspace plays a role similar to what nature and music once did.

Many of the experiences we once felt with "natural nature" now appear in cyberspace. Of course, the sensations are different, but what I noticed were the similarities in the patterns of experience. These similarities may help explain why the human race finds cyberspace so attractive and why our move into cyberspace is so inevitable. The lure of cyberspace does not arise solely from the convenience of organizing knowledge on computers nor from the way electronics enhances communications. Underneath the convenience hides, I think, a more profound affinity. Many people are finding in cyberspace a second nature, a new home. By nature I do not mean the object of physical science but the mythical romantic "Nature" that once attracted scientists to their profession and that once lured conquistadors to explore new continents.

Like the tea ceremony, cyberspace offers the allure of nature on another and different level. In a strange way, cyberspace restores a surrogate nature, reinstating the affective life at a level where the psychic framework of cyberspace absorbs nature. Cyberspace absorbs nature not only by transposing space exploration into electronics through telepresence, but by actually reviving certain experiential qualities that the human being once felt in nature and now feels in cyberspace. We can describe the experiential qualities of cyberspace/nature, but they only make sense if we first look more closely at the tenuous grip we have on "natural nature."

"All Natural"

Where, then, is nature anymore? I mean, for most of us urban dwellers? Aren't most of us caught in the artificial net? Is the garden in the front yard the only leftover?

As the technological system infiltrates every aspect of life, it is increasingly difficult to find natural life. In a college classroom, I once posed a puzzle. First I explained Aristotle's distinction between what is natural and what is artificial: Natural things are those that reproduce themselves; an artificial thing is something made according to a pattern extrinsic to the thing and produced by someone outside the material thing. Then I challenged the students: "Look around you, and name one piece of pure nature in this classroom." Students stared at doors, windows, blackboards, desks, tables. After a minute, some students finally looked at one another, their faces lighting up as they realized that their classmates are the remnants of non-manufactured reality. They discovered that they themselves, their human bodies, are the natural entities in the classroom because their bodies were generated by bodies of their own species and not fabricated by outside agency.

The thought experiment drives home two points.

- Most humans now dwell in an artificial environment nearly devoid of natural entities. Most urban trees grow according to the calculations and design of some city planner who has a horticultural file on the computer downtown. The human being remains a vestige of pure nature. By contrast, in pre-modern times, the human had always been the artificer, the shaper, the outstanding exception in a world of natural processes. Now the tables are turned. If, as Aristotle taught, natural beings are those that come from the reproductive actions of parents of the same species, then the remnant of nature we encounter in our daily lives remains other human beings. We find ourselves today surrounded by gadgets and fabrications, and even the birth of humans happens more and more through conscious planning and intervention. Some human hearts at this moment beat with the help of Pacemakers.

- Still, even in a totally planned world, as the Chinese Taoists remind us, nature can always be found "within" — if we quiet down and look further inside. Our subtle body energies and biorhythms reach down to cosmic connections of earth and sky, sun and wind. Our sexual and reproductive powers continually reclaim the force of natural cycles. Our awareness of subtle body processes, of weight distribution and balance, of dryness of mouth and relaxation of eyes, our holistic sense of well-being reveals the underlying, supportive movements of nature. Like the birds, deer, and fish, we humans still move in an invisible field of subtle, instinctive forces that underlie our conscious, calculating mentality. We should not be too quick to say that nature has vanished completely from our world.

The popular imagination, like the college students, tends to see a totally artificial environment, especially when talking about cyberspace. In the popular mind, computerized space excludes nature. Cyberspace epitomizes artificial contrivance, while real nature falls from the hand of God or emerges from the inscrutable depths of the universe itself. Most people believe that electronic culture belongs to artificial reality while natural things emerge from other natural things. Since antiquity, *natura* (from the Latin *nasciri*, "to be born") refers to entities emerging from parent entities that belong to the same species. Natural things, in the ancient and traditional views, are things that arise through the interaction of their own kind, of the male and female of their kind — however much the genders might vary among the different species. Whereas natural things spring from seeds within seed-bearing plants and animals, creations by artifice derive from the plans of an outside agent. Even God the Creator, according to medieval theology, works like an artist who designs the *natura naturans* ("nature doing its naturing") so that nature reproduces itself. Art has always gotten its meaning from completing, improving, or simply replacing nature, always by contrast to things that are natural. From this point of view, cyberspace is unnatural in the extreme. Cyberspace is pure human artifact.

Does the Human Being Fit?

How does the human being fit—if "fit" is the right word—into nature? The debate in the previous century harked back to modern intellectual giants like René Descartes. It was Descartes who in the seventeenth century sharply divided material quantifiable things, the *res extensae*, from the thinking things with souls, the *res cogitantes*. Descartes saw the physical world as a collection of inert material substances and he saw human beings as thinking substances that enjoy the power to mathematically measure and manipulate physical substances. Once Descartes had divided things in this way—thinking beings and material substances—the troubling question was not far behind: How—if at all—do thinking things belong to the quantifiable world that thinking things manipulate and conquer? How are thinking things linked to the material world that thinking things manipulate? Does our incarnation in physical bodies necessarily commit us as thinking things to a basic sympathy or connection or responsibility that thinking things should manifest toward the physical world?

Today we, the thinking things in physical bodies, have effectively moved the seventeenth-century Cartesian debate onto another footing. Our efforts have built an industrial system steered by information devices stretching over the earth and even reaching beyond the planet to probe alien life outside the galaxy. Our industrial system has turned into a technological system, a cybernetic, electronically self-steering system, so that the industrial age has given way to the age of information. When we apply our human tools with logical consistency, the result is technology. What enables us to apply tools thoroughly and logically is the computer. The computer weaves the actual web of logical consistency and coordinates our skill-based tools. Do computers and nature belong to each other? How does the technological world absorb the human body?

A Framework for Cyberspace

My personal catalog of the psychic properties of cyberspace was the upshot of a dialogue I had in 1993 with the environmentalist Svend Larsen, who directs the Humanities Research Center in Odense, Denmark. Scandinavians have over the centuries developed something of a theology of nature. Since the era of the Norsemen, the Scandinavian people have been fascinated by raw nature. This fascination with nature, Larsen points out, is shared by Americans. Both countries enjoyed, until recently, vast stretches of uncharted, wild land masses. In this period of the end of nature, Larsen described the gut feeling his people have for nature by listing the following features:

- Infinite

- Inaccessible

- Overwhelming in Power

- Fearsome

- Wild like "the moors of Jutland"

- Primal

In Larsen's six features of nature I saw a way of cataloging the psychic framework of cyberspace. If we see ourselves migrating from nature toward cyberspace—at least as I and many others experience it—we can describe the psychic framework of cyberspace as patterned on nature.

Infinite

Nature's infinity is fairly obvious. The feel of infinity draws us to the rivers, seashores, mountains, and forests. I walk along a river and my eyes flow effortlessly over an endless variety of colors and shapes under the rippling waves of the water. The forest presents my eyes with an unending feast of perspectives and my ears perceive an unpredictable mix of birdsong, cricket chirp, and insect buzz. A hike through the woods relieves our distracted spirits. The confines of our finite identities melt as narrow jobs and burdensome social roles vanish. Our perceptions fly free as the birds.

In his novel *Mona Lisa Overdrive*, William Gibson refers to cyberspace as "an infinite cage."[26] This paradoxical phrase suggests the infinity I have felt in cyberspace, an infinity not altogether unlike the infinity of nature. When first learning to use computer networks, we are stunned by the vast possibilities, we run down endless corridors of data, we seem unlimited in the universe of information. We can travel endlessly in cyberspace, without physical limits, for cyberspace is electronic. At present, our travel remains restricted by alphanumeric symbols whose words and numbers cannot replace the sights and sounds and smells of sensory immersion. Gibson's "infinite cage," reminds us that the physical side of our amphibious being can only feel trapped by electronic data as long as the data are colorless, tasteless, and disembodied. To a finite incarnate being, such an infinity constitutes a cage, a confinement to a nonphysical secondary realm.

As cyberspace fosters virtual reality, this finite confinement will expand. Our bodily senses will enjoy an expanded field of awareness. We will roam with graphics for the eyes, 3-D audio for the ears, and tactile feedback for the skin. A gap will, nonetheless, still exist between our primary biobodies and our newly evolved cyberbodies.

Inaccessibile

"Nature loves to hide," said Heraclitus, who himself loved to speak in obscure riddles. Some philosophers, like Heidegger, identify nature with the concealing, hiding aspects of the earth. Rock-bottom reality is, according to them, opaque as earth. When philosophers identify nature with earthy opacity, they rebel against the tradition of Aristotle, who anchored nature in lucid forms and substantial shapes (the genera and species of ancient science), and they rebel against reducing nature to the mathematical formulas of Postivism. Heidegger likes to point out how Aristotle's natural shapes belong to a process of growth, and that growth always protects a core seed of development hidden from outside access. Postmodern people tend to agree with Heidegger that life grows best out of the spotlight or shaded from the fluorescent lights of institutional corridors.

Where everything lies open to see, we have nothing to discover, no truths to call our own. We love the inaccessible because it invites us to explore and discover. It promises adventure. Nature calls us with its fresh pathways and untrodden trails.

So do computer networks. The Internet appeals to the adventurer in us because the Internet has no center, no unifying authority. You must learn the Internet on your own. It is not a single, top-down system. It consists of thousands of nodes linked horizontally. There is no single place or peak from which you can peer down to see everything. The experienced Internet user knows that any one session visits only a tiny corner of the Internet universe. You never cease exploring cyberspace. It beckons and fascinates, like the woods, like the underwater beds of offshore sea kelp.

Overwhelming

The first experience a computer user has with the Internet nearly always results in panic. "Panic," of course, comes from the Greek god "Pan," and "pan" in Greek means "everything." The ancient Greeks used the word to indicate their deep respect for the sudden panic that overwhelms a human being who confronts vast stretches of raw nature. Standing in a large meadow on a sunny afternoon or gazing over a twilit valley from a mountain top can overwhelm a human being. A feeling of "everything all at once" suddenly grabs us.

Similarly, panic usually overwhelms beginners on computer networks, not unlike the powerful feeling of the wide, open spaces. There is just so much to see and respond to: newsgroups and Internet mailing lists, FTP (File Transfer Protocol) and world libraries of information. The Internet's World Wide Web has gradually grown beyond the limited language of alphanumeric data. Electronically, we now cruise through video, photos, and graphic animation. We find all the prior media existing now in the electronic element. Tools for 3-D representation, like VRML, allow us to represent physical and imagined worlds. Such possibilities give users a creeping sense of panic.

Fearsome

Immanuel Kant developed the notion of the aesthetic sublime. He based the concept of the sublime on nature, specifically our experience of looking at the stars in the night sky. When our eyes wander over the face of the night sky, they tend to group the stars in clusters and patterns. The constellations of the classical Zodiac provide a way of grasping, of getting a hold of the night sky. When we relax our gaze and allow depth perception to read ever more deeply into the starry sky, the fixed constellations dissolve into the vastness of the ether. If we try to grasp the stars as a whole with our eyes, we grow dizzy with the effort. Kant says our vertigo comes from the contradiction of a finite sense organ coming up against an infinite object.

The sublime night sky often serves as a metaphor for cyberspace. There is something fearsome about it, something sublime. The whole notion of a separate "personal" computer dissolves as the desktop computer now connects to the Internet. Current operating systems are gradually erasing the lines that divide my files from the files of the information universe. The sheer size of the computer network is scary. With hundreds of thousands of users reading news groups, with millions of messages circling the globe every day, the matrix looms like a mountain on another planet. The Internet is so big that the user can never see the whole thing, never even begin to guess its true size. You surmise in your first month's experience that cyberspace holds a universe of information, far beyond anything you will ever be able to explore in your lifetime. Such vastness is awesome.

Wild

With sublimity comes wildness. In nature, the wilderness is where wild things grow, and where wild things happen. Wilderness is nature uncultivated, pre-civilized. In wilderness, wild things beget other wild things and bring forth the unexpected, the unpredictable, the growth that is unforced. When we are in the wild, we can—in Heraclitus' phrase—"expect the unexpected."

Many Americans today regard cyberspace as the new frontier. Groups like the Electronic Frontier Foundation aim to protect the wildness of cyberspace. Under the motto of Jeffersonian freedom—protection of personal privacy, respect for diversity, and the fostering of communities—the EFF produces policy recommendations and argues against the subordination of cyberspace to commercial or government interests. One of the EFF founders, Mitch Kapor, invented the electronic spreadsheet (*Lotus 1–2–3*), a personal computer application that brought PCs into the business world. Now Kapor worries about preserving the Jeffersonian qualities of cyberspace.[27] The EFF movement is, in a sense, an electronic equivalent of the ecological movement in the politics of the physical world.

The Net currently works on the mind like "the moors of Jutland" that still romance the civilized Scandinavians. City people can momentarily take a vacation from their social hierarchies, their polite manners, and their disciplined impulses. Cyberspace is a place of unexpected connections, of non-hierarchical meetings, and of communities that produce their own games, news, and social mores.

Primal

At bottom, cyberspace will always remain unintelligible to the human beings who inhabit its spaces. Cyberspace will remain fundamentally inscrutable because the computer is an essentially opaque technology. Unlike the bicycle or the typewriter, high technology means low transparency. The bike, as a mechanical device, is transparent to its users. When a stick gets caught in the bike chain or a brake wire snaps, the bike rider can look, analyze, and intervene. High technology, however, shuts the user out from the micro-world of electrons, microchips, and bit switches that make it work. More so with the worldwide system of computer networks where even experts remain in the dark about how certain things function in the mysterious guts of cyberspace.

To this extent, cyberspace recalls a theological property. The theological tradition refers to God as the mysterious origin, always inscrutable, beyond full human access and comprehension. Human nature was initially defined by its difference from the divine. God, as a term, remains undefined and tinged with mystery. No entity from the hand of God can reach back to grasp its divine source.

Of course, the traditional notion of divinity insists on the holiness of God. Which is to say that God is not only a primal origin, but also a fullness and wholeness toward which created things strive. The source functions as a mystery, and the mystery draws humans upward and onward. For theology, the source holds out the goal of eventual perfection, eventual participation in divinity. God's creations grow to become God's children.

What—if anything—draws us onward into cyberspace? Economic enrichment? Further evolution? Communication for a more peaceful world? More efficient planetary management? Does life in cyberspace imply any ideal of wholeness or holiness? Does artificial existence beckon the human race to a new level of existence?

Whoah!

Just a second! These questions must make us pause—not because they are unanswerable or meaningless, but because the questions conceal an assumption that the virtual can collapse what is real. This line of thinking floats into the stratosphere of idealism where the net and the web drift loose from all moorings. Like the thinking of the network idealists, this line of thinking makes cyberspace a realm apart. Reality gets transposed into cyberspace so that nothing outside cyberspace can regulate or define it. Computer vocabulary swallows the real world wholesale: "virtual communities," "virtual offices," and now "virtual nature." Net idealists identify reality with cyberspace, even to the extent of dreaming that virtual communities will redeem the human community. This line of thinking deifies cyberspace as a Teilhardian super intelligence.

From the standpoint of virtual realism, the notion of psychic frameworks conceals an idealist slant, even though it can play a useful role for inquiry. The very notion of psychic framework tilts toward subjective egos, toward how we feel. Western notions of psyche tend to disconnect from nature. Though valuable as a starting point, the notion of psychic framework needs grounding, needs to get outdoors. By taking the subjective mind so seriously, we may never find our way out. The notion of psychic framework has long ago left nature behind, because we began with human feelings, not with nature.

Osmose

A screen saver aglow on a monitor with a pretty nature motif will not get us outdoors. Blue skies and fleecy clouds may be restful and calming on a computer monitor when you are installing a Microsoft Windows operating system, but a company logo can hardly reconnect us to nature. Not even a live performance of Debussy's *La Mer* or oceanic symphonies by Sibelius can pull that off.

One extraordinary VR experiment reaches out to nature in the recent art work *OSMOSE* by Char Davies, who directs visual research at Montreal's SoftImage, a 3-D animation software company owned by Microsoft. After years of creating artistically stunning computer graphics, Char Davies decided to turn computers back to nature. She has thought long and hard about nature and cyberspace, and *OSMOSE* is an ongoing VR work that expresses her thoughts as well as those of her team: Georges Mauro in graphics, John Harrison in VR software, Rick Bidlack in music, and Dorota Blaszczak in design and sound processing. *OSMOSE* was first exhibited in Fall, 1995 in Montreal and New York City galleries, and it has been widely reviewed.

The gallery description of *OSMOSE* states:

> OSMOSE is an immersive virtual space exploring the interrelation between exterior Nature and interior Self. The work explores the potential of immersive virtual space as a medium for visual/aural expression and kinaesthetic experience of philosophical ideas. In biology, osmosis is a process involving passage from one side of a membrane to another. Osmosis as a metaphor means the transcendence of difference through mutual absorption, the dissolution of boundaries between inner and outer, the inter-mingling of self and world, the longing for the Other. OSMOSE as an art work seeks to heal the rational Cartesian mind/body subject/object split which has shaped so many of our cultural values, especially towards nature.

The hardware for *OSMOSE* uses a head-mounted display, but, in an important way, eliminates the data glove commonly used in conjunction with the HMD. Instead of navigating by pointing a finger or grasping objects with the hand, the immersed participant directs movement through a vest fitted with breathing and balance sensors.

By inhaling, the immersant floats up, and by exhaling the immersant sinks down, all the while body orientation—forward/backward and left/right—controls the direction. As we shall see, OSMOSE models VR on scuba diving. Char Davies abandoned the dataglove with clear intent. As I suggested in *The Metaphysics of Virtual Reality* (1993):

> Some date the advent of VR to the moment when the dataglove appeared on the computer screen. At that moment, the user became visible as an active, involved force in the digital world. This implies that VR tilts toward manipulation, even toward aggressive, first-person attitudes. The VR artist will need strategies for inducing a more receptive atmosphere, so that the user can be open in all directions, receiving signals from and having empathy for other beings. The user must be able to be touched, emotionally moved, by non-first-person entities in the virtual world. [28]

Precisely for these reasons, Char Davies avoids the computer gaming setup that typically makes virtual reality a hard-edged medium for shoot'em-up games. By controlling movement through breath and balance, the immersant slips out of the role of an isolated ego/eye that confronts, controls, and then dominates the entities of the world. With breath as a navigation tool, the immersant deepens the awareness of internal states, so that *OSMOSE* brings most participants to a state of meditation in about ten minutes. The drive to control things is gradually displaced by an awareness of simply being with things. Instead of moving toward objects to score them, the immersant swims with things in a state that merges proprioception with the things in the virtual world.

Conventional computer graphics consist of solid, textured, polygon blocks arrayed in empty space and rendered according to the Renaissance perspective that tapers the scene to fit the ego/eye (Cartesian ego). The isolated ego/eye has no alternative but to face off and oppose the hard-edged objects that present themselves before the eyes like targets. Instead of these solid polygon-based blocks, Davies introduces soft-edged, semi-transparent luminous particles (doubly appropriate for Microsoft's SoftImage). Not only the soft substances but the general types of these diaphanous entities melts the ego's sense of opposition. The entities in *OSMOSE* consist of a forest; a clearing; a pond; a leaf; some text and literature seen through a fog; and a world made of giant

See Figure 6.1

lines of green code. The soothing interaction with trees, clouds, water, and plants dissolves the boundary between inner sensations and outer environment. Nature, as reconstituted by Davies, recalls the peace and healing that we feel when visiting natural areas. The osmosis itself blurs the fluid lines between subject and object, self and world, between what I see before me and what I feel about what I see. One description of the experience runs:

> First I find myself in a 3-D Cartesian wireframe grid. I inhale and gradually begin to rise; if I lean forward I move forward. Lean back, and I move backwards. I'm flying. I have no physical form, yet I am whole. Gradually, a thick fog begins to rise over the grid. Leaves appear through the fog, and the grid is gone. Everywhere I look there are more leaves. I move through them, in them, around them. I fly over them, yet more appear above me. Am I lost? No, I am surrounded by a thick forest of leaves of all shapes and colors. It is dusk one minute, night the next. I float as if I am swimming deep in the ocean, yet I know I am in the air.
>
> There, on the edge, a clearing in the distance. I exhale and begin to descend into the clearing. Bend my knees and I fly faster. Finally, I am out of the dense forest and into a cozy clearing. Some leaves lie on the ground, a pond, a stream, and huge oak tree generously giving its shade. I drink it in. I cruise around this area, I want to touch the tree but because I have no physical form, I cannot. I glide up through the leaves of the tree and surround myself with their damp, exquisite beauty. There, look at that leaf. I'm going to go right through it. Inside a leaf. Look at this, I'm sliding along the inside of a leaf.[29]

See Figure 6.2

Although a head-mounted display seals the immersant in OSMOSE, an audience can vicariously witness the journey from within the larger installation space. The installation space remains relatively dark while two openings allow light to stream into the space: one light is a horizontal stereoscopic video projection showing the journey as the immersant perceives it; another light on a vertical screen projects the shadow of the immersant's silhouette sans cables and tracking devices. The same resonant, evocative sounds heard by the immersant—usually a re-mixed and synthesized male or female voice—fill the installation space. The view for the audience is not unlike watching a scuba diver swimming in an indoor tank—though the analogy should not diminish the poetic strangeness of the installation.

In fact, *OSMOSE* draws inspiration from Char Davies's own scuba diving. This virtual world floats the human being in a comforting fluid space not unlike undersea exploration. The scuba diver also dons encumbering gear to enter immersive space, and *OSMOSE* has no gravity, nor does the immersant need to remain vertical. The diver also moves through liquid space by affecting bodily buoyancy through subtle breath control. In both diving and *OSMOSE*, the horizontal spatial plane gains over the vertical gravitational plane. With lowered resistance, a harmony arises between the swimmer and what is met in the sea of experience. It is no accident that the French word *osmose* (in English "osmosis") connotes hydrotherapy, Jacuzzis, and health spas. The goal of total relaxation comes out in Davies's statement: "*OSMOSE* is a space where people who are stressed out from urban living can become re-sensitized to their own being. For me, this has important ecological implications."[30] The art work aims at creating a suspended, dream-like state of mind to encourage the immersant to let go, lose the urge for rational control, and allow the boundaries between inner mind and outer body to dissolve.

See Figure 6.3

The softening of hard space for the sake of an affect-laden environment was described by the French phenomenologist Gaston Bachelard in *The Poetics of Space*, cited frequently by Davies: "The space of intimacy and the space of the world blend through their 'immensity.' When human solitude deepens, then the two immensities touch and become identical."[31] This paradox makes a virtue out of the falcon-hood solitude of the head-mounted display. Excluding outside stimuli leads the solitary participant to experience a harmony prepared by the artist. The immersant's deepening solitude, like the lone undersea diver, opens a new relationship to the virtual environment. The harmony of the virtual environment arises from art and technology, not from any imitation of the actual outdoors. Osmosis occurs when the line softens between inner and outer sensory awareness.

Bachelard, like most postmodern philosophers, sought to undermine the walls of detached subjectivity. Since Edmund Husserl, the founder of the phenomenological movement, many twentieth-century thinkers have sought to break the bubble of ego-defined experience. Many thinkers even believe that the most basic of all questions revolves around the possible existence of "other minds." Ironically, most begin, like Husserl, with a study of Descartes' *Meditations*, where the *cogito sum* teaches them to doubt everything outside themselves. Even where the softened, amorphous ego learns to relax this initial suspicion, what it finds outside remains at best "the Other." The effort to purify subjectivity brought Husserl, at the end of his life, to study the "life world," but his idealist premise insured that the *Lebenswelt* would always remain an object of study rather than a place for pragmatic activity. Not surprisingly, the notion of psychic frameworks, as developed in *Electric Language* (1987), came out of studies in phenomenology.

Char Davies makes clear that *OSMOSE* is an art work—neither a representation of nature, nor a realistic surrogate:

> OSMOSE is not a replacement for walking in the woods. It is rather a filtering of Nature through an artist's vision, using technology to distill or amplify certain interpretive aspects, so that those who enter it can see freshly, can become re-sensitized, and can remember what it's like to feel wonder. [32]

OSMOSE is an art work that says as much about technology, and the potential of technology, as it says about nature. It provides only a little support for the eco-psychologists who claim that we must regain contact with the outdoors in order to retrain our sensory life, that aggression and civil violence relate to the fact that urban dwellers have literally lost touch with the healing experiences that come from spending a few hours a day in a natural environment. *OSMOSE* provides an ambivalent commentary on the fact that we are caught in the technological net while at the same time we sense that our healing lies elsewhere. The effect of *OSMOSE* is to make VR technology knock on our doors to remind us what lies outside. Like the tea ceremony, the art work can tune us for the real performance, but we do not want to stare at the finger and miss the moon to which it is pointing.

OSMOSE makes profound contributions to cyberspace. At a time when VRML and 3-D graphics are about to enrich the global visual language, *OSMOSE* extends the range of design and sets higher stan-

dards for VR. Unlike VRML, however, *OSMOSE* is not about communication but about self-transformation and about design that challenges communication technology to get outside itself. For virtual
realists, *OSMOSE* means fresh air.

Zen Sickness

The infinite cage breeds claustrophobia. Not immediately, but soon
enough. Long hours tied to a computer take their toll, even if you
find freedom online, even if you enjoy an osmotic float in software
ponds laced with friendly ferns.

To continue my personal odyssey through nature-and-cyberspace,
ten years ago, computers were pushing me to the brink where I had
either to find nature inside myself or face nervous breakdown. I would
eventually be lead by something inside me to re-discover nature outdoors—it's not Shawano Lake, but nature transfigured by changes in
me. Nature inside and out came through a discipline of grounding.
Nature emerged as felt ground, as supportive earth, as radiant center
in the ocean of information. But first I had to get sick. Let me explain.

In medieval China, the first Chinese Buddhists diagnosed something called "Zen sickness." The nervous disease arose from long hours
of concentrated work in a sedentary position. The Buddhists' work was
meditation (in Sanskrit *dhyana*; *Ch'an* in Chinese; *Zen* in Japanese).
The Indian teacher Bodhidarma had come to teach the Chinese
monks how to meditate, and he taught with a ferocious zeal. The Chinese responded with equal zeal, and soon enough many of the monks
began quitting the monastery from burnout. They became irritable, ill-
at-ease, insomniac, unbalanced. They had been exhausted by too
much head-and-eyes work combined with a sedentary lifestyle.

To remedy the situation, Bodhidarma developed a set of simple
physical movements based on what he knew of moving yoga. He led
the monks in a daily exercise routine and what he developed became
an Asian tradition later known as Chi Kung and Tai Chi Chuan.

Zen sickness means too much sitting, too much sitting with extensive use of the head. Zen sickness results from hours of overloading
the brain and eyes while immobilizing the lower body. The sickness
can come from sitting in meditation or from spending a long day in

front of the computer screen. Our machines, especially daily appliances, modify us as we use them. The computer has joined the automobile and the television in immobilizing our lower bodies while
overloading our upper nervous systems. The result is tiredness, irritability, and sleeplessness. Many people driving home in rush-hour
traffic after a long day at the computer come down with a case of Zen
disease. I was one of them.

The remedy is to re-arrange badly distributed energy. According to
Taoist physiology, the head of the healthy person runs cool while the
lower body is warm. In sickness or burnout, however, the bodily fire
moves up and heats the head while the lower body, the legs, and the
feet become cool. The eyes have a tendency, especially when they
stare for hours, of bringing too much heat to the brain. This illness
resembles the "video disease" in Wim Wenders' film *Until the End of
the World*. Recovery depends on re-heating the lower part of the body
through strong, deep breathing, in order to overcome the natural tendency of fire to rise and of water to sink. Certain gentle arm and leg
movements re-establish the lower body flexibility and energy. Sometimes herbs and diets are prescribed as well.

Another symptom of Zen sickness is imbalance. The attention
swings between introvert and extrovert. Either my mind pays too much
attention to the things around while I forget my own breath, balance,
and internal sensations, or my mind fixes too much on things outside
me as I struggle to control them.

The Tai Chi remedy for attention imbalance is the 50 percent rule.
The rule goes: 50 percent attention inside, 50 percent attention outside. Practice several minutes where you put half of your attention on
something outside, like a window or a tree, while at the same time
you put half of your attention on something inside, like breathing,
weight distribution, or warmth in the lower limbs. When attention
sinks to introversion, gently pull it back to something outside. When
attention fixes on something outside, gently pull it back to a half share
of inside awareness. A very difficult practice, maybe even impossible
to do perfectly for any length of time, but the practice effort itself balances and brings healing. Again, the danger is to indulge too much in
purely mental concentration.

To counter Zen sickness, physical exercises retrain the primal yoke between the upper-body nervous system and the lower body intestines and legs. The pressures of evolution disjoin the earth-based lower body from the "higher" brain activities. The head and the powers of volition pull out of alignment with the limbs and legs. Many of the exercises place the person in a semi-crouched position, half-way between the posture of four-footed and two-footed animals. The upper body learns to sink and relax into the lower body, which re-open channels of communication between the eye/brain and the involuntary nervous system of the stomach and bowels. The involuntary system—the lower, sedentary body—regains contact with the brain so the brain can in turn redistribute the efforts of the nervous system. The result is dynamic relaxation where any part of the body— say, the intestines—can send its strength into another part of the body, such as a fist. At its ultimate development, the training becomes a full-fledged martial art. The reestablished internal communication allows the head to draw on the strength of the gut and allows the involuntary processes like digestion and nervous reaction to become smarter and more conscious.

Most important in this revitalization of the individual is the sensation of grounding, of being grounded, of not floating. The Chinese Taoists call the sensation "earth energy." Unlike the Buddhists who treat incarnation as a prison for Pure Mind, the Taoists cultivate a healthy, earth-radiant body. A body rooted in earth energy means that the bones and joints align in such a way that they maximize the strength of the gravity vectors in the anatomical structure. Body weight drops into the aligned structure for maximum flexibility, coordination, and balance. Through hours of flexibility training and standing in alignment, martial artists can perform amazing feats. But the finest feat of these exercises is the sense of renewed harmony and refreshment: a cooling of the head and energizing of the lower body. Here is an excerpt from my training diary of ten years ago:

> The pre-dawn air was pale gray and the ocean breezes cool near Venice Beach in Los Angeles. Every morning for the past several months, I opened the same rickety wooden gate to walk into the backyard of Master Tung, Tai Chi man and Taoist teacher. Quietly, I took my position among the ten or fifteen human figures standing like statues under the fragrant eucalyptus trees.

Feet parallel, knees relaxed, spine straight, weight sunk into the balls of the feet, arms out-stretched with hands open but relaxed, eyelids nearly shut. Begin letting go of all thoughts, forgetting everything, listening only to the inhale and exhale of the breath. Sink down, letting go of muscle tension, releasing worries and desires, gradually merging the attention with the body. Every few minutes, teacher Tung makes the rounds to adjust the posture, and each time a burst of energy shoots from foot to crown of head. The attention wedded to a relaxed body generates a feeling of inner power, of expanding, radiant energy.

By the time the hour is over, the sun's patterns are flickering through the eucalyptus leaves onto the grass with an incredible but gentle brilliance. Sounds of birds and lawnmowers emerge slowly in the distance. Other students are stirring and moving about in the slow martial movements of Tai Chi Chuan. Awareness of the clock returns gradually.

Later that morning, driving on the freeway, or sitting at the computer, or lecturing in the classroom, I feel the sudden pull of body/mind unity reclaim my nervous system: unnecessarily taut muscles let go, clenched fingers release, breath comes full and sup-portive.

Or I catch myself in a moment of haste moving as if I were no more than a bundle of competing mental intentions, the body twisting with one limb this way and one limb that, without coordinating breath with action, and without making the most of my center of balance. The memory of Tung's garden adjusts me.

Now, when walking to the local park to teach Tai Chi, I find the balancing mechanism automatically come into play. I can no longer imagine working all day indoors in front of a computer and not tapping into that early morning hour when I lift my palms to the sun, feel its warmth spreading from eyelids to the energy channels, and finding my way back to the standing position that heals Zen sickness.

Tai Chi Telepresence

Every technology extends the reach of our physical senses, but networked virtual reality extends us to the maximum because it transports the sensory nervous system into the electronic environment. If contemporary culture already stresses and even overextends our finite capacities, then VR holds danger. If our bond with nature is weak, then VR strains it even more.

Art works like *OSMOSE* help offset the danger because they provide psycho-sensory tune-ups within the same powerful cyberspace
framework. But because time spent in HMDs tends to constrain
human attention into tunnel immersion, we should allot a corresponding amount of time for Spiral or CAVE VR. We should combine projection VR with HMD VR just as we combine a decompression chamber with scuba diving. Scuba divers check time tables to
find a ratio between time spent undersea and time in decompression.
They then spend the recommended time in the decompression
chamber so their deep-sea diving will not cause internal injuries. The
VR user should have a corresponding decompression procedure after
spending a couple hours in HMD VR. The CAVE VR provides a
decompression inasmuch as projected VR smoothens the transition
from cyberbody to primary body. Rather than feel an abrupt shock
between cyber and primary worlds, the immersant brings attention
back into the primary mind-body and re-integrates the nervous system. The next step, of course, would be a system that takes us to the
threshold of a transfigured nature outdoors.

The word "art" originally meant to join or harmonize, and the highest future art might be the art of joining tunnel and spiral VR, then
using them both to harmonize cyberspace with nature. Someday we
may learn to use Tai Chi—or something like it—to blend projection
VR and HMD VR, each with its appropriate range of applications,
both leading to a more productive, healthful life. If wisely applied, art
might meld the tunnel and the spiral into a single system that brings
humans to a higher state of well-being. The harmony of both types of
immersion could produce virtual environments for alert and self-aware
human beings. Ultimately, self-awareness could lead to a transformed
outdoors. The combination of HMD and CAVE might ward off Zen
sickness.

After breakfast you go to your home telepresence unit. There you
go to work by entering the corporate virtual workspace. For hours you
meet with colleagues, travel corridors of global data, help steer the
cybernetic industrial system. You never feel claustrophobic or bored
because the system designers have shaped the framework of cyberspace so that along the way, you time and again run up against the

infinity of this virtual world; a feeling of its overwhelming grandeur; its fearsome speed; its wild corners; its inaccessible and primal foundations. Its intensity and high speed allow only three or four hours of productive HMD immersion each day, so by noon you are switching to the *OSMOSE* program as you begin to relax. You feel yourself soften and recover your personal buoyancy. After ten minutes, the program prompts you to remove the encumbering data trackers. You take off the gear and the CAVE of your home unit awaits you.

A virtual Tai Chi expert invites you into the CAVE as you release your focus from HMD applications. The Tai Chi expert is a computer-generated composite that models the movements and postures of actual Tai Chi masters. The computer-generated master not only teaches a series of movements, but also adjusts meridian circulation, tests body structure, balance, and earth-energy strength. You play pushing hands, and even spar with the expert. An hour in the VR decompression chamber is a complete workout, and now you link smoothly to the primary world after reclaiming the integrity of conscious life in a biological body. The procedure offsets the disintegrating aspects of reality lags and Alternate World Syndrome. The VR experience becomes health-enhancing rather than health-compromising.

You leave the unit for lunch and notice that the patio door is open. The grass grows tall now where the asphalt highways used to be, and a pair of wild deer graze in the long grass. The breeze feels cool coming down from the mountains, and your heightened sensory awareness picks up the mountain rivers carried by the wind. In the distance, the mountains with their tall pines beckon you to take a walk this afternoon.

7

A W S a n d U F O s

Something. . . . —What?

—A phenomenon. Something intrusive, something vague but insistent, pushing itself upon us.

—Something outside? From afar? Something alien?

—Something descending in the night, standing in the shadows at the foot of the bed.

—An illusion? Hallucination maybe? A quirky twist of imagination?

—No, definitely a presence, something that might be a someone, a someone with wires and electric sensors, probing, penetrating, exploring private parts. Something lifting us off the familiar face of the planet we thought we knew so well, beaming us outside the orbit of our comfortable homes. Definitely something indefinite . . . or someone.

—We hear about them only from others who speak about sightings of unidentified objects in the sky, because we do not allow ourselves to be counted among the unstable few who acknowledge the possibility of something outside the circle of our sciences. Those unstable few accept belief in something standing in the shadows at the door. We listen closely to those speaking about incidents of the phenomenon. We do not look.

—Something IS out there. We've seen and heard it in the night. It's contacting us.

• • •

The phenomenon certainly exists in late-night chat like the above. It exists as metaphysical hearsay, as an internal dialogue between what we believe and what we think we are willing to believe. Popular descriptions of "the incident" waver between child-like awe and tongue-in-cheek tabloid humor. Here is where our knowledge, as a culturally defined certainty, becomes most vulnerable. Here we discover the soft edges of knowledge as an established and culturally underwritten form of belief. What a thrill to feel the tug of war on the thin thread of shared belief!

A blend of religious archetypes and science-fiction imagery supplies the words for those who tell about the incident. The stories often float up through hypnosis or "recovered memory" hypnotherapy, as in the famous case of Betty and Barney Hill who experienced abduction one September night in New Hampshire in 1961. Researchers have recently plotted consistently recurring patterns in thousands of stories, and the mythic dimension of the story line has not been lost on Hollywood. One of the biggest box-office hits in American entertainment history ($407 million) was the 1982 movie E.T. (*The Extra-Terrestrial*). A family stands against space invaders who in the end want nothing more than to make friends and "phone home." The alien remained alien only until we got to know it better, and then we came to love it.

Movie makers had a lesser but still notable success with *The Intruders* who mercilessly invade the inner recesses of the human body in their efforts to produce a human/alien hybrid. The intruders not only abduct sleeping victims but also probe them sexually with scientific instruments. The movie *Communion* supplied details about the intruders: their large black eyes, thin wiry bodies, gray complexion, and their spacecraft outfitted with high-tech labs. The same details appear in thousands of hypnotic sessions recorded in the case studies by ufologists like Budd Hopkins and Dr. John Mack at Harvard. Thousands of Americans have reported abduction incidents and millions believe them. Cults flourish around Nevada's "Area 51" near the U.S. Air Force base on Groom Lake off the official Nevada "Extra-Terrestrial Highway." The desert around Roswell, New Mexico, has been a locus for stories of alien spacecraft since 1947 when Lt. Walter Haut, public information officer at Roswell Army Air Field, issued a press release stating that the Army had recovered a crashed flying saucer from the desert in New Mexico. The Pentagon forced the incident into epistemological limbo until 1978 when witnesses to the crash began surfacing.[33]

The Dark Fortress

In the Summer of 1995, a flying machine set me down in Zurich, Switzerland, where I took a train to a small medieval town with high stone walls and story-book architecture known as Fribourg, Switzerland. Here was the site of "The Incident: A Symposium on Art, Technology, and Phenomena." The gathering was convened by the art curator Rob La Frenais in the ancient fortress called the Belluard. The Belluard's walls are mostly intact and its partial roof opens wide to the sky, letting celestial influence pour onto the old floor stones, dispelling some of the vaulting gothic shadows that clutter the fortress architecture. Seated under the skylight, I spent a day with a panel of speakers that included: Budd Hopkins, artist and author of *The Intruders*; Jacques Vallée, the French scientist who for decades applied science to UFO investigations; James Turrell, the artist who works with luminous phenomena; Rod Dickinson, artist and British crop circle hoaxer; Kathleen Rogers, who creates virtual reality installations related to parapsychology; Sergius Golowin, the distinguished Swiss writer on myth and folklore; Terence McKenna, the American ethnobotantist and messianic gadfly; and several other researchers from around the world.

The Belluard Fortress was an appropiate place to weigh the Fortean legacy of the Bronx philosopher, Charles Fort (1874–1932), who coined the term "teleportation" and who speculated that the mysterious lights in the sky were most likely craft from outer space. Fort is known abroad as the U.S. philosopher who believed mainstream science simply ignores the things it cannot explain. The Belluard made a perfect concert hall for John Williams's suite "Close Encounters of the Third Kind": a medieval city, a dark fortress, night falling. This was Rod Serling with the shades down, or the *X-Files*'s Fox Mulder on vacation.[See Figure 7.1]

The theme of the conference was the collaboration of art and technology in exploring the unknown. Art embraces things we can sense but do not know. The artist feels at home where intuition outruns reason. Paintings, music, and movies can expose the unconscious life of the mind, the sources of common fears and terrors, and the hopes that glow over the horizon of daily routine. In this sense, art is always extrasensory perception, because art exposes what lies behind our everyday mental maneuvers.

The Epistemology of the Peripheral

The artists of *The Incident* use technology to create works for contacting the unknown. Several artists at the symposium spoke about the thin line between art and hoax. Hoaxes, they explained, have historically walked hand-in-hand with modern art as artists seek to provoke, tease, and shock their audiences. From the "Wild Ones" (*Les Fauves*) to the notorious Andy Warhol, artists and hoaxers have shared a laugh at the gullibility of those who "follow" their work. The perceptions of the public have come to play an essential role in many art works, as in Christo's recent wrapping of Berlin's Reichstag building. The Reichstag, heavy with history, became the site of a street party where celebrants cheered the building's new airy look. The artist altered perceived history by altering the perception of a monument. The soft border between what we believe and what we are willing to believe becomes a theme for artists especially when scientists shun the unknown for fear of losing respectability and their hold on government grants.

Artists approach the credibility border in different ways. Some, like Rod Dickinson, aggressively document public reaction to the crop circles found mysteriously carved into Britain's corn fields near Stonehenge and then explained by tabloid journalists. (Dickinson and his friends did many of the cuttings themselves). Other artists move away from provoking public perceptions in an effort to lead perceptions to an internal shift. They approach the unknown head-on by using technology to probe cosmic elements.

James Turrell, for instance, makes technology reveal what we perceive but never notice. He isolates pure light. Light, of course, forms the backdrop and necessary condition for seeing anything at all. Yet

Figure 7.1 **The Belluard.** Photo courtesy of Eliane Laubscher.

we hardly ever notice light in its purity. Light usually functions to illuminate things other than itself, and all the while light forms the hidden horizon of our viewing things. Yet all our lighting devices are designed to put light to work and make it reflect off something we want to see, whether a book or the people in a room. Light itself seldom becomes the object of our vision. In that sense, light is the Great Unknown and Unseen.

Turrell's technology brings light to light. His machines invite us to step into an environment where the whole point is to see light itself, and to enhance our awareness of light, in its full spectrum, with a wide range of color and luminosity, by handling light controls. Without showing anything in particular, Turrell's art displays the presence of pure light—no longer as background for something else, but as central phenomenon. What we normally take for backdrop or ambient condition, Turrell puts front and center.

Turrell's technology frees light from its usual task of illumination. His installation "Change of State" in the Belluard invites the viewer to enter a small colorless booth where wall controls allow modulation of hue and intensity throughout the spectrum. Playing with the dials, you begin to see what your vision usually misses because of vision's thing-oriented focus: luminosity itself. Turrell compares this strategy to Heidegger's notion of the Clearing of Being (*die Lichtung*), where the philosophic person apprehends not the things in the environment, but the conditioning environment itself—as that environment shifts. Like the sun which Plato dubs "the Good," the light makes anything seen capable of being seen. Turrell energizes the viewer by opening an experience that largely sleeps in the unconscious. As the viewer makes each adjustment of light, the eyes register a "change of state" which marks a shift in the total environment.

By activating background awareness, Turrell does more than simply make background into foreground. He advances what I call the epistemology of the peripheral.

The difference between centrally focused and peripheral vision is crucial for certain activities. The hunter and the martial artist, for instance, train themselves to switch deliberately between central and peripheral modes of vision. Peripheral vision notices changes in the environment much more quickly than central or spot perception. The fovea, the retinal center spot of the eye, connects to the logic processing of the brain, while the more diffuse peripheral vision links more directly to the subconscious nervous system. If the martial artist maintains a relaxed attention with a full field of view—everything all at once with no fixation—then reaction time to any change or movement in the field of view is much quicker than the reaction filtered through a focused, ego-aware, centrally fixed stare. A stare provides more discrimination of details because the brain will process through central fixation and sort the colors and motions for pattern identification, but this optical processing slows the response to stimuli. Slower processing is imperative for the higher skills of survival, and whenever we turn our heads to see better, we prove the importance of central focus. But every skill we develop takes its toll on our full potential. A higher stage of civilization requires that we consciously undo what survival training has done to us in order to transform and adapt anew.

The difference in vision between peripheral and central modes has its analogy in electronic tracking. Radar engineers discovered a similar difference when they developed early-warning systems. The almost instantaneous detection of approaching air targets requires very different electronic systems from the pin-pointing searchlight that zooms in with great precision to identify the nature of an incoming flying object. Radar splits into two types of tracking: one works to alert the system that something, anything, has appeared on screen; the other zooms in to determine what kind of pattern the incoming object might match. Likewise with human eyes. Human eyes can detect a brief warning flash of less than 150 milliseconds spread through the entire visual field, but at that speed the eyes are unable to tell apart individual objects. When objects are inspected with focal attention, the eyes can discriminate many fine distinctions in the objects.[34]

The epistemology of the peripheral picks up flashes that appear faster than any discriminating cognitive attention can analyze. The important shift between central and peripheral focus has an ontological dimension. It goes beyond eyesight to our reality awareness itself. The world itself, as a totality, flashes its changes only to alert peripheral vision. Being as a whole reveals itself prior to any of the beings we encounter. The flash of light is not itself a thing to be looked at directly. James Turrell makes the point dramatically in his early projection pieces. In the early pieces, Turrell makes pure light a sculpted object standing before us. The background of light has become an incandescent thing placed against dark nothingness. The normal background of vision becomes a sculpted object to see. In his Afrum-Proto series, a specially designed projector throws massive geometrical light structures onto a public space.

The quintessence of Turrell's art arrives in the year 2001. That is the finish date for his Roden Crater project. Roden Crater is a dead volcano near Flagstaff, Arizona. Turrell has been modifying the volcano so that shafts of pure starlight will slip through the rock walls of the volanic structure and spread through the dark interior of the mountain in specific configurations. The entry angles of the starlight and the patterns of the light shafts derive from complex computer astronomy. In this way, Turrell hopes to make conscious the unconscious foundations of the universe as a phenomenon. The peripheral will come into focus without losing its essential mystery.

Another artist working at the edges of conscious life is Kathleen Rogers. Rogers combines parapsychology with the elemental features of country life. Her video art scans the seances and magical practices of rural folk. The primal and the spooky belong together in her art. At the Belluard, Rogers created an installation in a gloomy corner loft high inside the fortress. On the creaky wooden floor of the loft stand elaborate patterns of glass bottles each filled with water. Candles flicker on the bottle glass, making the water shine and sparkle. Video monitors around the edges of the room reflect the scene and put it into fluid motion. The theme of Rogers's *The Memory of Water* is the elemental energy patterns inherent in water. The power of the water element that usually goes unnoticed now hovers ghost-like through the room. The phenomenon can be literally true yet keep its essential mystery.

Kathleen Rogers's *The Memory of Water* fuses thick darkness with an array of light patterns—computerized and elemental—to coax the viewer into peripheral vision. She also uses sound patterns to gradually widen the edges of the experience. The end effect on the viewer resembles Turrell's luminosity. Both affect the feeling of the space/time dimension. Peripheral awareness renders the present spacious and non-temporal. Relaxing into our physical center and letting attention sink into the gut, the eyes soften and the attention spreads throughout the entire field of view. The awareness lives in open space as opposed to the brain's linear time sequence. A wide-angle view slows down the frantic race of the logical chains of thought. We find ourselves visited by those cosmologically primal elements in which we live: water and light. They manifest themselves under artfully prepared conditions.

See Figure 7.2

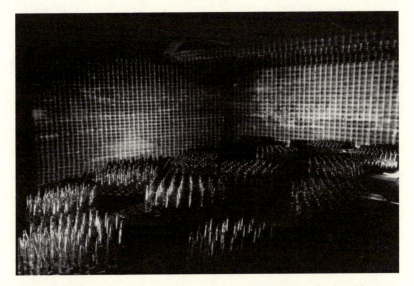

Figure 7.2 Installation "The Memory of Water" by Kathleen Rogers. Photo courtesy of Kathleen Rogers.

AWS and AWD

Each speaker at the Belluard Fortress brought another piece of the unknown. Some, like Turrell and Rogers, brought art works to explore the outer perimeters of awareness. Others, like Budd Hopkins and Jacques Vallée, brought stories of close encounters and various ways of interpreting those stories. Hopkins interpreted the stories with a credulity based on hundreds of first-hand interviews with abductees. Vallée interpreted the phenomena with a skepticism based on suspected government strategies of disinformation (arguing, for instance, that crop circles may be designed to distract from government experiments at nearby research sites). Some, like myself, brought speculation about the dark corners of the psyche out of which the stories emerge. I presented my theory in the context of VR technology.

The theory first appeared in a previous book, *The Metaphysics of Virtual Reality*, where I touched briefly on AWS (Alternate World Syndrome). AWS or AWD (Alternate World Disorder) is the darker side of virtual reality that I first noted on encountering VR art works at the Banff Center for the Arts. My Banff notes on AWS became part of my account of the VR experience. When psychotherapists ran across AWS in my book, they immediately connected it with their own work counseling abductees. Certain similarities between AWS and the abduction accounts intrigued them, and they invited me to explore the connection. So in 1994, I published an article in *The Bulletin of Anomalous Experience* where I connected virtual reality with the UFO experience. Vicki Cooper of *UFO Magazine* read the article and wanted the idea developed for the magazine.

The reader will find my Banff notes on AWS sprinkled throughout Chapter 3 "The Art of Virtual Reality." But let me summarize the notes here and then explain AWS in the context of the UFO phenomenon.

In the broadest sense, AWS (Alternate World Syndrome) is technology sickness. AWS is the relativity sickness that comes from switching back-and-forth between the primary and virtual worlds. The ontological oscillation creates a nervous state that makes one hypersensitive to sights and sounds and prone to make mistakes in mismatched contexts. After hours of VR immersion, everything seems brighter, even slightly illusory. Primary reality afterwards seems hidden underneath a thin film of appearance. Your perceptions seem to float over a darker, unknowable truth. The world vibrates with tension, as if something big were imminent, as if you were about to break through a veil of illusion. The tension can be accompanied by irritability, headaches, insomnia, or disorientation. Flashbacks from the virtual world pop up unexpectedly, or features of the real world that resemble the virtual suddenly balloon out of proportion.

AWS has predecessors in simulator sickness and motion sickness. Certain technologies have negative health effects on a percentage of the population. Some people find that long automobile rides, jet travel, or time in a flight simulator produces discomfort or intermittent illness. The symptoms of the discomfort vary. Some people experience nausea and sweatiness; some headaches, eyestrain, and insomnia; some feel a general malaise or mild depression. Clusters of the symptoms are classified as motion sickness, or jet lag, or simulator sickness. These illnesses are related to AWS, but they are more local in their impact. AWS is technology sickness writ large because virtual reality (in the strict sense used by virtual realists) brings the human being over the threshold into the artificial world. The human being entering a full-blown virtual habitat for work or play must exit and reconfigure the senses in order to resume life in the primary world, then later reconfigure when reentering the virtual world, etc. The psycho-physiological stress is greater than in previous technology syndromes. The mind and body become fully engaged in the artificial world and then they must reconfigure for the primary world. AWS occurs when the virtual world later obtrudes on the user's experience of the actual world, or vice versa. AWS is technology sickness, a lag between the natural and artificial environments.

In this sense, AWS sums up the other syndromes, much as VR sums up a whole phase of technology evolution. When the mind/body stretches long-term over virtual and primary worlds, then the acute AWS can turn into the chronic existential AWD (Alternate World Disorder). In AWD, the felt kinesthetic body loses its relative coherence and balance, and the disintegration depletes somatic energy. AWD is the imbalance that John Dewey, writing during the early evolution of technological society, feared: "There is an internecine warfare at the heart of our civilization between the functions of the brain and the nervous system on one side and the functions of digestion, circulation, respiration and the muscular system on the other."[35] From a cultural evolutionary perspective, the debate between naïve realists and network idealists springs from their common premonition of AWD. AWD is the rupture of the kinesthetic from the visual senses of self-identity.

Simulator sickness was a problem long before the advent of virtual reality, but simulators were used by only a tiny portion of the population, mostly military and commercial pilots. In recent decades, military researchers have done extensive studies of simulator sickness. These studies however, take into account only a narrow range of virtual world phenomena, and their observations are based on a select portion of the general population. Compared to virtual reality, simulators are a limited and controlled mock scenario. Nevertheless, the AWS syndrome has a younger cousin in simulator sickness.

Simulators play a major role in training U.S. military personnel. Pilots learn to take-off and land aircraft through motion-platform flight simulators, and tank crews learn to coordinate their action through distributed-network simulations coupled with mock-up tank vehicles. More recently, individual dismounted soldiers train in combat simulations called "the electronic battlefield." Although AWS runs much deeper than simulator sickness, the military studies provide some landmarks for understanding AWS.

The military studies show recurrent patterns or syndromes in simulator-sickness.[36] While the symptoms vary with the individual, they typically include eyestrain, nausea, headaches, flashbacks, loss of postural balance, and disorientation. Sometimes sweating or vomiting occurs, but these symptoms are not as frequent as disorientation or a general malaise. About half of the pilots using military simulators report symptoms. Because of acute symptoms, many pilots cannot use simulators, and even those who train in simulators are grounded for days afterwards. Distance vision is adversely affected by simulator sickness, and so is postural stability. Simulator experience counts toward upgrading a pilot's license to more powerful aircraft, but the hazards of simulator sickness exclude a large portion of pilots from upgrading their licenses in this way.

Simulator sickness has been studied as a form of motion sickness. Scientists are not sure whether the two syndromes share the identical etiology, but some of the same anatomy and physiology seems involved in both syndromes. The brain detects motion by receiving cues from several senses: the eyes, the ears (binaural sound location), the inner ear (vestibular system), the skin (temperature), and the kinesthetic and proprioceptive senses. Motion sickness appears to come from conflicting cues based on the body's felt memory and current expectations. Inconsistency in the cues creates disharmony. If you are sitting in a car and your kinesthetic sense signals to the brain that you are not moving, while at the same time your eyes signal that you are moving at high speed through a landscape, a dissonance occurs and motion sickness can result. If you are in a simulator and the horizon of your field of view says that you have just leveled off and are flying parallel to the ground while at the same time the simulator's motion platform has not yet quite synchronized with the control panel, then you have a internal dissonance. Even slight, unnoticeable discrepancies can induce subtle, subconscious miscues. Motion sickness and simulator sickness occur when the brain fails to make sense out of the sensory cues as the entire organism seeks a holistic interpretation based on past experience.

Likewise with jet lag. When the sun goes down, the darkness activates certain enzymes in the pineal gland and sleep results. As morning approaches and daylight intensifies, levels of substances like melatonin decrease in the body and we awaken. The melatonin levels can be interrupted artificially as in jet travel when several time zones are traversed in one day. The result is jet lag. The body's production of melatonin gets out of sync with the circadian rhythms of the new environment. Some people remedy jet lag by ingesting melatonin during a flight. People working swing shifts may have trouble getting used to sleeping during the day for the same reason. Again, the dissonance comes from mismatched cues to the biopsychic body.

Similarly with AWS. The VR experience can mix images and expectations from alternate worlds so as to distort our perception of the primary world, making us prone to errors in mismatched contexts. The virtual world obtrudes upon our activities in the primary world, and vice versa. AWS should not be confused with the symptoms caused by the lag in current head-mounted VR displays that produce jerky graphics as the user moves head and hands. This widely known problem with current HMDs comes from discrepancy between the user's movements and the response time needed for current computers to re-paint the appropriate graphic images on the miniature display screens in the helmet. The jerky rendering of graphics often causes headaches and discomfort. But these problems will eventually be solved as the speed of computing power catches up with user feedback. HMDs also create eye pain because of the illusion involved in stereoscopic visual accommodation: focusing on a screen one inch in front of the eyes while the brain processes a virtual object thirty yards away in the virtual distance can create subtle dissonance. But these physiological problems of current HMDs are internal to its system of technology; the problems do not touch the more fundamental issue of AWS. AWS concerns not the system per se, but the system within the broader context of world entrance and exit. AWS concerns how the responses ingrained in the one world step out of phase with the other. AWS shows the human being merging, yet still out of sync, with the machine.

Experienced users become accustomed to hopping over the rift. Dr. Stephen Ellis, scientist at NASA/Ames and at the UC Berkeley School of Optics, says that his work in VR often has him unconsciously gesturing in the primary world in ways that function in the virtual world. He points a finger half expecting to fly (as his cyberbody does under the conventions of the virtual world). His biobody needs to re-calibrate to the primary world.

Observe someone coming out of a VR system such as W Industries' *Virtuality* arcade games. Watch the first hand movements. Invariably, the user stands in place a few moments (unless hurried by the arcade administrator), takes in the surroundings, and then pats torso and buttocks with the hands—as if to secure a firm landing and return to presence in the primary body ("Am I really here?" and "Where's my wallet?"). The user feels a discrepancy on returning to the primary world. The discrepancy marks the gap between the virtual and the biopsychic bodies. The virtual body still lingers in the afterimages and the newly formed neural pathways while the primary body resumes involvement in the actual, non-virtual world.

Research on simulators used in the military throws a shadow over the popular enthusiasm for VR. The military studies of simulators suggest that the population at large might suffer serious side effects if regularly exposed for long hours to virtual environments. The side effects of AWS would not be avoidable like the hazards of radiation exposure. The side effects of virtual world systems come from the intrinsic power of technological immersion. Because of their powerful immersion techniques, VR systems retrain the user's autonomic nervous system. In learning to respond smoothly to the virtual environment, the user adapts to the technology in ways that confuse the psyche and even affect subsequent actions in the primary world.

AWS is stress from the pressures on biological structures and rhythms. It is a technology sickness that springs from accelerated evolution. To improve the technology alone will not remedy AWS. It is our relationship to technology that must come into balance. Because we are mutating with the technology, we need flexibility to adjust.

Our Western medicine is good for treating specific illnesses but not so good at preserving a state of well-being and preventing illness. Chinese herbalists invented something called "adaptogens." An adaptogen comes from herbs like Ginseng or wild Asparagus root. The purpose of the adaptogen is not to cure acute illness but to regulate the bodily processes so that stress is dealt with more resiliently. The adaptogens do not cure but they function as tonics for maintaining balance under changing circumstances. Asparagus root, for instance, is prescribed as a tonic for keeping the spirit in flight. The saying goes, "You cannot consider yourself healthy unless your spirit (*shen*) can fly." "Flying" means being able to rise above circumstances and situations, being able to see many sides of a situation or issue. Only when you can fly, will you be able to survive changing circumstances. Asparagus root, the Chinese herbalists say, "grows wings on the heart," meaning that the person who consumes the adaptogen will regularly rise above pressures and be able to see things from all sides and perspectives. To offset AWS, we need something like an adaptogen, though it may not come so much in the form of a pill or tea as in the form of a meditative practice.

There is growing awareness of AWS in popular culture. The troubling shift between alternate worlds runs through science fiction and movies. From *Jacob's Ladder* to *Twelve Monkeys*, film writers probe the troubling jump between worlds. Many episodes of *Star Trek: The Next Generation* rework the anomalies in the space/time continuum, and so do television programs like *Sliders*. The naïve realists and the network idealists see one another over the fence of different worlds. Anxiety about AWS becomes so central that we begin looking for adaptogenic aids outside our solar system. Maybe evolutionary help will come from aliens in another star system? That's why we scan the skies for UFOs.

Fast-Forward Jung

Virtual reality is a key for understanding contemporary culture. It reveals as much about contemporary lives and conflicts as traditional psychiatry. Twentieth-century philosophers—from Dewey and Mumford to McLuhan and Heidegger—saw technology plaguing us not as

a HAL mainframe (from the film 2001) whose artificial intelligence
outsmarts us, nor as a Frankenstein monster looming menacingly over
its creators. Rather, these philosophers saw technology as a source of
internal stress brought on by the complexity of this stage of human
evolution. They realized that the inner tension would grow and install
itself into our daily routines as we use everyday appliances. When the
appliances lead to a full-flown virtual reality, then you see a corre-
spondingly large crack open in the biopsychic body. Write this conflict large, look at where our actual use of technology is taking us, and
you have AWS and AWD.

UFO abduction belongs, I think, to the peripheral perception of
our evolutionary destiny. It belongs to the rocky marriage of human
and technology. The psychopathology of abduction reveals what is
written large in AWS and AWD. The hallucinatory intrusion of technology belongs to the unsteady, out-of-kilter grafting of technology on
the human species. The naïve realists and the network idealists are
therefore both correct in believing that this era stands at a high-risk
crossroads. Virtual reality gives us a clue to the UFO experience
because VR represents the culmination of the artificial, technology-
driven world we already inhabit but which we have not yet assimilated. At this point in evolution, we experience our full technological
selves as alien visitors, as threatening beings who are mutants of ourselves and who are immersed and transformed by technology to a
higher degree than we think comfortable and who about to operate,
we sense, on the innards of our present-day selves. The visitors from
outer space descend from our own future.

The Swiss psychoanalyst Carl Jung had a persistent and continuous
interest in the UFO phenomenon throughout his lifetime. He even
wrote a book about it. In *Flying Saucers: A Modern Myth of Things
Seen in the Skies*. Jung repeatedly warns us that he does not have
enough evidence and has never seen a UFO himself, so he cannot
address the physical existence of the unidentified flying objects. Working from UFO reports, Jung insisted that "something is seen, but we
don't know what."[37] He also wrote that "a purely psychological explanation is illusory, for a large number of observations point to a natural
phenomenon, or even a physical one."[38] Yet because of his limited

evidence and because the visitors from outer space seemed important, Jung studied UFOs as psychological patterns. His interest was in the psychology of the phenomenon, though he believed there was more to the phenomenon than the psychological.

Jung applied his psychology of personal integration to the reported incidents. The unidentified flying object, he conjectured, represents the aspiration of the individual to become whole — the same aspiration he saw in the dreams, hallucinations, and recurrent mental obsessions that the human species has expressed throughout the recorded history of art and religion. Jung saw images of alien visitors in powerful spacecraft as symbols of the human ascent to a richer, more complete personal life. He compared the role of the saucers in contemporary life to the role that angels played in the Middle Ages. Jung saw the whole panoply of spiritual symbols recurring in the twentieth century, not under the auspices of the Church, but in the dreams and late night experiences of secular modern Western people, whom Jung considered to be sundered from primal roots and overly intellectualized.

Jung saw the UFO phenomenon as the psyche's projection of a longing for a more complete life. His book treats UFOs in the hearsay of popular culture, in modern painting, and in reports dating back to the 1500s. He found alien spacecraft in the spiritual and artistic legacy of the past — in the Bible and in older art forms. In all his sources, Jung saw a pantheon of recurring archetypes which he postulated to belong to the symbolic language of the collective psyche. Today's Close Encounter is yesterday's Angelic Visitation. Jung caught the influence of the past on the present. The flying saucer itself was a symbol with religious meaning:

> If the round shining objects that appear in the sky be regarded as visions, we can hardly avoid interpreting them as archetypal images. They would then be involuntary, automatic projections based on instinct, and as little as any other psychic manifestations or symptoms can they be dismissed as meaningless and merely fortuitous. Anyone with the historical and psychological knowledge knows that circular symbols have played an important role in every age; in our own sphere of culture, for instance, they were not only soul symbols but "God-images." There is an old saying that "God is a circle whose center is everywhere and the circumference nowhere." God in his omniscience, omnipotence, and omnipresence is a totality

symbol **par excellence**, something round, complete, and perfect. Epiphanies of this sort are, in the tradition, often associated with fire and light. On the ancient level, therefore, the UFOs could easily be conceived as "gods." They are impressive manifestations of totality whose simple, round form portrays the archetype of the self, which as we know from experience plays the chief role in uniting apparently irreconcilable opposites and is therefore best suited to compensate the split-mindedness of our age.[39]

Here Jung draws on his experience interpreting the symbols that appear in his patients' dreams. He applies a profound understanding of the religious meaning of traditional symbols as they flicker through dreams. The circle, for instance, conveys aspirations for a felt completeness and fulfillment.

The upshot of Jung's analysis is to interpret UFOs as entities from the deep past, as gods or angels. His references to numinous, divine, awesome powers tend to come from antiquity. The strongest influence on dreams and hallucinations, as Jung sees it, comes from the past. UFOs carry the ancient human aspiration for completeness. Flying saucers appear in the same symbol set used by the worshipper bowing before the perfection of divinity. As humans in the past worshipped perfect divinity, so too, Jung believed, humans now stand in awe before celestial phenomena. Jung sees in the phenomena the divine perfection for which we long. The past helps Jung understand the present.

Carl Jung was only partly right about UFOs. What Jung missed was the future. His eyes turned to the past, not the future. The influence of the future on the present is nowadays stronger than the influence of the past. Today we are influenced by the technology of the future. We are drawn forward by it as our internal telos or underlying goal. We are evolving, and our evolution inscribes in us a technological destiny, an intimate relationship to information systems. The technological mutants of our own future evolution influence us now. They summon us forward and upward. Their summons comes from within, and it speaks with terror as well as hope.

Jung did recognize the connection between the UFO phenomenon and the high-stress life in a technological society. He wrote: "The saucer sightings can be found in many reports that go back to antiquity, though not with the same overwhelming frequency. But then, the possibility of global destruction, which is now in the hands of our so-called politicians, did not exist in those days. McCarthyism and its influence are evidence of the deep and anxious apprehensions of the American public. Therefore most of the signs in the skies will be seen in North America."[40] And Jung refers to the widespread media interest in UFOs as connected to the Cold War's nuclear threat, as "psychic compensation for the collective fear weighing on our hearts."[41]

Here Jung brings the phenomenon closer to the present. He paints the background of the phenomenon in colors of present-day anxiety. Still, he does not address the technostress future that increasingly drives the present. Jung himself belonged to a century before the merger of humans with technology. He did not realize that the UFO experience derives as much from deep technostress as it does from the urgings of archetypes from past experiences of the human species. He did not realize that what we see in the UFO is a glimpse of the *homo technicus*: the thoroughly technological mutant standing at the edges of our peripheral vision, haunting us as an alien intelligence, threatening to probe our guts and reorganize our psyches. The Unidentified Flying Object conveys our future selves to us more than it bears mythic stories from the past. The alien haunting us is already modifying the children of the future.

The human race is not stupid. There is something like a peripheral vision by which humans glimpse their future from the corners of the eye. Peripheral knowledge of the future does not register clearly on the central focus. The logic of the fovea reacts later and more slowly, once the details have surfaced for cognitive analysis. Peripheral awareness catches the first outlines of the future much earlier. The biopsychic body continually collects information about present trends and future adjustments; it constantly projects patterns for adaptation; it alerts us through dreams, art, and creative contemplation. For the mind's central focus, the truth is out there; for the peripheral mind, the truth has already landed—within.

We are not surprised, then, when the UFO abductee Betty Luca explains that the gray aliens who frequently abduct her and her husband are actually "biological robots." The robots, she says, are con-

trolled by a group of higher entities that resemble humans.[42] The
biobots lack the freedom of will that would make them responsive
and approachable, while the higher entities who control the biobots
do not carry out abductions themselves. These higher entities Luca
calls the "Elders." The Elders have a notion of what is best for the
human species and they continually watch us. The watchers use samples drawn from humans to determine what we are made of and to aid
production of a new version of human beings. The human race is an
experiment. We are an experiment worth worrying about, and we
exist under the watchful eyes of an intelligence that remains out of
our control. Minions of that intelligence hover in the skies if we look
for them. What peripheral awareness then tells us is to adapt, stay flexible, be prepared to mutate. We are evolving, and technology belongs
to that evolution.

Telepresence Evolution

Jung misread our evolutionary destiny, but his search for the inner
meaning of outer experience helps us understand AWS in its relation to UFOs. Throughout his life, Jung studied the literature of
alchemy. Before modern science broke from its Renaissance roots,
the chemist walked hand-in-hand with the alchemist. Alchemy is the
technology of self-transformation. Although alchemists often got
sidetracked into spurious experiments, many alchemists sought the
inner meaning of outward events, the human correlate of minerals
and vegetables. When they believed they had found the correlate,
alchemists tried transforming themselves by applying the techniques
they had learned from nature. Alchemists and astronomers like Gior-
dano Bruno mapped the cosmos in order to understand the many
layers of the human mind. "As above, so below" meant that the
macrocosm could reveal the microcosm and vice versa. Much of the
alchemists' visionary material intrigued Jung, and Jungian psychotherapists today are looking closely at VR as a tool for inner
alchemy. Virtual reality, by empowering inner vision, extends the
tradition of alchemy.

   Some Jungian psychiatrists make a direct correlation between
inner and outer technologies, between dream analysis and VR, as I

learned from a discussion with Dr. Robert Romanyshyn, author of *Technology As Symptom and Dream*.[43] In the glossary to *The Metaphysics of Virtual Reality*, under the entry "virtual reality" I once wrote the following: "Virtual Reality convinces the participant that he or she is actually in another place, by substituting the normal sensory input received by the participant with information produced by a computer" (p. 180). Reading this passage closely, Romanyshyn wrote me that my definition could be slightly altered to make an alchemical point. All we need do is substitute two phrases: "Dreams [instead of VR] convince the participant that he or she is actually in another place, by substituting the normal sensory input received by the participant with unconscious wishes and desires [instead of information produced by a computer]." In other words, VR parallels the functions of dream life. Both are profound forms of visualization that blend inner vision and outer scenes.

VR transforms reality through visualization. The alchemists studied by Jung had practiced elaborate techniques for self-transformation (searching for youth or personal power). VR extends and enhances the evolutionary powers of transformation. So great is the promise of VR for self-transformation that pundits compare the invention of virtual reality to the invention of fire. Fire helped nourish our division of labor (tending the fire, controlling it, working by the fire). And fire fostered our meditative and contemplative powers (watching the flickering flames at night, acknowledging the danger from the camp fire, resting in a bright circle where dangerous animals fear to enter).[44] Both fire and cyberspace phosphor support the effort to build memory palaces in the mind. Cyberspace itself is a gigantic memory palace. Instead of ink drawings, our contemporary memory maps have hardware support.

Yet we should not forget that underneath the hardware evolution lies a magical power within us. Inside us we have the power to transport ourselves elsewhere. This inner power propels us forward into the future or backward into the past. Call it memory or expectation, teleportation lies at the basis of virtual reality. Teleportation is also a key for understanding our evolution and for mitigating its technostress. If VR is to serve as adaptogen, we must not forget that its remedy enhances, not supplants, our own intrinsic internal power.

Electronic equipment depends ultimately on the intrinsic human capacity for telepresence. The vast communication networks on the planet would collapse in a second without the human skill to teleport ourselves mentally and emotionally. Usually we take for granted the fact that we can project ourselves to remote times and places, that we can create internal images of locations we know only through past acquaintance or by reading and hearsay. We humans conjure up distant realities out of a few slim leads, map an entire world with a scrawl of lines on paper, and think "universe" at the sound of a single word. At least since the archaic Greece of Anaximander, the use of globes, maps, and compasses have stamped humans as natural teleoperatives. The word "imagination" fails to convey this rich telepresence ability.

To appreciate how naturally we achieve presence at a distance, think for a moment about pure presence. When are we ever Fully Present? We are typically elsewhere, divided, on the way somewhere. We're going towards, underway, or wishing we were. Birds sit warbling on the wires. Cats luxuriate and lick fur in the sunshine. But us? We're on the move, thinking back, or planning ahead. Elsewhere runs in our blood. Whole religions are built on the pledge to get us to sit still. Rituals and formalities offer momentary respite from instability, but we relentlessly push beyond ourselves—even to the point of exhaustion. If telepresence means "presence at a distance," then we are already half-way there.

Anywhere else can become home. At the slightest cue, we spin out and latch onto a world. Our senses take a bit of information about something that might exist and we're there! We see it, we believe it— until we decide not to believe it. Our minds scan for reality occasions. Advertisers know this: we hear what someone says and we take it for truth, unless we make a deliberate effort to doubt it. Someone says something, and that's the way it is—until we stop to question. If it even only looks like information, we buy it. We love reality and want to find it everywhere. Our senses, like horses nearing the barn, speed to a gallop when they smell reality around the bend. We want to land right now in a world we call home where we move securely from one thing to another and where we receive attention and nourishment. Then, quick, off to another home in a world elsewhere!

Because of this itch for telepresence and this yen for world-building, we have a history of producing endless devices for simulation, all in the name of Realism. Art history boasts the sensory realism of the Fifth-Century Athenian vase painter, Zeuxis, who first used shading to give depth to two-dimensional drawings. His painted grapes attracted birds who tried to peck at them—or at least so the friendly critics report. Realistic painters like Courbet and Daumier portrayed hard-to-watch misery that would otherwise remain blurry to the flint-eyed squint of law and morality. In literature, Flaubert and Balzac described fading, commonplace lives without idealizing or romanticizing them. These art works take us somewhere to "see with our own eyes" instead of having us look through the haze of general ideas. And with photography in the twentieth century, the lust for realistic images created the motion-picture studios as well as the home video camera. Science, too, now fuses its realism with instruments—from the scanning/tunneling microscope that inspects molecules to the satellite dishes of radio astronomy—all displaying the realities that have become intertwined with the technology that offers them for our study.

Computers supercharge this world-building drive of ours. Computers are not only the instruments but also the objects of that drive. Hardware and software now help us transform and upgrade computer hardware and software. Recall the rapid evolution of personal computers. First, users had no monitors but used punch cards and teletypes to bring data in and out of the data processors. Then the CRT (cathode ray tube), similar to a television screen, presented the data. Soon typewriter-style keyboards replaced the punch cards, and then the mouse pointing device took over for some of the keyboard. Storage media grew from big tapes to tiny disk drives with huge capacities. All the while, software was bringing human beings closer to the data. The clueless command line gave way to the look of a desktop, with data conveniently labeled in files which fit into folders, and graphic icons helped sustain the feel of a desktop with folders, trash cans, and even windows.

With Windows software, the user came to a transition. Previously, software suggested a set of tools that were extensions of the user, as a hammer might extend the power of the arm or the magnifying glass the power of the eye. Software as a window onto data, means that the data itself becomes a space we look into, and eventually a place we might enter. Instead of peripheral tools, the software becomes a center from which we work. Windows allows us to look into an area that is now evolving into its own virtual reality. The next step is to walk through the glass, climb in through the window, and find ourselves in wonderland.

Getting ourselves inside the data does not necessarily pull us away from life on planet earth. Sometimes you feel more present when you're absent. My opera-partner and I listen to a digital recording and she remarks, "That sounds a lot better than when we heard it from row thirty in the balcony!" Even a pair of good headphones can help you enjoy a piece of music you might otherwise avoid if it were amplified in concert. The physical world puts up parking problems and pillars, hats and noisy neighbors, so that the ideal setting might be the headroom of your own audio equipment. Computers may soon bring us closer to many places if we first enter the computer.

The evolution of computers pulls us further into it whether we like it or not. Many of us hesitated to upgrade our machines to run Windows because of the cost in time and energy required by upgrades. It's painful. It means messing with confusing new features, memory "solutions," and touchy configuration puzzles. But evolve we did, and later we felt the leap in power and convenience. In fact, we have little choice as individuals, because the evolutionary flow draws us inevitably through the computer screen from Windows to VR. The steps of evolution invite us to make ourselves at home in the computer. Which is not to say that the steps are painless or without anxiety.

VR telepresence shows an evolution similar to the evolution of hardware and software. Telepresence can be as easy as picking up the phone. Walking on the moon gets more complicated. A complex VR system may require total immersion. Total Immersion allows us to experience all the sights and sounds of another place and even join people to interact with the things in that virtual place. Total immersion is the holy grail of VR, the equivalent of the Holodeck from *Star Trek: The Next Generation*.

The example this book began with—the moon explorer—offers total immersion with the added bonus of teleoperation.

Teleoperation allows us to affect the physical lunar landscape. But we are intrinsically teleoperatives even before we ever use robotic arms to move a barrel or even before we toss our bait line on a long fishing pole out into the lake. Our thoughts and desires go forward to affect things.

This power of ours will come into prominence with the widespread use of VR. The technology will augment that already characteristic power of human beings. The power will evolve, and with its evolution, human presence will be stretched ever more in coming centuries. Technostress is the dark side of evolution. The human mind-body structure will undergo shifts with the pressures of evolution. Jung was right in seeing the human task as one of balance, of continually seeking integrity for feelings and intellect, of assimilating experience into a harmonious whole. The fascination and pain of the UFO phenomenon shows us only the first glimpse of our ultimate merger with technology. The assault of change means that we must listen to those whispering elders who show us how technologies like VR can be used to cure the sickness they cause, or at least help us adapt. As we proceed with the merger, we should actively embrace the disciplines that can restore us to balance and heal our inner divisions. We need to turn our telepresence abilities inwards.

Riding the Boomerang

The Belluard panel included a Swiss anthropologist, Robert A. Fischer, who had been living with and studying Australian Pintupi aborigines for several years. His special interest is the evolution of aboriginal technology, and his studies yielded insight, I think, into the possible direction of telepresence evolution. By looking to archaic origins, we can teleport ourselves further down our own evolutionary path—only in the opposite direction.

The racial origin of the Australian Aborigines remains uncertain. Some ethnologists classify the aborigines as a separate race of Australoids while others view them as archaic Caucasoids from the prehistoric Asian mainland. The aborigines number around 200,000 and constitute one percent of Australia's population. Their language is related to no other language. Before settling on reservations, they lived as nomads. One-third of their population still lives as nomads. In their native condition, the aborigines hunt and fish, and they show great skill in using the boomerang, the waddy (a war club), and the throwing stick (which throws spears). They are known for their bold colorful rock paintings, but the most widely known aborigine invention is the boomerang.

The return boomerang is a hardwood, V-shaped missile used for hunting small birds and for sport. The boomerang's arms are slightly skewed, with the angles ranging from 90 to 160 degrees. Both edges of the arm are sharpened, one surface flat and the other slightly convex. The aborigine holds the boomerang vertically in the right hand and throws it spinning on a line parallel to the ground. The missile flies at the same level; then inclines to its flat side, rises, curves to the left, and, still curving, glides back to the thrower. Throws of more than 91 meters (300 feet) have been made with the return boomerang. The boomerang is a unique technology among these unique people on the face of the earth.

Living with the aborigines, Robert Fischer studied the boomerang as a technology. He tried to piece together the evolution of this remarkable invention, and he wanted to find out why the aborigines had stopped inventing devices after the boomerang. Why did aboriginal evolution stop after the boomerang? Did evolution bypass them, or did they take a detour along another evolutionary path? From his studies, Fischer concluded that once the aborigines had developed the boomerang as a physical technology, the boomerang then later emerged as a tool for self-transformation. It ceased being a physical tool and began leveraging an interior power.

After the Pintupi aborigines had developed the boomerang, according to Fischer, they later began to internalize the spiritual meaning of its trajectory. Their skill at sending the missile through the air increased, and they began observing the principles of the boomerang. So taken were they with the principles of the boomerang flight that the Pintupi began experimenting inside themselves. They invented spirit travel, a part of aboriginal culture that also appears in archaic world cultures. The flight of the soul became a higher kind of boomerang. The soul, they discovered, could transport itself through space and time, with at least as much magic as the boomerang. The outer technology found an inner correlate. The boomerang got translated into spirit flight.

Soul travel for the Pintupi resembles the "dragon ride" exercises of Taoist meditation. In soul travel, the traveler closes the eyes to leave present physical space. The spirit sinks into darkness, letting go the cares and needs of the moment. Breathing and energy techniques pump strength into the soul. And the journey begins. The soul flies to people, places, and things that need attention. Unfinished business, things unsaid that need to be said, draw the spirit onward in its mission. The traveler moves along, lifted by the night wind instead of by the dictates of daylight. The soul knows of itself where to travel, and skill develops over time. The awareness of internal body currents dissolves the ego-mind's boundaries between inner world and outer space, and the spirit collects and absorbs energy from the cosmic elements, the sun, the moon, and the stars. To return from soul travel much skill is needed. Here the guidance of a more experienced traveler is necessary. (Don't try this at home.) The soul traveler arrives back in the body slowly. On return, the body rejoices. The fulfilled soul brings joy to the body. In Taoism, the inner organs—liver, heart, lungs, and stomach—are each greeted in turn, and the organism as a whole enjoys a boost of well-being.

Fischer claims that the spirit's boomerang ended the outward evolution of aboriginal technology. He believes that the inward impact of the boomerang was so strong that the Pintupi ceased developing their physical technology. The Pintupi, we might say, found an alternate route for technological development. Humans can direct a technology onto another plane, a spirit plane, if they are inspired to do so. The new plane may not be entirely new, because, like the boomerang, it returns home on a recursive spiral. We can use the technology to begin a journey, and the journey may then lead out of the tunnel of entrapment and estrangement.

Ascent of the Belluard

The UFO Elders may be lending us guidance through the gift of VR. If VR becomes a tool for transformation, our intrinsic telep-

resence ability can begin operating on a spirit level. VR might
become our strongest adaptogen. It might teach us to return to
our earth rather than destroy or escape it. We might create communication systems with new depth, with greater scope and intimacy, greater respect and distance than ever before. That system
might lend grace to our bodily selves and healing to our planetary
anxieties.

Look again at the photo of the Belluard Fortress so lovingly composed by Eliane Laubscher. The photographer intuitively captures
the Belluard Fortress as a site of the UFO gift. The photo suggests a
spirit journey.

First, the two lines of the pathway lead over hard stones. The path
drawing us inward is a long road, and we must not rush but walk each
stepping stone. Proceed cautiously, with conscience.

As we pass between the bright pillars that support our inner structure, the darkness descends. The doors of darkness fade to ebony
emptiness all around.

We wait in the dark. We remain open and welcome any advance
into the unknown. Our work is to release anxiety and abandon the
desire for certainty and control. Our breathing expands with every
breath. We drop any fixed intentions to see something specific. Peripheral awareness gradually takes over.

Many breaths pass through us. At long last, there, up above, the
roof space opens, and on the edge of vision, a circular light emits its
rays. The light grows and expands.

We are uplifted. A radiant reality captures us. We are present to a
higher self.

Now we must become that vision and find our way back home.

Notes on Artists and Works

Artists and Works in Chapter 3

Dancing with the Virtual Dervish   Marcos Novak directs the graduate Advanced Design Research Program at the School of Architecture, University of Texas at Austin. He also teaches advanced design and theory. Professor Diane Gromala is Director of the New Media Lab in the School of Communications at the University of Washington in Seattle. Yacov Sharir is the founder and artistic director of resident professional dance company of the University of Texas at Austin, and he teaches dance, choreography, computer animation, and interdisciplinary art and technology courses.

Topological Slide   Michael Scroggins currently teaches both video and computer graphic animation at the California Institute of the Arts. Stewart Dickson is a sculptor and programmer currently employed as Technical Director at Walt Disney Pictures in Burbank, California.

PlaceHolder   Brenda Laurel works at Interval Research Corporation in Palo Alto, California, where she coordinates a project for designing interactive systems that accommodate individual and cultural diversity. Rachel Strickland is an architect who has focused on the cinematic dimensions of the sense of place, and she has taught film and video production at the Massachusetts Institute of Technology, the University of California, Santa Cruz, and the Southern California Institute of Architecture.

Bar Code Hotel   Perry Hoberman lives in Brooklyn and teaches at the Cooper Union School of Art. He has presented installations, spectacles, sculptures and performances throughout the United States and Europe.

See Banff   Michael Naimark works at Interval Research in Palo Alto, California, where he develops computer interfaces. He has taught at San Francisco Art Institute, San Francisco State University, California Institute of the Arts, Massachusetts Institute of Technology, and the University of Michigan.

VR on Five Dollars a Day   Ron Kuivila performs and exhibits installations throughout the United States, Canada, and Europe, collaborating with composers, artists and choreographers, including Anthony Braxton and Merce Cunningham. Recordings of his work are available from Lovely Music Ltd, Nonesuch, Slowscan Editions, and Tellus.

Inherent Right, Inherent Vision   Laurence Paul Yuxweluptun is a native artist from northern British Columbia. His drawings stylize the Northwest Coast Native Canadian traditional images.

Artists and Works in Chapter 4

Videoplace   Myron Krueger has been called the "Father of Virtual Reality" because he worked on many of the principles of VR since the early 1970s. *Videoplace* shows a characteristic technique of reading the participant's body with cameras and projecting it onto a graphic environment so the participant can interact in real time with a computerized entities. Today, television weather forecasters and professional sports enthusiasts put many of Krueger's visual ideas into practice.

Hidden in Plane Sight   Clarence Major is a multimedia environmental designer in the Los Angeles area who has worked for several years in the film industry. He bases much of his current work on the *trompe l'oeil* paintings of the middle Renaissance. His expositions mix the traditional gallery space with what he calls "hyper-real paintings" that combine 3-D sound, 3-D photography, and a variety of computerized sensing devices.

Elective Affinities   Sara Roberts collaborated with Lynn Hershman on the internationally exhibited interactive installation *A Room of One's Own* (1992). She worked in feature film at Lucasfilm's Skywalker Ranch, and has done several commissioned interactive sculptures in both San Francisco and Los Angeles. She now teaches at the California Institute of the Arts in Los Angeles.

The Family Portrait and Portrait One   Luc Courchesne has found support for his work in Canada, France, and Germany. Influenced by experimental cinema in the 1960s and by video in the 1970s, he started combining computers and television in the early 1980s while doing graduate studies at the Center for Advanced Visual Studies at the Massachusetts Institute of Technology. He currently teaches information design at the School of Industrial Design at the University of Montreal.

Silicon Remembers Carbon   David Rokeby is an interactive sound and video artist based in Toronto. He was an artist-in-residence at the Bioapparatus Session at the Banff Center for the Arts in 1991. His interactive installations have been exhibited internationally, and he has shown work at *Ars Electronica*, the *MuuMedia* Festival, SIGGRAPH, the Venice *Biennale*, and other international festivals.

Bridge at Remagen   John Massey is a Toronto artist who exhibits internationally. He is one of two artists representing Canada in the 1996 Sydney Bienniale.

Virtual Reality Simulator   Robert Wedemeyer is a professional photographer and multimedia artist who explores the paradoxes of the virtual dimension. He works in Los Angeles, and his *Virtual Reality Simulator* appeared in a 1993 exhibit at the El Camino College Art Gallery in Torrance, California.

Artists and Works in Chapter 5

James Cracraft   James Cracraft helped develop the application of photogrammetry to virtual worlds at the TRW facility in Redondo Beach in the early 1990s under the direction of Dr. Chuck Wuller. Cracraft now develops virtual reality at Dreamworks, Inc., in Marina Del Rey, Southern California. Wuller continues the project at TRW.

Artists and Works in Chapter 6

Char Davies   Char Davies is the director of visual research at SoftImage in Montreal, Québec. She directed the overall concept and design of *OSMOSE*, and has won awards for many other computer graphics projects. Georges Mauro did the graphics for *OSMOSE*. John Harrison developed the custom VR software. Musical composition and programming was done by Rick Bidlack, and the sound was designed and programmed by Dorota Blaszczak.

Artists and Works in Chapter 7

Water Memory   Kathleen Rogers teaches at the School of Television and Imaging at the University of Dundee in Scotland. Besides the installation at the Incident in Switzerland, her work includes "Psi-Net," a 1994 exhibit of live-broadcast psychic experiments with mediums and sensitives in rural England. Using biofeedback, thermographic-optical scanning, and microwave transmitters, Rogers probes the peripheries of networked consciousness.

James Turrell   James Turrell is a video artist who works with technology and light. His work ranges from indoor projection installations of artificial light to the outdoor Roden Crater project begun in 1979, which involves moonlight, a dead volcano in Arizona, and celestial mathematics. One of the founders of the California Museum of Photography, Turrell has established an international audience for his video work.

Notes

1 The moon example in Chapter 1 was adapted from the planetary exploration projects at the NASA-Ames Research Center. Since 1984, NASA's Virtual Planetary Exploration project has used billions of bytes of data about Mars retrieved by the Viking 1 and 2 spacecraft. Drs. Michael McGreevy, Stephen Ellis, and Lewis Hitchner developed this project and I am indebted to them for helping me understand it to the extent that I do. I shifted the model from Mars to the moon for poetic purposes, and the reader must bear in mind that my purpose is to explain the concept of VR and that any errors in the description are mine.

2 James Jerome Gibson, *The Ecological Approach to Visual Perception* (Boston: Houghton Mifflin, 1979).

3 *Prosthetic Territories: Politics and Hypertechnologies*, edited by Gabriel Brahm and Mark Driscoll (Boulder: Westview Press, 1995), 106. The citation of the author's *The Metaphysics of Virtual Reality* (Oxford and New York: Oxford University Press, 1993) is found on page 85.

4 Matthew Arnold cites the Joubert quotation in his *Essays In Criticism: First Series* (New York: Macmillan, 1898), from the essay "Joubert."

5 Gibson, *The Ecological Approach to Visual Perception*.

6 Originally in *High Fidelity*, April 1966; now available in *The Glenn Gould Reader*, edited by Tim Page (New York: Vintage Books, 1990), p. 331 ff.

7 See Page, xii–xiii. Geoffrey Payzant also covered "Gould's New Philosophy of Music" in *Glenn Gould: Music & Mind* (Toronto: Key Porter Books, 1992).

8 Katherine McCoy of McCoy & McCoy Associates describes this history in the *Visual Proceedings of the Computer Graphics 1993 Annual Conference of ACM SIGGRAPH*, 54.

9 Jim Morrison, *The Lords and the New Creatures*, (New York: Simon and Schuster, 1969), 29.

10 Ibid., 39.

11 Wallace Fowlie relates: "Jim performed acrobatically. He moved more on stage or talked to people in the balcony and jumped off the stage. As the crowds got bigger, Jim felt he had to do more, such as falling on the stage and writhing like a snake. He usually succeeded in getting responses from the audience. Ray

[Manzarek] once called Jim 'an electric shaman.'" *Rimbaud and Jim Morrison: The Rebel as Poet*, (Durham: Duke University Press, 1993), 81.

12 Statistics from "Dream Machines,"*Los Angeles Times*, 22 August 1995.

13 See Richard Coyne's valuable article "Heidegger and Virtual Reality: The Implications of Heidegger's Thinking for Computer Representations" in *Leonardo: Journal of the International Society for the Arts, Sciences and Technology* 27, no. 1 (1994): 65–73. Coyne criticizes the tendency of VR researchers to suggest that they will ultimately "picture" the primary sensory world. Instead, he suggests Heidegger's theory of truth as "disclosure" is a more appropriate model. I agree with this suggestion insofar as the reconstruction I describe does not pretend to re-present the primary world.

14 The whole passage runs: "My calling it a "symphony" is really inaccurate, for it doesn't keep to the traditional form in any way. But to me symphony' means constructing a world with all the technical means at one's disposal. The eternally new and changing content determines its own form. In this sense I must forever learn anew how to forge new means of expression for myself—however completely I may have mastered technical problems, as I think I may claim to have done." Cited by Peter Franklin, "Genesis and Design," chapter 3 in *Mahler: Symphony No. 3* (Cambridge: Cambridge University Press, 1991), 37.

15 In describing Mahler's music, I often rely on musicologists like Peter Franklin, *Mahler* and Constantin Floros, *Gustav Mahler: The Symphonies*, translated from German by Vernon and Jutta Wicker (Portand: Amadeus Press, 1993, original German copyright 1985).

16 Deryck Cooke, *Gustav Mahler: An Introduction to His Music* (Cambridge: Cambridge University Press, 1988), 12.

17 See the program notes in Foros (*Ibid.*), 63.

18 Myron Krueger, "The Experience Society" in *Presence: Teleoperators and Virtual Environments*, 2, no. 2, (Spring 1993), 162.

19 David Constantine, translated with an introduction and notes, *Elective Affinities: A Novel*, (New York: Oxford University Press, 1994).

20 *Portrait One* debuted at the *Ted2* conference in 1991 in Monterey, California.

21 Derrick de Kerckhove in the catalog of *Press/Enter: Between Seduction and Disbelief* (Toronto: Power Plant Contemporary Art Gallery, 1995), 95.

22 Daniel J. Boorstin, *The Republic of Technology: Reflections on Our Future Community*, (New York: Harper and Row, 1978), 47–8.

23 Bill McKibben, "The End of Nature," *The New Yorker*, (11 September 1989), 47–05.

24 Daisetz T. Suzuki, *Zen and Japanese Culture*, Bollingen Series (New York: Princeton University Press, 1959), 295-6.

25 *The Collected Poems of Dylan Thomas: 1934-1952* (New York: New Directions, 1971), 178.

26 William Gibson, *Mona Lisa Overdrive* (New York: Bantam Books, 1988), 49.

27 See Mitchell Kapor, "Where is the Digital Highway Really Heading? The Case for Jeffersonian Information Policy," in *WIRED*, (July/August 1993), 53-59.

28 *The Metaphysics of Virtual Reality*, 127.

29 Excerpts from a personal account by Mark J. Jones in *CyberStage*, (Fall 1995), 24.

30 Jones, from an interview with the artist.

31 "C'est par leur 'immensité' que les deux espaces: l'espace de l'intimité et l'espace du monde deviennent consonants. Quand s'approfondit la grande solitude de l'homme, les deux immensités se touchent, se confondent." Gaston Bachelard, *La Poétique de l'espace*, (Paris: Presses Universitaires de France, 1974), 184.

32 Char Davies, "OSMOSE: Notes on 'Being' in Immersive Virtual Space," (unpublished research notes at Microsoft SoftImage), October 1995.

33 Detailed accounts of these events appear in several books, including Stanton T. Friedman and Don Berliner, *Crash at Corona* (New York: Paragon House, 1992) and Kevin D. Randle and Donald R. Schmitt, *UFO Crash at Roswell* (New York: Avon Books, 1991).

34 See Richard L. Gregory, ed."Vision: The Early Warning System" in *The Oxford Companion to the Mind*, (Oxford and New York: Oxford University Press, 1987), 787–92.

35 John Dewey, preface to *The Resurrection of the Body: The Writings of F.M. Alexander*, Frederick Matthias Alexander, ed. Edward Maisel (New York: University Books, 1969), 169.

36 Some studies to read include: Eugenia M. Kolasinski's "Simulator Sickness in Virtual Environments," (Technical Report #1027, U.S. Army Research Institute for the Behavioral and Social Sciences, May 1995), and the entire Volume 1, no. 3 of the journal *Presence: Teleoperators and Virtual Environments*, (Cambridge: MIT Press, 1993).

37 Carl G. Jung, *Flying Saucers: A Modern Myth of Things Seen in the Skies*, Bollingen Series, translated by R.F.C. Hull (Princeton: Princeton University Press, 1978), 136.

38 Jung, 132.

39 Jung, 21.

40 Jung, 136.

41 Jung, 81.

42 See Raymond E. Fowler's account of Betty and Bob Luca in *The Watchers: The Secret Design behind UFO Abduction*, (New York: Bantam, 1990).

43 Robert Romanyshyn, *Technology as Symptom and Dream* (New York: Routledge and Kegan Paul, 1989).

44 The speculative pre-history of human invention touches, of course, values more than it does facts, since facts and artifacts from pre-history are rare. My favorite speculation comes from Willard Johnson's *Riding the Ox Home: A History of Meditation from Shamanism to Science* (Boston: Beacon Press, 1982), 24ff, and 84 ff..

Vocabulary of Virtual Realism

This glossary provides terms for concepts related to VR, as well as terms relevant to the art of emerging technology. The glossary is not exhaustive, but it updates the glossary in *The Metaphysics of Virtual Reality*. Additions or corrections will be gratefully received at any of the following addresses: mike@mheim.com, mheim@artcenter.edu, or mheim@usc.edu.

3-D Sound   Sound reproduction in the space of a virtual world occurs at all its digital points, allowing a sense of precise source locations. The sounds seem to occur above, below, in front of, and to either side of the listener. Such omni-directional sound produces an "acoustic photograph" of a sound environment. VR sound has emerged with advances in psychoacoustic research combined with the development of digital signal processing.

adaptogen   A tonic used to enhance flexibility and balance under rapidly changing circumstances. Adaptogens like Ginseng root moderate the metabolism so the body can better deal with stress. Chinese herbalists prescribe some adaptogens, like asparagus root, to maintain emotional resilience. Internal energy exercises, like Tai Chi Chuan or Chi Kung, are broadly classified as adaptogens in the context of technological evolution.

aesthetics   The branch of philosophy investigating questions such as: what makes something a work of art? Are there absolute values in art, or are aesthetic values relative? Are aesthetic arguments based only on personal preference? VR realism mixes traditional aesthetic criticism with additional questions of immersion, interactivity, and information intensity.

agents   Software entities that perform actions in virtual worlds. They can change, evolve, and learn. The creation of software agents draws on techniques from computer animation, artificial intelligence, neural networks, genetic algorithms, artificial life, and chaos theory.

Altered States   An emphasis in psychology focusing on paranormal states of consciousness, such as drug-induced hallucinations, isolation tanks, and religious rapture. Altered-states research interprets VR as a pattern of private perception rather than a real-world connection.

Analytic/Synthetic   Whereas analytic thinking takes things apart, synthetic thinking brings things together. Much of early-twentieth-century philosophy emphasized the analytic process and the need for telling details. With the advent of
computer support, philosophy has become free for holism, for connections and
associations, for ways to assemble illuminating combinations. Multimedia,
hypertext, and virtual reality express and reinforce the search for synthetic
wholes.

Artificial Life   Computerized agents that simulate biological life have artificial
life, or a-life. Such agents reproduce, evolve, and carry out the dynamic
processes of organic life. Not to be confused with Myron Krueger's "Artificial
Reality" (AR).

Artificial Reality (AR)   AR has a precise meaning in the work of Myron Krueger.
Krueger's "computer-controlled responsive environment" (p.ooo) means an
unencumbered involvement in a computerized environment. Computerized
sensors "perceive human actions in terms of the body's relationship to a simulated world. The computer then generates sights, sounds, and other sensations
that make the illusion of participating in that world convincing" (p.ooo).
Artificial reality belongs to VR in the sense that participants aesthetically enter
a computer-enhanced environment but AR systems do not require goggles or
datagloves, and such systems involve full-body motion without wiring humans
to an interface. The Cave at the University of Illinois exemplifies recent offshoots of AR. For details, see Myron Krueger, *Artificial Reality*, 2nd ed.
(Reading, Mass.: Addison-Wesley, 1991).

Augmented Reality   The superimposition of computer-generated data over the primary visual field. An operating surgeon, for instance, may wear dataglasses to
augment the perception of the patient's body, thereby gaining continually updated information on vital signs. The jet fighter's heads-up display is an early form
of augmented reality.

AWS (Alternate World Syndrome), AWD (Alternate World Disorder)   Flight
simulators can cause nausea and disorientation because of the discrepancies
between the pilot's actual physical movement (or lack of movement) and the
perceived motion in the simulator. The delay between the user's head motion
and the computer-simulated motion also adds to the "barfogenic zone."
Similarly in VR, a conflict of attention can arise between the cyberbody and the
biobody. In this case, an ontological rift appears as the felt world swings out of
kilter, not unlike jet lag. In Alternate World Syndrome, images and expectations
from an alternate world upset the current world, increasing the likelihood of
human errors. If the Alternate World Syndrome (AWS) becomes chronic, the
user suffers Alternate World Disorder (AWD), a more serious rupture of the
kinesthetic from the visual senses of self-identity. Treatments for AWS or AWD
range from de-linking exercises in cyberspace to more demanding disciplines,
such as Tai Chi and Yoga, that restore the integrity of somatic experience.

bandwidth   The amount of data that can be transmitted per second through the
lines of an electronic network. VR requires a bandwidth equal to the amount of
realism required for the particular application. Realism ranges from photorealistic representation to a softer evocative realism to a sharp-focus-soft-edges realism.
The relationship of bandwidth to realism remains a disputed question in the VR
field. Experiments with different applications will provide pragmatic answers

over time, but a full grasp of the question awaits an in-depth understanding of realism and presence.

BOOM (binocular omni-orientational monitor) A stereoscopic box mounted on a desktop that floats like a periscope and provides a wraparound three-dimensional imagery.

CAD/CAM (Computer-aided design or computer-aided manufacture) Software for computerizing the industrial-design process so that the initial planning stages of a product have greater precision and flexibility than when drawn by hand. The two-dimensional screen of CAD/CAM software limits the user to perspective drawing that only suggests three dimensions. The CAD software company Autodesk, producer of AutoCAD™ software, develops virtual reality and cyberspace software with "6 degrees of freedom" (x, y; and z axes, plus the three orientations of roll, pitch, and yaw).

CAVE The CAVE is a system for projection-room immersion. SID is a domed projection system that has long been used for tactical jet flight simulators. Some "reality centers," such as those built by Silicon Graphics, Inc., use panoramic projection screens. Multiple video projectors can create a single display with wide field-of-view. The CAVE and the SID (Spatially Immersive Display) have several advantages over HMDs: collaborative group viewing, simultaneously high resolution and wide field-of-view, no cumbersome headgear, low viewer fatigue, user mobility, single and multi-user interactivity, stereoscopic viewing, applicability to augmented reality, collaborative sense of presence.

cyber A prefix used throughout the literature of VR. The root reference comes from cybernetics, the science of self-regulating systems (the Greek *cybernein* means "to control or steer"). The term expanded to refer to mainframe computers (the Cyber 960) and now connotes the human involvement with computers (the cyborg, or cybernetic organism). For instance, the primary human body becomes a cyberbody when appearing in the cyberspace of a virtual environment.

cyberglove Another form of the dataglove, or device for monitoring hand movements so that the user's position and gestures can be calculated and the computer can adjust the graphic virtual environment accordingly.

cybernation The application of computers and automatic machinery to carry out complex operations. Managers in government and industry cybernate complex, repetitive tasks by introducing computers.

cyberpunk A literary-cultural style that projects a computerized future. The future is dominated by private corporations that use information technology and drugs to control individuals. Cyberpunk stories are told from the criminal perspective and portray a widespread use of biotechnology, computers, drugs, and a paranoid life-style. Individuals increasingly merge with electronic devices, and hallucinations rule public life. Cyberpunk is based on a dystopian brand of science fiction whose patron saint is Philip K. Dick and whose manifesto is William Gibson's novel *Neuromancer*. The term was coined by the science fiction writer Bruce Bepkie and became a literary critical term with Gardner Dozois, the editor of *Isaac Asimov's Science Fiction Magazine*.

cyberspace The juncture of digital information and human perception, the "matrix" of civilization where banks exchange credit and where information seekers navigate layers of data stored and represented in virtual space. Buildings in cyberspace may have more dimensions than physical buildings, and cyberspace may reflect different laws of existence. It has been said that cyberspace is where you are when you are having a phone conversation or where your ATM money exists. It is where electronic mail travels, and it resembles the Toontown in the movie *Roger Rabbit*.

dataglove, cyberglove   A sensor-laced nylon glove that provides manual access to objects in virtual environments, sometimes also enabling a variety of gestures to initiate movements in the virtual world. That is, the glove has fiber-optic sensors to track hand and finger positions, permitting the user to reach out, grab, and alter objects in the virtual world. Present-day datagloves register the hand positions and the degree of movement of each finger but do not yet register the somatics, the inner kinesthetic of movement that is difficult to measure.

datasuit   A sensor-equipped garment like the dataglove but covering the whole body in order to track the user's movements and to provide instant input into the host computer so the computer-generated graphic environment and the cyberbody can be updated according the user's gestures and orientation. The discomfort of body suits can be avoided by using a variety of spot sensors to track movement and to perform biofeedback.

determinism   The view that every event occurs necessarily, following inevitably from preceding events that cause it. Determinism rejects randomness, considering freedom to be either an illusion (hard determinism) or subject in some way to necessity (soft determinism). Soft determinism might be applied to technological change in the following way: the introduction of a technology inevitably transforms society, and as a working individual in society, I have no real choice but to participate in using the new technology; the manner in which I implement the technology, however, can be thoughtful or reflective, critical or conservative, depending on the attitude I consciously adopt. Hence, the how of my individual response is neither reactionary (rejecting technology wholesale) nor utopian (heralding technology as a panacea). Such technological determinism is variant of soft determinism.

dualism   The view, stemming from the seventeenth-century philosopher René Descartes, that mind (thinking substance) can work on its own, apart from matter (extended substance), to constitute a fullness of reality. According to this view, matter exists only in inert substances and cannot be understood outside the sciences. Descartes founded analytic geometry and contributed to geometrical optics in his *Discourse on Method* (1637). Cartesian philosophy continues to have an influence on the debate about virtual realism. Some see Cartesian solipsism in the single-user VR system.

e-mail, electronic mail   Messages delivered by networked computers. An e-mail network may be local within a single corporation, or it may extend to hundreds of nodes throughout the world, such as the Internet. Users receive and answer mail messages at a terminal or personal computer, and the system relays the messages in seconds to the address where they arrive for the receiver to view at a convenient time. Such systems are asynchronous rather than real time because the users need not be present at the time of delivery.

enhanced virtual vision   Continuous three-dimensional data superimposed over video images and pumped across a workstation into eyephones helps locate missing graphic elements or disparities. It is similar to augmented reality but without the direct contact with the primary visual world.

entity   Something that registers as ontologically present or that has an effect on a world. Entities include virtual objects as well as expert systems functioning as agents in the virtual world. Entities need not reflect real-world metaphysics but may draw on imaginary and/or spiritual traditions, such as the Loas of Voudun (Gibson) or the myth systems of the great religions (Rogers's "Mythseeker").

epistemology   The traditional study of human knowledge, its sources, its validation, and its implications for other aspects of life.

existential, existentialism   A philosophical emphasis on presence and making present, on action and human choice. Existentialism was a movement in early-twentieth-century philosophy that rejected static, essentialist worldviews in favor of pragmatic, risk-taking encounters with history and change. Its main proponents were Martin Heidegger, Jean-Paul Sartre, Simone de Beauvoir, and Karl Jaspers. Philosophers like Maurice Merleau-Ponty emphasized the role of human body in achieving presence. The interactivism of the late twentieth century carries on certain themes of existentialism.

eyephones   A head-mounted display that links the user's visual field with the computer-generated images of a virtual world. Eyephones shut out the primary visual world and supply the user with a continuous stream of computer-generated three-dimensional images. A variety of devices, from stereoscopic booms to virtual retinal displays, feed input into the user's optic sense.

eye-scanning devices   The host computer needs information about the user's eye movements in order to generate and constantly update appropriate visual images. A variety of devices, from head tracking to low-level lasers, are used to supply and compute the user's visual activity. As Aristotle pointed out in *Metaphysics* over two thousand years ago, humans have tended to learn more about the outside world from their sense of vision than from any of their other senses, because eyes deliver the most detailed and differentiated field of information. Existentialist philosophy, however, has meanwhile challenged the primacy of vision by pointing out the importance of presence and the nonvisual cues that alert us to presence.

flight simulator   A precursor of VR that emerged before World War II as an aid to pilot training. The earliest simulators used photographs coupled with motion machines to imitate the feel of flying an aircraft.

glass-bead game   A fictional game described by Hermann Hesse's novel *Das Glasperlenspiel* (1943), translated in English as *Magister Ludi* (the game master). Discussions of VR often evoke references to the glass-bead game because the game's players combine all the symbols of world cultures so as to devise surprising configurations that convey novel insights. Each player organizes the cultural symbols somewhat like a musician improvising on an organ that can mimic any instrument. The glass-bead game's synthetic, non-linear information play is a conceptual forerunner of hypertext and virtual worlds. Hesse's fiction also touches on some of the human problems underlying the advent of cyberspace and virtual reality, such as the role of the body and of disciplines for deepening the human spirit immersed in technology.

GUI (graphical user interface)   A term used by the computer industry to distinguish one specific approach to interacting with a computer. GUI is distinguished from the Command Line Language (CML). The alphanumeric symbols of a computer's command line (such as the C prompt on MS-DOS personal computers) present more abstract, less body-relevant symbols than GUI does (such as on Apple computers or on Windows PCs). GUI dramatizes the user's bodily action by making the delete command, for example, into the motion of carrying files (with a mouse) out to the (icon of a) trash can.

HCI (human-computer interaction)   HCI studies how to access computer power. The computer industry developed "human factors engineering" to explore different kinds of input ranging from binary code to alphanumeric keyboards to touchscreens and the mouse or track ball. Seen from the HCI viewpoint, VR is a latest development in "user friendliness." The HCI approach, however, misses the broad implications of the human entrance into virtual reality.

head-mounted display (HMD)   Also known as virtual-reality goggles or eyephones or, sardonically, "the Facesucker." The device covers both eyes and renders real-time stereoscopic graphics generated by the host computer. The HMD also provides head-tracking information so that the computer can generate perspectives of the virtual world appropriate to the user's bodily orientation and head/eye movements. Some HMDs also come equipped with headphones for audio tracking virtual entities. "Visette" is the British term for the HMD manufactured by W Industries of the United Kingdom. More advanced techniques include the use of low-level laser lights to send beams directly onto the retina, creating holographic representations. See VRD.

heads-up display (HUD)   A visor that, combined with head-positioning sensors, augments the visual field of the user. The visor superimposes a virtual floating window display that acts as an electronic associate, providing image projections of assembly instructions or blueprints to guide workers during their manufacturing tasks.

Holodeck   An idealized computer-to-human interface from the science fiction television series *Star Trek: The Next Generation*. The Holodeck is a room where spoken commands call up images in realistic landscapes populated by walking, talking "humans" (artificial personalities) and detailed artifacts that appear so lifelike that they are indistinguishable from reality. Used by the crew of the Starship Enterprise to re-create and to visit such times and places as medieval England and 1920s America.

hyper   The prefix hyper means "extended." Hyperspace is space extending beyond three dimensions. Hypersystems are nonlinear linked systems in which one link may route directly to a link on an entirely different plane or dimension. Hypermedia can cross-reference information in text, graphics, audio, and video.

hyperinstruments   Musical instruments modified for virtual realism. A traditional acoustic violincello, for example, can be wired so that the instrument's wooden body and perlon strings respond to the player's body parts in other than traditional ways. The hypercello allows the cellist to control an extensive array of sounds through performance nuance. Special techniques (wrist measurements, bow pressure and position sensors, left-hand fingering position indicators, direct sound analysis and processing) enable the computer to measure, evaluate, and respond to as many aspects of the performance as possible. This response is used in different ways at different moments of a piece: at times the cellist's playing controls electronic transformations of his own sound; at other times the interrelationship is more indirect and mysterious. Tod Machover, who created the first hypercello for Yo-Yo Ma, states "The entire sound world is conceived as an extension of the soloist—not as a dichotomy, but as a new kind of instrument."

hypertext   An approach to navigating information. From the computer science point of view, hypertext is a database with nodes (screens) connected with links (mechanical connections) and link icons (to designate where the links exist in the text). The semantics of hypertext allows the user to link text freely with audio and video, which leads to hypermedia, a multimedia approach to information. Many prototype hypertext systems, such as KNS, IBIS, INTERMEDIA and NOTECARDS, used the model of computer index cards (which later became Hypertext "Stacks") containing data such as text, graphics, animation, and video. In 1982, the ZOG hypertext was installed as a computer-assisted information management system on the USS Carl Vinson, a nuclear-powered aircraft carrier. ZOG is the most fully tested hypertext system to date. Its hypertext features include filtering through points of view or subjects, aggregative structures rather than shared logical structure, and versioning that keeps the history of the modifications to the database. The term hypertext was coined by Theodore Nelson in 1964. The disadvantages of hypertext include disorientation and cognitive overload.

IA (intelligence amplification)   The sum of the interface of human and computer. The human being intuits patterns, relations, and values, and the computer processes and generates data that include the sensory input for human senses. IA replaces the AI paradigm of human-computer rivalry by focusing on the interdependence of human and computer.

idealism   The ontological view that in the final analysis, every existing thing can be shown to be mental or spiritual. In the West, this view is usually associated with the views of George Berkeley and Georg Hegel. Asian philosophy also has its proponents of idealism, especially in the Hindu metaphysics that denies the reality of the material universe.

immersion   A key feature of VR systems. The virtual environment submerges the user in the sights and sounds and tactility specific to that environment. Immersion creates the sense of being present in a virtual world, a sense that goes beyond physical input and output. Immersion clearly has psychological components, but it involves sensory input in ways that surpass purely mental imagination. How presence and immersion coalesce remains an open question in VR research.

InfoEcology   The study of the humane adaptation of information systems. InfoEcology examines the points where information systems intersect human cultures, and the infoecologist suggests ways of preserving the organic balance of techno-cultures.

infonaut, cybernaut   Terms used to describe those who "swim" among virtual polymer molecules, who enter the virtual interior of galactic black holes, and who explore scientific data by moving through representations in a virtual world.

input   Information supplied to a computer through a variety of devices like keyboards, a mouse, a joystick, voice recognition, and position trackers such as helmets, BOOMs, and datagloves.

interface   The locus of communication between two systems, applied to either hardware or software or a combination of both. A graphical interface, for example, may use visual metaphors such as a desktop or a house with a garbage pail, paintbrush, or yardstick. An alphanumeric interface, such as that of the early MS-DOS personal computers, consists of a monitor, a keyboard, and the appropriate software for input and output. Interface is a key term in the philosophy of technology because it designates the connecting point between human and digital machine. See Chapter 6 of *The Metaphysics of Virtual Reality*.

irrealism   The view that "world" is a plural concept. According to irrealism, each world is a variant of related worlds, and each world makes its own context and rules of intelligibility. There is a world of sports and a world of art and a world of religion and a world of science. There are also times and places when we have a need for making ourselves present in a single world. This is irreal because it undermines the uncritical affirmation of a single world. Irrealism parallels Heidegger's existentialist notion of world in *Being and Time* (1927).

kinesthetic   The kinesthetic sense is the awareness of body position conveyed by muscle sensitivity and by feedback from joint and tendon membranes. With eyes closed, we continue to know the position of body parts because of our kinesthetic sense. Gestures, pressures, and tensions come to the brain through the kinesthetic sense. The kinesthetic sense is the warp of the fabric of sensation, and it often goes unnoticed in Western culture because of the dominance of the outward visual sense. Disciplines like Yoga and Tai Chi work largely with kinesthetic awareness.

materialism   The ontological view that in the final analysis, everything can be shown to be material and that mental and spiritual phenomena either are nonexistent or have no existence independent of matter. In the West this view is usually associated with Democritus, Thomas Hobbes, and Karl Marx.

metaphysics, metaphysical   The study of the first principles of realit,. including speculation on epistemology (knowledge), ontology (being), ethics (goodness), and aesthetics (beauty). The metaphysics of VR treats issues such as presence, degrees of reality, objectification (first person, third person),. simulation versus reality, the ratio of mental to sensory material, the ethics of simulation, the evaluation of virtual environments, and the central coordination of virtual realities. Traditional metaphysics also treats topics such as possible worlds, intrinsic goals (teleology), and umbrella concepts like meaning and final purpose.

mirror worlds   A software concept developed by David Gelernter at Yale in which the computer creates real-time miniature maps that mirror the larger world in which the user is present. Mirror worlds appear in some measure on the bird's-eye view of the jet pilot's radar screen, and they were also foreshadowed earlier by prototypes in ancient philosophy and art.

mobility devices   Stationary bikes, track balls, flying mice, treadmills, and other hardware connecting human motions with computer-generated environments.

network, the net, the matrix   A network connecting computers through cables, telephone lines, or satellite transmission. The global Internet connects institutions of all kinds: military and government, commercial and educational. Networks also exist in local areas such as in businesses and on commercial mainframe computers, such as those used by CompuServe and America Online. Most often, gateways exist through which one network opens onto another.

neural interface   Projected by science fiction, the notion of connecting human-computer input and output by tapping immediately into the nervous system of the human user. Discouraged by neurologists because of its obvious dangers, the notion still persists among scientists looking for an "ultimate interface."

nihilism, nihilistic   The view that either nothing truly exists or nothing deserves to exist.

object-oriented programming (OOP)   Programming languages such as C and C++ offer solutions to the complex problem of programming virtual worlds. Each situation in a virtual world requires a complex logical calculus. For example, if X number of agents exist in a world and all can have one interaction with one another, then the interactions will multiply to $X`2 - X$. If a variety of interactions are possible, say 9, then 10 agents will require 90 interactions; 100 agents, 9,900; and so on. OOP reduces the exponential growth of software complexity. The qualities of OOP languages — encapsulation, association, and polymorphism — reduce the complexity of programming virtual worlds, since multiple interactions do not have to be programmed individually.

ontology, ontological   The study of the relative reality of things. An ontology ranks some things as "more real" or "actually existing," as opposed what is unreal, phony, fadish, illusory, ephemeral, or purely perceptual. Ontology locates the difference between real and unreal and then develops the implications of that way of differentiating the real from the unreal. Traditional ontology studies entities or beings by observing the conditions under which we ascribe reality to beings. Ontology in the existential sense goes beyond traditional ontology by noticing the holistic background against which entities appear. The existential "world" in which entities appear also changes over time. The ontological shift constitutes a change of context according to which the realness of entities must be recalibrated. Epistemology, the study of knowledge, takes its bearings from clearly known entities and so does not dig down to the field of ontology. Because knowledge is based on assertions and propositions, the results of epistemology can stand up to greater logical scrutiny. Ontology, on the contrary, relies more on intuitive awareness and peripheral noticing than on argument and logic — which is not to say that ontology rejects argument and logic.

pragmatic   A classical position in American philosophy emphasizing the point of view of the user. The important questions are not separable from questions of human action. Pragmatism is the metaphysics of human factors.

presence   A notion crucial to early-twentieth-century philosophy. In Heidegger's *Being and Time* (1927), presence is synonymous with being and is a function of temporality. The entire history of reality, according to Heidegger, must be reconsidered from the standpoint of essence. Presence is also a key term in VR, with researchers seeking to define and quantify the presence that a given system will deliver.

primary reality   As opposed to virtual reality, primary reality refers to the earth-based somatic body of first-person experience. First-person experience includes bodily currents and energies that lie outside conscious ego control. Balance, breathing, and peripheral awareness of the environment remain outside ego control and constitute the somatic root of primary experience. The notion of primary reality functions to limit the idealism that would upload the mind to silicon or treat the somatic body as a carbon-based vehicle for artificial experience.

primary world   The world (the context of human involvement) outside the computer-generated world. The primary world has distinguishing properties such as natality or mortality, fragility or vulnerability to pain and injury, and personal care. The ontology of the primary world limits the realism of the virtual world.

psychological atomism   The view that all knowledge is built from simple, discrete psychological data, such as primitive sensations of color, sound, and taste. In the West, this view is usually associated with John Locke, George Berkeley, and David Hume.

realism   In a technical sense, realism refers to metaphysical theories that attribute priority to abstract entities. Platonism, for instance, is a kind of realism in maintaining that mathematical patterns are more real than are their instances in the physical world. Platonism finds the reality of things in their stability, intelligibility, and their reliability for the knower. In a related sense, realism is the approach that treats cyberspace as an actual phenomenological world with its own particular kind of entities. Non-realists approach cyberspace and VR as hardware and/or software configurations separate from the user's experience. Pragmatists speak of the Net as an actual place but also as one layer of reality resting ultimately on the primary world of the users.

real time   Simultaneity in the occurrence and registering of an event, sometimes called synchronous processing, as opposed to asynchronous processing in which the event remains at a distance from its registration as data.

robotic telepresence   The science of driving robots remotely and attaching video cameras to them to perform building inspection and other tasks with a human user's presence. Robotization has begun in underwater and space construction as well as in the handling of nuclear waste.

SIMNET   A three-dimensional visual simulator developed for virtual-world exploration in the military. SIMNET is a distributed interactive simulation (DIS) that links numerous simulation sites at one time so that the users can interact with users at other sites. SIMNET originally helped trained tank combat crews practicing communication techniques. One team drives its tank over a simulated terrain and encounters the tank driven by another crew on a remote or near site. Developed at the Naval Postgraduate School, NPSNET is an offshoot of SIMNET. NPSNET allows the participant to select a vehicle by means of a button box and to drive the vehicle over the ground or in the air in real time with a space ball that allows control with 6 degrees of freedom. The displays show on-ground cultural features such as roads, buildings, soil types, and elevations. It supports a full complement of vehicles, houses, trees, signs, water towers, and cows; and it can represent environmental effects such as San Francisco-like fog and Los Angeles-like smog.

solipsism   The view that the only true knowledge one can posses is the knowledge of one's own consciousness. Solipsism maintains that there is no good reason to believe that anything exists other than oneself.

somatics, somatic   An inside view of the human body taken from the first-person point of view, as opposed to a third-person point of view that looks at the body from the outside. The term somatic comes from the Greek *soma*, meaning "body," and derives from Thomas Hanna's studies of integral body experience. Non-Western approaches to health and medicine, including Yoga and Tai Chi, begin with somatic assumptions. Terms such as energy (*chi*, *ki*, and *prana*) gain their phenomenological meaning from the application of attention to the sensation of first-person physical processes. Western medicine insists on a split between the observer and the observed, the mind and the body, whereas the Eastern approach seeks a fuller presence that harmonizes the mind with the body.

spacemaker A designer of cyberspace constructs, like a filmmaker. The term was first introduced at Autodesk to indicate the unity of design and construction, because to plan something in cyberspace is tantamount to building it.

substance A traditional term referring to what is considered to be the most basic, independent reality. For Aristotle, the color of a horse is not a substance because the color cannot exist independently, but the horse is indeed a substance because it can exist independently of its color or size. For Spinoza, only God can be said to truly exist because only God is a completely independent being. George Berkeley believed that material things cannot exist independently of perception, and Immanuel Kant relegated substance to a category of human thinking.

Taoism, Taoist A stream of psycho-physical practices emerging in ancient China. Taoists conceive Nature as a continual balancing of yin/yang energies, as an unfathomable source of emerging patterns. More important than the theory are the practices that define Taoism. Taoists invented hundreds of practices, from acupuncture to Tai Chi movement, from specific "inner body" meditation to healing and artistic skills. These ancient practices still carry Taoism through the world, always on the periphery of the Western scientific systems of thought.

teleology, teleological An explanation in terms of goals or purposes (Greek *teloi*). The intention may be distant (Greek, *telê*) from the action, but the intention informs the action, giving it teleological reality. Teleological thinkers tend to equate reality and meaning.

telepresence Operations carried out remotely while the user remain immersed in a simulation of the remote location. (The Greek word *telê* means "at a distance," and so telepresence means "presence at distance.") Robotic mechanisms make telepresence effective at a remote site. Telepresence surgery, for example, allows surgeons to combine robotic instruments with endoscopy (cameras inserted in the patient's body). NASA uses slightly asynchronous transmissions to achieve telepresence outside terrestrial space.

telerobotics The technique of using mechanical devices to do work (Russian *robotayu*) at a distance. Add the cybernetics of information systems and the telerobot becomes a component of telepresence.

trackers Position-tracking devices that constantly monitor the user's physical body motions — hand, head, or eye movements — so as to feed the user's actions into the host computer, in which motions are interpreted as changes in the computer-generated environment. Some of the earliest devices for tracking head position, and hence visual perspective, are the 3Space Isotrak by Polhemus, Inc. and the Bird by Ascension Technology. Position-tracking devices by themselves do not register the user's somatic states.

transhuman Through repeated exposure, the most visionary moments can shrink to banal facts. This tendency of human perception is countered by the transhuman. The transhuman consists of artistic and psychological strategies to break through well-worn perceptions. The transhuman counteracts the all-too-human.

Turing test   A procedure for testing whether a computer is capable of thinking at the human level. As proposed (1950) by British mathematician Alan Turing, a person sits with a teletype machine isolated from two correspondents. One correspondent is another human, the other is a computer. By asking questions through the teletype and studying the responses, the isolated person tries to determine which correspondent is human and which the computer. If that proves impossible, the computer is considered to have passed the test.

Unabomber Manifesto   The manifesto "Industrial Society and Its Future" was first published by the *Washington Post* on September 19, 1995. The 56-page insert was published under threat from an anonymous serial bomber known to law enforcement agencies as the "Unabomber." (The bomber's first victims were university and airline employees). The bomber eluded capture while killing three people and injuring twenty-three during an anti-technology bombing campaign between 1978 and 1995. A reclusive Harvard-educated mathematician who had taught at Berkeley, Theodore John Kaczynski was apprehended in a remote Montana cabin on April 3, 1996, for possession of bomb components. On June 18, 1996, a Federal Grand Jury in Sacramento, California, returned a ten-count indictment charging Kaczynski with four separate bombings that killed two individuals and injured two others.

VRD   (Virtual Retinal Display) directs tiny beams of light through the iris and onto the eye's retina. By scanning at the rate of 18 millions pixels per second, the VRD provides enough infomation for the brain to fill in color images or lines of text. The VRD can fit onto eyeglasses, into headsets, or in miniature standalone devices.

virtual   A philosophical term meaning "not actually, but as if." It came into recent vogue with the use of computer techniques to enhance computer memory. Virtual-memory techniques multiply the data storage capacity of a computer without adding any hardware to it, so that the computer functions as if it had more memory. On a personal computer, for example, virtual memory can be a part of RAM used as though it were a hard disk storage device. Such a virtual disk can be used like a hard disk, but does not have the physical limitations of an actual mechanical disk. Similarly, something can be present in virtual reality without its usual physical limitations. The ancient Roman term *virtus*, from which virtual derives, meant the powers of a human being. The later Christian meaning of "virtue," as Nietzsche pointed out, inverted the Roman value system and eliminated the overtones of power. A virtual presence is one where the power of the person is not simply represented but makes itself felt.

virtual realism   The pragmatic interpretation of virtual reality as a functional, non-representational phenomenon that gains ontological weight through its practical applications. Virtual realism steers a course between the idealists who believe computerized life represents a higher form of existence and the down-to-earth realists who fear that computer simulations threaten ecological and local values. See Chapter 2.

virtual reality (VR)   Virtual reality is a technology that convinces the participant that he or she is actually in another place by substituting the primary sensory input with data received produced by a computer. The substitution is usually done through three-dimensional graphics and input-output devices that close-ly resemble the participant's normal interface with the physical world. The most common input-output devices are gloves, which transmit information about the participant's hand (position, orientation, and finger-bend angles), and head-mounted displays, which give the user a stereoscopic view of the vir-tual world via two computer-controlled display screens, as well as providing something on which to mount a position/ orientation tracker. The "as-if" qual-ity of virtuality becomes a pragmatic reality when the virtual world becomes a workspace and the user identifies with the virtual body and feels a sense of belonging to a virtual community. The definition of VR includes the three key factors of immersion, interactivity, and information intensity. The meaning of VR includes: artificial reality, as when the user's full-body actions combine with computer-generated images to forge a single presence; interactivity, as when the user enters a building by means of a mouse traveling on a screen or grabs a virtual entity; immersion, as when the user dons a head-mounted display enabling a view of a three-dimensional animated world or enters a cave-like projection room; networked environments, in which several people can enter a virtual world at the same time; telepresence, in which the user feels present in a virtual world while robot machines effect the user's agency at a remote location in the actual primary world. See Chapter 1.

virtual world, virtual environment   A scene or an experience with which a par-ticipant can interact by using computer-controlled input-output devices. Most virtual worlds attempt to resemble physical reality, but controversy continues about the value of various level of resemblance. Virtual worlds are not tied to physical reality, since any information that can be visualized can also be made into a virtual world that a participant can experience. Cyberspace in other words contains many kinds of virtual worlds. Even if a virtual world initiates a physical world, a decision has to be made whether the VR should imitate the perceived world of human phenomena or the world known to physical sciences (which often defies the everyday assumptions of human perception).

VRML (Virtual Reality Modeling Language)   A set of Internet protocols for building a 2D version of virtual reality (desktop VR). VRML defines a more complex graphic layer than the HyperText Markup Language (HTML) that defines the current visual environment of the Internet's World Wide Web. VRML is the next step of interface design where networked information will reside in 3-D visualizations.

Web, WWW, W3, the World Wide Web   A hypertext interface for the Internet that allows multimedia links so that the user can access information in textual references, audio, video, or real-time interactive communication. Since 1993, the Web has become the most creative area of computing. The Web goes beyond text-based electronic mail and binary-coded programming information to offer a mosaic of text, images, video, audio, and real-time interaction. The Web's protocol (http) absorbed previous Unix utilities like Gopher, File Transfer Protocol (FTP), and Archie, and it provided networking with an easy-to-use hyperlink framework for navigating multimedia information. Users of the Web have graphical access to global information. The Web's VRML (Virtual Reality Modeling Language) builds a 2-D version of VR, in the popular sense, and builds a more complex layer on the underlying HTML (HyperText Markup Language) that defines the shape of the Web. The Web was invented in late 1990 by Tim Berners-Lee at CERN, the European Particle Physics Laboratory.

world A world, either virtual or real, is a total environment for human involvement, such as the "world of sports" or the "world of the Otavalo Indians," or the "world of nuclear physics." The world in a singular sense refers to the horizon or totality of all involvement. A virtual world represents things so that they have an artificial presence. To prune exaggerated expectations, research laboratories often prefer to speak of virtual worlds rather than virtual reality (University of Washington) or virtual environments rather than virtual worlds (MIT and the military).

Suggested Readings

Abramson, Jeffrey B., F. Christopher Arterton, and Gary R. Orren. *The Electronic Commonwealth: The Impact of New Media Technologies on Democratic Politics.* New York: Basic Books, 1988.

Alexander, Frederick Matthias. *The Resurrection of the Body: The Writings of F. M. Alexander.* with a preface by John Dewey. Edited by Edward Maisel. New York: University Books, 1969.

Aukstakalnis, Steve, and David Blatner. *Silicon Mirage: The Art and Science of Virtual Reality.* Berkeley, California: Peachpit Press, 1992.

Barfield, Woodrow, and Thomas A. Furness, eds. *Virtual Environments and Advanced Interface Design.* New York & Oxford: Oxford University Press, 1995.

Barrett, Edward, ed. *The Society of Text: Hypertext, Hypermedia and the Social Construction of Information.* Cambridge, Mass.: MIT Press, 1989.

_____, ed. *Text, Context and Hypertext: Writing with and for the Computer.* Cambridge, Mass.: MIT Press, 1988.

Benedikt, Michael, ed. *Cyberspace: First Steps.* Cambridge, Massachusetts: MIT Press, 1991.

Benjamin, Walter. "The Work of Art in the Age of Mechanical Reproduction." In *Illuminations,* edited by Hannah Arendt. New York: Schocken Books, 1969.

Berk, Emily, and Joseph Devlin, eds. *The Hypertext/Hypermedia Handbook.* New York: McGraw-Hill, 1991.

Berman, Morris. *Coming to Our Senses: Body and Spirit in the Hidden History of the West.* New York: Bantam Books, 1989.

Berreby, David. "Get on Line for Plato's Cave." *New York Times,* June 25 1995.

Biocca, Frank. "Will Simulation Sickness Slow Down the Diffusion of VE Technology?" *Presence: Teleoperators and Virtual Environments* (MIT Press) I, no. 3 (Summer 1992): 334–43.

_____, and Mark R. Levy, eds. *Communication in the Age of Virtual Reality.* Hillsdale, N.J.: Lawrence Erlbaum Associates, 1995.

Birkerts, Sven. *The Gutenberg Elegies.* Boston: Faber & Faber, 1994.

Bolter, Jay David. *Writing Space: The Computer, Hypertext, and the History of Writing*. Fairlawn, N.J.: Erlbaum, 1990.

Boorstin, Daniel J. *The Republic of Technology: Reflections on Our Future Community*. New York: Harper & Row, 1978.

Borgmann, Albert. *Crossing the Postmodern Divide*. Chicago: University of Chicago Press, 1992.

———. *Technology and the Character of Contemporary Life: A Philosophical Inquiry*. Chicago: University of Chicago Press, 1984.

Brahm, Gabriel, and Mark Driscoll. *Prosthetic Territories: Politics and Hypertechnologies*. Boulder: Westview Press, 1995.

Brook, James, and Iain Boal. *Resisting the Virtual Life*. San Francisco: City Lights Books, 1995.

Burdea, Grigore C. *Force and Touch Feedback for Virtual Reality*. New York: John Wiley & Sons, 1996.

Burdea, Grigore, and Philippe Coiffet. *Virtual Reality Technology*. New York: John Wiley & Sons, 1994.

———, and Philippe Coiffet. *Virtual Reality Technology*. New York: John Wiley & Sons, 1994.

Bush, Vannevar. "As We May Think." *Atlantic Monthly*, July 1945, 106–07.

———. *Science Is Not Enough*. New York: Morrow, 1967.

Carande, Robert. *Information Sources for Virtual Reality: A Research Guide*. Westport, Conn.: Greenwood Press, 1993.

Chia, Mantak, and Maneewan Chia. *Awaken Healing Light of the Tao*. Huntington, N.Y.: Healing Tao Books (Tao Books, P.O. Box 1194, Huntington, NY 11743), 1993.

Colford, Ian. *Writing in the Electronic Environment : Electronic Text and the Future of Creativity and Knowledge*. Halifax, N.S.: Dalhousie University, School of Library and Information Studies, 1996.

Cooke, Deryck. *Gustav Mahler: An Introduction to His Music*. Cambridge: Cambridge University Press, 1988.

Coyne, Richard. *Designing Information Technology in the Postmodern Age: From Method to Metaphor*. Cambridge, Mass.: MIT Press, 1995.

———. "Heidegger and Virtual Reality: The Implications of Heidegger's Thinking for Computer Representations." *Leonardo: Journal of the International Society for the Arts, Sciences and Technology* 27, no. 1 (1994): 65–73.

Cyberspace: First Steps. Michael Benedikt, ed. Cambridge, Massachusetts: MIT Press, 1991.

De Kerckhove, Derrick. *The Skin of Culture: Investigating the New Electronic Reality*. Toronto: Somerville House, 1995.

———. "A Volcanic Theory of Art." In *Press/Enter: Between Seduction and Disbelief*, edited by Louise Dompierre, 87–99. Toronto: Power Plant Contemporary Art Gallery, 1995.

Delany, Paul, and George P. Landow, eds. *Hypermedia and Literary Studies*. Cambridge, Mass.: MIT Press.

Dewey, John. "Preface." In *The Resurrection of the Body: The Writings of F.M. Alexander*, edited by Edward Maisel, vii–xlviii. New York: University Books, 1969.

Doheny-Farina, Stephen. *The Wired Neighborhood*. New Haven: Yale University Press, 1996.

Dunlop, Charles, and Rob Kling, eds. *Computerization & Controversy*. San Diego: Academic Press, 1991.

Durlach, Nathaniel I., and Mavor Anne S., eds. *Virtual Reality: Scientific and Technological Challenges*. Washington, D.C.: National Academy Press, 1995.

Eddings, Joshua. *How Virtual Reality Works*. Emeryville, Calif.: Ziff-Davis Press, 1994.

Edwards, Deborah M., and Lynda Hardman. "Lost in Hyperspace: Cognitive Mapping and Navigation in a Hypertext Environment." In *Hypertext: Theory Into Practice*, edited by Ray McAleese. Norwood, NJ: Ablex Pub. Corp., 1989.

Ellis, Stephen R., Mary K. Kaiser, and Arthur C. Grunwald, eds. *Pictorial Communication in Virtual and Real Environments*. New York and London: Taylor & Francis, 1991.

Flim, Leona. "Bookish Versus Electronic Text: Ivan Illich and Michael Heim." Diss. Calgary, Canada: University of Calgary, 1991.

Floros, Constantin. *Gustav Mahler: The Symphonies*. Translated by Vernon and Jutta Wicker. Portand: Amadeus Press, 1993.

Foltz, Bruce V. *Inhabiting the Earth: Heidegger, Environmental Ethics, and the Metaphysics of Nature*. Atlantic Highlands, N.J.: Humanities Press International, 1995.

Fowler, Raymond E. *The Watchers: The Secret Design Behind UFO Abduction*. New York: Bantam, 1990.

Fowlie, Wallace. *Rimbaud and Jim Morrison: The Rebel as Poet*. Durham & London: Duke University Press, 1993.

Franklin, Peter. *Mahler: Symphony No. 3*. Cambridge: Cambridge University Press, 1991.

Friedman, Stanton T., and Don Berliner. *Crash at Corona*. New York: Paragon House, 1992.

Gelernter, David. Mirror Worlds: *The Day Software Puts the Universe in a Shoebox*. New York: Oxford University Press, 1992.

Georgopoulos, N., and Michael Heim, editors. *Being Human in the Ultimate: Studies in the Thought of John M. Anderson*. Value Inquiry Book Series, vol. 23. Amsterdam and Atlanta, GA: Rodopi Publishers, 1995.

Gibson, James Jerome. *The Ecological Approach to Visual Perception*. Boston: Houghton Mifflin, 1979.

Gibson, William. *Burning Chrome*. New York: Ace, 1987.

_____. *Mona Lisa Overdrive*. New York: Bantam Books, 1988.

_____. *Neuromancer*. New York: Ace Books, 1984.

Gould, Glenn. *The Glenn Gould Reader*. Edited by Tim Page. New York: Vintage, 1990.

Gray, Susan H. *Hypertext and the Technology of Conversation: Orderly Situational Choice*. Westport, Conn.: Greenwood Press, 1993.

Gregory, Richard L. "Vision: The Early Warning System." In *The Oxford Companion to the Mind*, edited by Richard L. Gregory, 787–92. New York and London: Oxford University Press, 1987.

Hanna, Thomas. *Bodies in Revolt: A Primer in Somatic Thinking*. New York: Holt, Rinehart and Winston, 1970.

_____. *Somatics: Reawakening the Mind's Control of Movement, Flexibility, and Health.* Reading, Mass.: Addison-Wesley, 1988.

Hardison, O.B. *Disappearing Through the Skylight: Culture and Technology in the Twentieth Century.* New York: Viking, 1989.

Heidegger, Martin. *Holzwege.* Frankfurt am Main: Vittorio Klostermann, 1950.

_____. *On the Way to Language.* Translated by Peter D. Hertz. San Francisco: Harper & Row, 1971.

_____. *Poetry, Language, Thought.* Translated by Albert Hofstadter. New York: Harper Colophon, 1971.

_____. *The Question Concerning Technology and Other Essays.* Translated by William Lovitt. New York: Harper Colophon Books, 1977.

Heim, Michael. "The Art of Virtual Reality." *Virtual Reality Special Report* 1, no. 4 (Winter 1994): 9–22.

_____. "The Computer As Component: Heidegger and McLuhan." *Philosophy and Literature,* October 1992, 33–44.

_____. "Cybersage Does Tai Chi." In *Falling in Love with Wisdom: American Philosophers Talk About Their Calling,* edited by David Darnos and Robert Shoemaker, 205–09. New York: Oxford University Press, 1993.

_____. "The Design of Virtual Reality." In *Cyberspace/Cyberbodies/Cyberpunk: Cultures of Technological Embodiment,* edited by Mike Featherstone and Roger Burrows, 65–77. London: SAGE Publications, 1995.

_____. "The Design of Virtual Reality." In *Press/Enter: Between Seduction and Disbelief,* edited by Louise Dompierre, 57–76. Toronto: The Power Plant Contemporary Art Gallery at Harbourfront Centre, 1995.

_____. "The Design of Virtual Reality." *Body & Society* 1, no. 3–4 (November, 1995 1995): 65–77.

_____. *Electric Language: A Philosophical Study of Word Processing.* New Haven: Yale University Press, 1987, 2nd edition 1997.

_____. "The Erotic Ontology of Cyberspace." In *Cyberspace: First Steps,* edited by Michael Benedikt, 59–80. Cambridge, Massachusetts: MIT Press, 1991.

_____. "Infomania." In *The State of the Language,* edited by Christopher Ricks and Leonard Michaels, 300–06. Berkeley: University of California Press, 1990.

_____. "The Metaphysics of Virtual Reality." In *Virtual Reality: Theory, Practice, and Promise,* edited by Sandra K. Helsel and Judith Paris Roth, 27–34. Westport, Connecticut: Meckler Publishing, 1991.

_____. *The Metaphysics of Virtual Reality.* New York: Oxford University Press, 1993.

_____. "Nature & Cyberspace." In *Bodyscapes: Body and Discourse,* edited by Svend Larsen, Mette Bryld, Jacques Caron, Nina Lykke and Niels Nielsen, 183–203. Odense, Denmark: Odense University Press, 1995.

_____. "Remembering the Body Temple." *The Healing Tao Journal* (Tao Books, P.O. Box 1194, Huntington, NY 11743) 1, no. 4 (1991): 10–12.

_____. "Searching for the Essence of Tai Chi." *The Healing Tao Journal* (Tao Books, P.O. Box 1194, Huntington, NY 11743) 1, no. 2 (Winter 1989): 10–12.

_____. "The Sound of Being's Body." *Man and World: An International Philosophical Review* 21, no. 1 (1988): 48–59.

————. "VR for Real-World Ecology." *Virtual Reality Special Report* 2, no. 4 (September/October 1995): 50–57.

————. ""The Erotic Ontology of Cyberspace."." In *Cyberspace: First Steps*, edited by Michael Benedikt, 59–80. Cambridge, Massachusetts: MIT Press, 1991.

Illich, Ivan, and Barry Sanders. *ABC: The Alphabetization of the Popular Mind*. San Francisco: North Point Press, 1988.

Jacobson, Linda, ed. *CyberArts: Exploring Art and Technology*. San Francisco: Miller Freeman, 1992.

Johnson, Willard. *Riding the Ox Home: A History of Meditation from Shamanism to Science*. Boston: Beacon Press, 1982.

Jou, Tsung Hwa. *The Tao of I Ching: Way to Divination*. Piscataway, N.J.: Tai Chi Foundation, 1984.

————. *The Tao of Meditation : Way to Enlightenment*. Piscataway, N.J.: Tai Chi Foundation, 1983.

————. *The Tao of Tai-Chi Chuan: Way to Rejuvenation*. Edited by Shoshana Shapiro. Piscataway, N.J.: Tai Chi Foundation, 1980.

Joyce, Michael. *Of Two Minds : Hypertext Pedagogy and Poetics*. Ann Arbor: University of Michigan Press, 1995.

————. "Selfish Interaction: Subversive Texts And The Multiple Novel." In *The Hypertext/Hypermedia Handbook*, edited by Emily Berk and Joseph Devlin. New York: McGraw-Hill, 1991.

Jung, Carl G. *Flying Saucers: A Modern Myth of Things Seen in the Skies*. Translated by R.F.C. Hull. Princeton, NJ: Princeton University Press, Bollingen Series, 1978.

Kalawsky, Roy S. *The Science of Virtual Reality and Virtual Environments: A Technical, Scientific and Engineering Reference on Virtual Environments*. Reading, Mass.: Addison-Wesley, 1993.

Kennedy, Robert S., et al. "Profile Analysis of Simulator Sickness Symptoms: Application to Virtual Environment Systems." *Presence: Teleoperators and Virtual Environments* (MIT Press) I, no. 3 (Summer 1992): 295–301.

Kolasinski, Eugenia M. Simulator *Sickness in Virtual Environments*. Alexandria, Virginia: U.S. Army Research Institute for the Behavioral and Social Sciences, 1995.

Koren, Leonard. *Wabi-Sabi for Artists, Designers, Poets & Philosophers*. Berkeley, California: Stone Bridge Press, 1994.

Kroker, Arthur, and Michael W. Weinstein. *Data Trash*. New York: St. Martin's Press, 1994.

Krueger, Myron. "The Experience Society." *Presence: Teleoperators and Virtual Environments* (MIT Press) 2, no. 2 (Spring 1993): 162.

————. *Artificial Reality II*. Reading, Massachusetts: Addison-Wesley, 1991.

Landow, George, P. *Hypertext: The Convergence of Contemporary Critical Theory and Technology*. Baltimore: Johns Hopkins University Press, 1992.

————, ed. *Hyper/Text/Theory*. Baltimore, Maryland: Johns Hopkins University Press, 1994.

————, and Paul Delany, eds. *The Digital Word : Text-Based Computing in the Humanities*. Cambridge, Mass.: MIT Press, 1993.

Levinson, Paul. *Mind at Large: Knowing in the Technological Age*. Greenwich, Conn.: Jai Press, 1988.

Lewis, Dennis. *The Tao of Natural Breathing*. San Francisco: Mountain Wind
  Publishing, 1997.
McCauley, Michael E., and Thomas J. Sharkey. "Cybersickness: Perception of
  Self-Motion in Virtual Environments." *Presence: Teleoperators and Virtual
  Environments* (MIT Press) I, no. 3 (Summer 1992): 311–17.
McKibben, Bill. *The Age of Missing Information*. New York: Plume, 1992.
McKnight, C., A. Dillon, and Richardson J., eds. *Hypertext : A Psychological
  Perspective*. New York: E. Horwood, 1993.
McLuhan, H. Marshall. *The Gutenberg Galaxy: The Making of Typographic
  Man*. Toronto: University of Toronto Press, 1962.
_____. *Understanding Media: The Extensions of Man*. New York: McGraw-
  Hill, 1964.
Mitchell, Donald. *The Language of Modern Music*. 1964. Philadelphia:
  University of Pennsylvania Press, 1994.
Morrison, Jim. *The Lords and the New Creatures*. New York: Simon and
  Schuster, 1969.
Nelson, Theodor Holm. *Computer Lib/Dream Machines*. Redmond, Wash.:
  Tempus Books, 1987.
_____. "Computopia Now!" In *Digital Deli*, edited by Steve Ditlea. San
  Francisco: Workman, 1984.
_____. *Literary Machines*. Sausalito Calif.: Mindful Press, 1990.
Nielsen, Jakob. *Hypertext and Hypermedia*. San Diego: Academic Press, 1990.
Payzant, Geoffrey. *Glenn Gould: Music & Mind*. Toronto: Key Porter Books,
  1992.
Pimental, Ken, and Kevin Teixeira. *Virtual Reality: Through the New Looking
  Glass*. New York: Intel/Windcrest, 1993.
Po-tuan, Chang. "The Secret of Opening the Passes." In *Vitality, Energy, Spirit:
  A Taoist Sourcebook*, edited by Thomas F. Cleary, 124–29. Boston,
  Massachusetts: Shambhala Publications, 1991.
_____. *Understanding Reality. Translation of: Wu chen p'ien*. Translated by
  Thomas F. Cleary. Honolulu: University of Hawaii Press, 1987.
Poster, Mark. *Critical Theory and Poststructuralism: In Search of a Context*.
  Ithaca, New York: Cornell University Press, 1989.
_____. *The Mode of Information: Poststructuralism and Social Context*.
  Chicago: University of Chicago Press, 1990.
_____. *The Second Media Age*. Cambridge, Massachusetts: Blackwell, 1995.
Randle, Kevin D., and Donald R. Schmitt. *UFO Crash at Roswell*. New York:
  Avon Books, 1991.
Rheingold, Howard. *Virtual Reality*. New York: Summit Books, 1991.
Robinett, Warren. "Synthetic Experience: A Proposed Taxonomy." *Presence:
  Teleoperators and Virtual Environments* (MIT Press) I, no. 2 (Spring 1992
  1992).
Romanyshyn, Robert. *Technology as Symptom and Dream*. New York: Routledge
  & Kegan Paul, 1989.
Rorty, Richard. *Philosophy and the Mirror of Nature*. Princeton, N.J.: Princeton
  University Press, 1980.
Rothenberg, David. *Hand's End: Technology and the Limits of Nature*. Berkeley,
  Los Angeles, and London: University of California Press, 1993.

Rouet, Jean-Francois, and et al., eds. *Hypertext and Cognition*. Mahwah, N.J.: Lawrence Erlbaum, 1996.

Rushkoff, Douglas. *Media Virus*. New York: Ballantine Books, 1994.

Sale, Kirkpatrick. *Rebels Against the Future: The Luddites and Their War on the Industrial Revolution*. Reading, Massachusetts: Addison-Wesley, 1995.

Schipper, Kristofer. *The Taoist Body*. Translated by Karen C. Duval. Berkeley: University of California Press, 1993.

Schroeder, Ralph. *Possible Worlds: The Social Dynamic of Virtual Reality Technology*. Boulder, Colo.: Westview Press, 1996.

Slouka, Mark. *War of the Worlds: Cyberspace and the High-Tech Assault on Reality*. New York: Basic Books, 1995.

Stoll, Clifford. *Silicon Snake Oil: Second Thoughts on the Information Highway*. New York: Doubleday, 1995.

Streitz, N., A. Rizk, and J. André, eds. *Hypertext: Concepts, Systems and Applications: Proceedings of the First European Conference on Hypertext*. The Cambridge Series on Electronic Publishing. Cambridge, Mass.: Cambridge University Press, 1990.

Suzuki, Daisetz Teitaro. *Studies in Zen*. Edited by Christmas Humphreys. New York: Dell Publishing Company, 1955.

Talbott, Stephen L. *The Future Does Not Compute: Transcending the Machines in Our Midst*. Sebastopol, California: O'Reilly & Associates, 1995.

The Taoist I Ching. Translated by Thomas Cleary. Boston: Shambhala.

Taoists (Chuan Chen). *The Jade Emperor's Mind Seal Classic: A Taoist Guide to Health, Longevity and Immortality*. Translated by Stuart Alve Olson. St. Paul, Minnesota: Dragon Door Publications, 1992.

Vinge, Vernor. *True Names and Other Dangers*. New York: Baen Books, 1987.

Virtual Environments and Advanced Interface Design. Edited by Woodrow Barfield and Thomas A. Furness. New York & Oxford: Oxford University Press, 1995.

Weghorst, Suzanne J., Hans B. Sieburg, and Karen S. Morgan, eds. *Medicine Meets Virtual Reality: Health Care in the Information Age*. Studies in Health Technology and Informatics, vol. 29. Washington, D.C.: IOS Press, 1996.

Woolley, Benjamin. *Virtual Worlds: A Journey Into Hype and Hyperreality*. Cambridge, Massachusetts: Blackwell Publishers, 1992.

Wu, Eleanor B., Morris. *Human Efflorescence: A Study in Man's Evolutionary and Historical Development*. St. Louis, Missouri: Warren H. Green, 1983.

Wurman, Richard Saul. *Information Anxiety*. New York: Bantam, 1989.

Yuasa, Yasuo. *The Body: Toward an Eastern Mind-Body Theory*. Edited by Thomas P. Kasulis and translated by Nagatomo Shigenori and Thomas P. Kasulis. Albany: State University of New York Press, 1987.

Index

Page numbers in italics refer to pages in the Vocabulary for Virtual Realism.